PRAISE FOR *RAW SURVIVAL*

"In an era of reality stories, it is rare to find the truth, clarity of experiences, and memories as shared by Jan Rozga in her new book, *Raw Survival*. While I was only a small part of this story of a mother's joy turned to heartache, I can testify that all of what is recorded in this riveting book is true, and the emotions are real. If you have your own teenagers, hug them every day and tell them you love them, because life can change in an instant."

—*ANTHONY J. SCALZO, MD, Director, Division of Toxicology, Saint Louis University School of Medicine*

"Incredibly well-written and vulnerable. I felt the hope and love of God as I read *Raw Survival*. Each passage of Scripture shared connects powerfully to surviving grief, regardless of the type of loss experienced by the reader. Very, very important guidance throughout the book. This needs to be shared!"

—*SUSIE SHER, Iowa Governor's Office of Drug Control Policy*

"Jan speaks directly from her broken heart into the grieving hearts of those devastated by the sudden, tragic death of someone they love. Masterfully written, this book not only pulls the reader in closely as Jan shares her own compelling and devastating story, but it challenges the reader to consider their own grief journey, bringing hope and healing through thought-provoking questions, poignant Scripture passages, and comforting prayers that the reader can personalize as their own when there just are no words."

—*SASHA J. MUDLAFF, Vice President, Hamilton's Funeral Home, Des Moines, Iowa*

"When we wander through grief valleys of despair, we doubt anybody understands. Oh, sweet soul, my friend Jan does. Her book *Raw Survival* is a heartbreaking, hope-gushing story about the healing love of Jesus. She doesn't sugarcoat the hard; instead, she shares with brave transparency, beautiful authenticity, and a kindred vibe. By inviting us into her own raw survival, Jan helps us discover healing and hope in ours. What a gift."

—*TINA SAVANT GIBSON, contributing author to Let Your Light Shine: Being a Light in a Dark World*

"This book is really well done and it's going to bless, comfort, and impact so many people at their point of need. I love the balance of spiritual elements and the raw, honest trust in our God. It is boldly transparent and clearly presents the Gospel."

—KAREN LANGSTRAAT, *Regional Director, Stonecroft*

"I definitely recommend this book to others. It takes a poignant look at the grieving process and gives readers important strategies needed to navigate it: counseling, journaling, prayer, connecting with others who are grieving, self-care, etc. *Raw Survival* is a tool that will positively impact the mental health of readers."

—TINA CHAPLIN, *School Counselor*

"I'm beyond amazed. As I read *Raw Survival*, I tried to put my own grief aside, but it was simply impossible. Time and time again, I felt God saying, 'Come to me, trust me,' and I found courage and hope that I will be able to look back after a few years and see progress in my own battle with grief. The realism and raw emotion pour off the pages."

—VICKY OHNEMUS, *grieving parent*

"God is going to use this book to minister to so many who need the hope and truth of Jesus Christ in their moments of deepest pain and loss."

—MIKE SHIELDS, *District Superintendent, Evangelical Free Church of America*

"This book is real, it's truth, and it offers *hope*! There is a tremendous ministry between its covers, making it a great gift to share with someone who has lost a loved one! The reader sees how God can (and will) meet us where we're at and continue to bring healing. Great guidance for dealing with the thoughts and emotions of grief."

—SANDY BLOEM, *grieving grandparent*

"I am dealing with the emotional loss of a close family relationship. Although I would never compare my struggle with the loss of a child, I find great hope in the words and scriptures in *Raw Survival* and appreciate Jan's transparency in sharing personal struggles, like needing a nightcap before bed to keep her mind from wandering. It is relatable and makes me feel less alone."

—JAKE LETTINGTON, *friend of David Rozga*

"Jan brings to life an unfathomable loss and how God steps in and 'carries' us through our biggest struggles. *Raw Survival* shows how he gives us our daily bread by speaking through his word and the special people he has put in our lives. Jesus is the only hope and peace in these times!"

—ADAM TIMMERMAN, *Director, Northwest Iowa Fellowship of Christian Athletes*

"A wonderfully inspiring book that is a real page-turner! The information is presented in a straightforward manner that is easy to read, well organized, and Jesus centered. 'The Truth Companion' is a tremendous asset to help readers distinguish the lies that come to them and turn them around with the power of God's truth. Powerful!"

—MARGE THOMPSON, *author of I Love You Anyhow*

"Exceptional content that is worthy of publishing. Specific guidance for walking through grief, encouragement for readers to lean on God's Word as a foundation for healing, and the 'First Aid for Your Grieving Heart' sections, with prayers and journal prompts, make this book extremely practical for anyone suffering from loss."

—LINTON LUNDEEN, *Pastor of Care & Counseling, Valley Church*

"With profound vulnerability Jan ushers the reader through the depths of her loss and the truths she found along the way. *Raw Survival* is a beacon of hope and healing for the grieving and non-grieving alike."

—ZACH SIKORA, *Licensed Clinical Psychologist*

"I believe the deepest teaching is drawn from the well of one's lived experience—particularly painful experience. Jan has survived the greatest pain any parent can imagine. *Raw Survival* is her gift to us. It contains the lived lessons that will sustain each of us through our own dark night of the soul. More than a book, it's a lifeline and it's an honor to commend it to you."

—RYAN HUGULEY, *author of 8 Hours, or Less: Writing Faithful Sermons Faster*

"Jan Rozga's stirring book is a gift of heart-rending transparency and ultimate hope for anyone who has suffered deep loss—and for those who seek to support them. The chapters are not theory. Each one is intensely honest and real. The depth and breadth of her empathy and wisdom are truly life-giving. Highly recommended!"

—QUINTIN STIEFF, *Lead Pastor, Valley Church, Des Moines, Iowa*

Raw Survival

Raw Survival

A Practical Guide to Living through Loss

JAN ROZGA

Foreword by Jon Duey

RESOURCE *Publications* · Eugene, Oregon

RAW SURVIVAL
A Practical Guide to Living through Loss

Resource Publications
An Imprint of Wipf and Stock Publishers
199 W. 8th Ave., Suite 3
Eugene, OR 97401

www.wipfandstock.com

PAPERBACK ISBN: 978-1-7252-9987-0
HARDCOVER ISBN: 978-1-7252-9988-7
EBOOK ISBN: 978-1-7252-9989-4

07/14/21

For my David.
These pages hold the shattered pieces of my heart,
left in the wake of your death.
They hold the messy details of my journey to survive life without you.
And incredibly, they hold the joy of keeping the promise I made to you
(and to God) under the stars in the wee hours of that horrible night.
Forever your mom—I love you, sweet boy.

"My God is my rock, in whom I take refuge.

The waves of death swirled about me;

the torrents of destruction overwhelmed me.

The cords of the grave coiled around me;

the snares of death confronted me.

In my distress I called to the Lord; I called out to my God.

He reached down from on high and took hold of me;

he drew me out of deep waters.

You, Lord, are my lamp; the Lord turns my darkness into light.

It is God who arms me with strength and keeps my way secure.

The Lord lives! Praise be to my Rock!

Exalted be my God, the Rock, my Savior!"

2 SAMUEL 22:3, 5–7, 17, 29, 33, 47

Contents

PART V: REDISCOVERING JOY

PART VI: THE TRUTH COMPANION

Foreword

by Jon Duey
David's youth pastor, worship partner, and friend

Dear David, I miss you.
Wow, that's hard to say.
What I wouldn't give to sit down and talk with you.
To hear you laugh. To play guitar together.
To pray over your friends. To talk football.
I still like the Bears. Come on, you knew that wasn't going to change! And I never learned those guitar leads, even after all the lessons you gave me. Nope. I don't know a single one. As I think about it, I wonder if I ever really cared about learning those leads or if the lessons were far more about spending time together!
David, you would be proud.
Proud of your brother for growing into a mature, caring, funny, intentional man of God.
Proud of who he is. Proud of what he is doing, and of what he stands for.
And you would be so proud of your parents.
Losing you has been hard on them. But wow, God is using them in amazing ways. They have chosen to intentionally lean into their grief and pain so God can use their story–your story–for his glory. It's pretty incredible to watch.

As I read this book and relive the moments that I shared with David's family in those first frantic hours of losing him, and in the years to follow, two words come to mind. Hard and Hopeful.

It is HARD for me to read. It's hard because it reminds me of that day. Of the phone call from Dan and the scene at the Rozga home. Of the blur and pain and numbness of that week, that month, that summer. As David's youth pastor, I was shattered. As youth pastor to the dozens of broken kids and families left with only questions, I had to push through. It is hard to read because being reminded of their pain, brings back my own. Pain of loss. Pain of rejection. Pain of abandonment. Pain of life.

Yet, it is HOPEFUL.

God's faithfulness.

His nearness.

His provision.

Right in the middle of the mess, the hurt, the impossible. . .there is so much HOPE.

If God can redeem even this; then there is nowhere and no situation where he cannot bring beauty from ashes. Even mine. Even yours.

As you read the pages of this book, you will be confronted with your own brokenness, your own hurt and your own pain. I was. Not only did it stir up the grief of losing David, it stirred-up the heartache of my parents' divorce, of miscarriage, of the tragic death of my brother-in-law and the too-soon loss of my father-in-law. It stirred the pain of seeing loved ones struggle with deep depression and anxiety. . .of seeing people I love take their own lives.

Left on my own, I have default reactions to such grief.

I IGNORE IT. Just pretend it isn't there. Pretend it didn't happen. Pretend it doesn't affect me. When in reality, I am wounded at the core. And because I choose to ignore it, I develop all sorts of unhealthy habits and actions to mask my grief.

OR I GIVE IN TO IT. The grief becomes so overwhelming and all-encompassing that I let it take over; my emotions, my actions, how I react to people, how I work.

Ignore it? Give in to it? Either way, grief holds me captive.

BUT, God's Word (and this book) remind me that there IS another way.

A BETTER way.

There is a way to WALK THROUGH IT.

I've read that one of the unique things about bison is that they are made to walk through storms. If you picture them, they've got lots of fur covering them. When they sense a storm coming, they gather together and walk straight into it. They charge through the storm to the other side of it. Because all storms pass. Cows, on the other hand, try to escape by running away from the storm. And instead of escaping, they find themselves running right along with it. Stuck in the intensity. Unable to get away. When we face our storm head-on and walk straight into it, like the buffalo, we find ourselves closer to the other side; closer to peace and calm.

I am learning that the same is true with grief and hardship.

Don't ignore it. Don't pretend it away. Don't linger in it.

Gird yourself up in the strength of the Lord.

Gather your people around you.

And walk straight toward it.

Limp through the storm.

Crawl through the storm.

Just keep moving.

You can't shortcut recovery, so choose to walk through the storm.

And know that hope and healing is ultimately only found in Jesus.

I know it's a church answer.

For you, it may be a hollow answer.

But it's true. Trying to find hope or healing anywhere else is like trying to catch the wind.

Hope and healing is found in the PRESENCE of Jesus. He is near. Scripture tells us that he is not far. He's not somewhere else. Rather, he is near. He's as close as your next breath. And for the believer, he's not just near you; he's in you. At the very center and core of who you are.

Hope and healing are found in the PROMISE of Jesus. God keeps his word. He fulfills his promises. And he promises so many things to his children:

All things work together.

Your story isn't over.

Victory is yours in him.

Goodness will follow you.

Blessings and favor are yours.

His promises will carry you through all situations and all circumstances.

Hope and healing are found in the POWER of Jesus.

The cross is empty. The grave is empty. Jesus has power over sin.

Power over brokenness.

Over grief.

Over desperation.

Jesus HAS power. And that power is IN you.

His PRESENCE, his PROMISE, and his Power are made known by his Word.

By his Spirit. And by his people.

These truths, along with so many practical tools for living through loss, are explained in Raw Survival. This book delivers the ANCHOR and LIFE VEST your grieving heart needs.

Are pain and grief causing you to feel like you are drifting aimlessly, with nothing to tether you to life, to hope, or to healing? Let the words in this book be your ANCHOR. An anchor to the truth of God's Word. An anchor to the promises of God's Word.

Are pain and grief causing you to feel like you're drowning in deep waves? Are the hurt, the emotion, the grief just too overwhelming? Allow the following pages to throw you a LIFE VEST. To remind you that there is more life to live. There is healing to be found. There is a path to restoration. And a vision for life that is bigger than your immediate suffering.

Do you need hope?

Real. Tangible. Earthy. Messy. Hope?

Take time to read this book. More than that, work through it.

Read it slow.

When you get to the hard parts, take time to sit in it.

Ask people to surround you with prayer as you read it.

Do the work. Answer the questions. Especially the ones you don't want to answer.

As you read . . . as you work . . . as you pray . . . know that hope is on the way.

Darkness is but a fleeting shadow.

And light is on the horizon.

Acknowledgments

To my husband Mike. I could never have imagined when we said our vows so long ago that we would experience the profound loss of our son. Living without him will continue to challenge us until we meet him again face to face. I'm so thankful for your love and support through it all. Thank you for consoling me when I was down, encouraging me when I doubted myself, praying for me always and believing in me. I love you.

To my son Daniel. I can't imagine what it was like to lose your brother at such a young age. You could have chosen many unhealthy alternatives to cope with grief, but you chose to cling to Jesus. God gave you wisdom and you took it to heart. You'll never know how much you've ministered to me during this journey. David is proud of you, Daniel, and I know he would love Savannah.

To our parents and extended family. Spending time with family was so important to David and he loved you all so much. I will always be thankful for the precious memories you shared with him. Thank you, Mom, for encouraging me when I questioned whether or not I was strong enough to relive and share the most intimate parts of my broken heart. You said, "David's worth it Jan. He would want you to help others and I know he's saying, 'Go Mom go.'" Thank you so much for that.

To Kristi Dusenbery, my editor and one of my very best friends. Through this whole process you've given me an abundance of emotional encouragement so that I could keep my head above water. You reminded me of the 'why' when I doubted myself; to honor David's life and record God's faithfulness. The following pages wouldn't be possible without your love, wisdom and support. God knew I needed you and we make a good team. You are truly a gifted editor and a forever friend.

To our dear friends. Lori and Jerry Lehr, thank you for loving David as one of your own and grieving alongside us. DeDe Rankin, thank you for feeding me saltines when I was too weak to eat. And yes, for sitting beside me and watching, to ensure I actually ate them! Martha Miller, your example of survival after losing your Sam inspired me so many years before I lost David. I love you friend. We are forever connected.

To Dawn Johnson, thank you for all of your "hello friend" texts, and encouraging me to earn "'checkmarks" as I faced life's challenges without David. Thank you for capturing the joy of David's high school graduation celebration and for taking our last family pictures with him. I will cherish them forever.

To Pastor Jon Duey. I thank God for you, Jon. You've made an eternal impact on David and Daniel as their youth pastor and friend. I've not met anyone as passionate about young people as you. David loved laughing with you, worshiping with you, and razzing you about the Bears, and he would be so proud that you authored the Foreword of this book.

To Dave Turnball and Adam Timmerman. Dave, thank you for introducing me to Adam, Green Bay Packer alum. And Adam, thank you for providing input on the manuscript and for your encouragement. David would be thrilled that his Mom is hobnobbing with a Green Bay Packer and that most of our correspondence ended with "Go Pack Go!" The Green Bay Packer fanatics in the Rozga family are over the moon.

To so many others. Carrie Leimbach, you will always have a special place in my heart! Jake and Holly, Sean and Shelby, Anne Woodward, and Cheryl–thank you for letting me share. Joel, your counsel continues to be a godsend. Our GriefShare family, your support and honesty and shared-struggle continue to get us through. The staff of Overton Funeral Home, the emotional tenderness you offered during our darkest days meant more than you can imagine. An amazing group of Beta Readers, your support and meaningful feedback greatly enhanced the content of this book. Mike Shields and Ryan Huguley, thank you for your spiritual wisdom and professional guidance. To the *Wild Bible Study Girls of Warren County, Iowa*–we're not really wild but I love you and I'm forever blessed by your love and prayers.

Our mission to protect others from the devastating effects of synthetic drugs introduced us to so many government officials and passionate citizens who care deeply about the wellbeing of others. After David died, Governor Culver initiated a formal public campaign to educate Iowans of the dangers of K2 and other synthetic drugs. Governor Branstad's support led to the signing of Iowa's first synthetic drug bill into law. U.S. Senator Charles Grassley led a bipartisan effort, with the support of Senator Dianne Feinstein, to share David's story and to introduce and see signed into law the David Mitchell Rozga Act, which bans the chemicals used to make K2. Additional thanks goes to Judge Mark Schlenker, Brian and Susie Sher, Chief Steve Bonnett, Kent Sorenson, Gary Kendell, Mark Schouten, Dale Woolery, Peter Komendowski, Linda Kalin, Dr. Edward Bottei, Mark Ryan, Dr. Anthony Scalzo, and Veronica and Devin Eckhardt.

Finally, and perhaps most of all, to every parent who has buried a child. To every person grieving a precious friend or family member. To every family who has lost a child to K2 or equally dangerous substances. May God bless you and keep you as you walk this long and difficult road. You are not alone. There is hope for healing. And even though I don't know you, I will always pray for you.

PART I

SURVIVING THE FIRST DAYS

Chapter 1

Oh God!

It was springtime. The snow was finally gone and green shoots were just beginning to peek up through the cold ground. High school seniors could taste the freedom of graduation and were anxious for the future. Parents of high school seniors were planning the graduation parties they'd been anticipating for years: the right decorations, the right photos, invitations, senior pictures, cake, and (of course) getting the house just right. Such an exciting time.

It was no different for us. Our oldest son, David, was a senior and we were scrambling. *March 2010. Already? Where did the years go? He's graduating in three months?* Not gonna lie, I was emotional. So, there I was, at the party store, list in hand. The mission was to find purple and gold plates, napkins, tablecloths, decorations, cutlery . . . you name it. *Focus. Okay, everything purple and gold. Should all of the napkins be purple? All gold? A mix of the two? Why is this such a difficult decision? It's napkins!* The ugly lip–tremors came first, and then the tears. I was overwhelmed. Not with napkins, but with the idea of buying stuff for his going–away party. Yes, I know it was a celebration, but it was also "goodbye."

A few people stared at me from the card aisle but I didn't care. I knew I'd still have my husband Mike and our younger son Daniel at home, but the anticipation of missing David was too much. He was already enrolled at the University of Northern Iowa, where he would study business and room with one of his best friends from high school. They had big plans for the dorm room and they were so excited. We were excited for them too . . . and so proud. Still, I couldn't imagine not seeing him every morning. Not going to band concerts or baseball games. Not having to yell at him for having laundry all over his bedroom or leaving the kitchen a mess. Not eating together every night. Maybe it was selfish, but it was real. I would miss all of it.

Enough with the pity party, Jan. It's time to buy napkins. I took a deep breath, brushed away the tears, and finished shopping. But who was I kidding? If the cashier asked anything about the party, I was toast.

The party was awesome. My parents came and my brother drove in from Colorado with my niece, Anna. Mike's whole family came from Wisconsin. Dozens of friends showed up. And David greeted each one with a hug and smile. The camera captured it all.

David with grandpa and grandma Rozga.

David with grandpa and grandma Mitchell.

I'm pretty sure I set a personal record that day by not peeing for several hours. Seriously. I know, TMI, but I didn't want to miss anything. . .. Not one single photo . . . not one. *Someday, he'll appreciate my cat–like paparazzi skills. You're welcome.* I took hundreds of photos. So many special memories for him to remember. Special memories for us to remember, too.

A treasured father-son moment.

One detail David cared about most was the food. It had to be BBQ and it had to be catered by a local guy who made the best. So we hired him, along with a local gal who made the best sugar cookies, each frosted in purple or gold . . . of course. No cake, which was weird to me, but we wanted it to be all about what David wanted that day. He chose bottled water with flavored add–in packets, cups of purple and gold M&Ms at each table, and a soft–serve ice cream machine . . . which was a huge hit.

As for the decorations—or more specifically, *thee* decoration—it was standing proudly between the tables of food and the tables of all–things–David. It was a life–size cardboard cutout of Green Bay Packer legend Brett Favre. That's right. Too much? Oh yeah! Most guests just smiled and shook their heads because they knew David was an extreme Packer fan. By the end of the party, there were no unwanted drawings on Brett's face, so I considered it a win. Let's just say, in addition to being the official photographer that afternoon, I also kept a close eye out for any disgruntled Vikings or Bears fans. It was all part of the job that day.

David with his favorite guest of the day.

David's favorite gift arrived in the back of a pickup truck, delivered by his friends. A refrigerator. No, not a dorm fridge for college, as one might expect. This was a full–sized (rescued from somebody's curb) refrigerator. Why? I have absolutely no idea, but David laughed so hard. His friends laughed so hard. And everyone at the party roared. We never did find out why they did it, but I'm pretty sure it had everything to do with the priceless look on David's face when it was delivered. Mike, on the other hand, stood there wondering how the heck we were going to get rid of it. I just kept snapping pictures. It was awesome!

As the last guest drove away, David told me that his mouth hurt from smiling. So did mine. It was a cloud–nine sort of day, and it left us with so much joy. We were incredibly proud of the young man he had become and excited to see him chase his dreams. But the festivities weren't over. David thought all the pictures had been taken, but wait, there's more!

Knowing our extended families would be in town for the weekend, I made plans for family pictures to be taken after graduation. The only photographer I trusted for the job was my friend Dawn. She has twin boys who went to school and played sports with our younger son, Daniel, and her photos always amaze me. Not only does she take great photos; she also has what it takes to keep our families in check, which is no easy task. I warned everyone in advance about getting photos taken and made it clear that there would be no eye–rolls allowed; before, during, or after the shoot, thank you very much.

It turned out to be a gorgeous day. Everyone was there and they were all good sports about it. Dawn took hundreds of pictures: this family, that family, the whole family, posed, candid, and action shots. The results were incredible and timeless reminders of a perfect weekend. We had no idea they would be our last family portraits ever taken . . . with David.

Our last family photo with David.

The following Saturday, he left home early to drive to St. Louis, where he would join his girlfriend, Carrie. Her family had lived in St. Louis prior to moving to Iowa and most of her friends and extended family still lived there, so that is where they would have her graduation party. It was a big deal for David to make such a long drive alone, but we knew it was a great chance for him to get to know her family and for them to get to know him. After all, it was a week of cutting apron strings, right? He made it there without a problem, and he and Carrie returned home the next afternoon. Again, I was proud (and relieved) to have him back safely. . .and without a speeding ticket! After taking Carrie home and visiting with her mom about mowing their lawn for the summer, he came home briefly before heading out to spend some time with friends. He'd be home later so I could catch up with him and hear all about it.

I was enjoying the afternoon sun on the deck, talking on the phone with a friend, when I heard him pulling up the driveway, so I headed inside to let him know that I was finishing a call and then we could talk about his weekend. *But, where was he?* I looked out the front window and saw his red truck parked in the usual spot. But he was nowhere to be seen, so I stepped outside to look. He was walking near the prairie grass that borders our yard so I held the phone to my chest, to ask what he was doing. He waved his finger in a circular motion, his lips saying, "Just walking around." I didn't think much of that either, so I went back to the deck to finish my phone conversation.

Several minutes later, I heard a pop. "I'm sure it was just a firecracker," I told my friend. I mean, he just got back from the fireworks capital of the Midwest and it wouldn't be uncommon for him to light fireworks off in the yard, just to annoy me. *Of course it was a firecracker.* I shrugged it off.

But as quickly as I dismissed it, I was flooded with a sinking, sick feeling. *Was it a firecracker?* I ran to look where he'd been walking. He wasn't there. I went inside. I didn't see him. Room by room, I yelled his name. Nothing. *He should hear me.* And then I smelled it. . .smoke. I continued to call his name, but now I was frantic. *Where are you, David!* The sinking feeling was gone and horror made it hard to breathe.

I opened the basement door. Gunpowder. *What? Gunpowder?* The smell got stronger as I walked down the stairs. And then I saw him. And I saw what happened. *Oh God!* He had taken his life. I didn't have to take another step to know that he was gone. He was gone and there was nothing I could do. I was hysterical as I stumbled up the stairs, the phone still in my hand. *Oh God! Oh my God!*

What I experienced in that room was horrific. And the crushing truth of it will stay between God, David, and me. I only shared it with two people, Mike and my counselor. . .and it took a long time to get there.

Everything about me was overwhelmed. Somehow, I got to the deck and yelled for our neighbor, hoping he was working outside and would hear my cries. He wasn't. I dialed 911. My fingers felt like lead. I could barely press the buttons. It was unreal. I told them to hurry . . . even though I knew it was too late.

I needed to call Mike. He and Daniel were fishing at a friend's farm pond, 45 minutes away. *How do I tell my husband that his son is dead? How do I tell him he took his own life? How does he tell Daniel that his brother is gone? How?* There are no words for that. I knew what I saw was real, but how could any of this be real? I can't imagine what the ride home was like for them.

Sirens howled in the distance, getting louder and louder. I couldn't move. Ambulance and police lights flew over the crest of the hill, screaming down the long road that leads to our driveway. I still couldn't move. It was like I was being pulled under by ocean waves, fighting to breathe.

When Mike and Daniel arrived, we just held each other and cried, in absolute disbelief. What else could we do? Nothing. I don't even think we spoke. There was nothing to say. The paramedics finished what they had to do. The police asked the questions they had to ask. And then we stood in the yard and watched the ambulance drive away. No sirens this time. No speeding. They just drove off . . . in silence. With my son. He was gone.

RAW JOURNAL ENTRY

October 2010–Five months after burying our son

It is a cold, blustery day and I finally feel like I can jot down some of the feelings I am experiencing. I have kept a journal off and on since I was in elementary school. When in the writing mode I found it to be a great release. A place to put my heart on paper. My hands shake as I write this now. After David died, I thought about writing down my thoughts, but I just couldn't bring myself to verbalize them, let alone write them. I wasn't capable of either it seemed. I couldn't even pray for the longest time. All I could say was, "Oh God," with the heaviest heart I have ever felt, and somehow that was the best prayer I could pray to the Lord. Just "Oh God." It spoke a thousand words from my heart to his.

My prayers continued to be short words. Nothing more, because that's all I was capable of. I realized after a few weeks of this that even though my prayers were merely a few short words at a time, the Lord heard every last syllable uttered. And then one of God's promises hit me. . .Romans 8:26–27, "In the same way, the Spirit helps us in our weakness. We do not know what we ought to pray for, but the Spirit himself intercedes for us with groans that words cannot express. And he who searches our hearts, knows the mind of the Spirit, because the Spirit intercedes for the saints in accordance with God's will."

I had heard this scripture a million times during sermons at our church or in Bible studies, but I had never personally owned this myself because I had never experienced this before. I am usually never at a loss for words. Why should my prayer life be any different? But at this time in my life, losing my precious David, I could better understand the profound truth of this scripture, and believe me, I was banking on it. It was the only glimmer of hope I had.

FIRST AID FOR YOUR GRIEVING HEART

Healing Prayer

Dear Jesus, I don't understand why my loved one is gone or how to move forward. You are the one who knows the beginning and the end (Isaiah 46:10) and you also know the pain of my heart (Psalm 56:8). I need your help, Lord, hold me in your arms and bring peace to my frightened heart.

Healing Truth

Go to page 157 to access scripture and daily prayers to help you crush the lie that *you can't pray*, and to unleash the healing power of God's truth.

Healing Words

Embrace your grieving heart today by writing the raw details of your own story. It will pierce your heart to relive it, but it will also bring relief as you express your raw emotion in writing. What do you remember about the day your loved one died? What about the days or weeks just before and after?

Chapter 2

Our David

On October 4, 1991, Mike and I were overjoyed when the doctor put our firstborn son in our arms and we looked at his sweet face for the first time. What a miracle! The next eighteen years held too many memories to count . . . good ones, funny ones, and ones we'd rather forget. There were all of the *firsts*: the first tooth, first haircut, first bike without training wheels, first trip to the ER, first day of school, and the first date. There were vacations and injuries and baseball games. There were Christmas mornings, birthday parties, and Easter egg hunts.

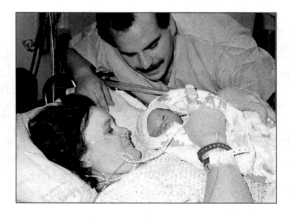

David's birth–October 4, 1991.

Mostly, there was laughter. David was born with an amazing sense of humor and he filled our home with joy. At a very young age, he picked up on the sarcasm and jokes in Disney movies (you know, the ones that are thrown in to entertain the parents) which led to some interesting debriefing. And he came by it honestly, learning the value of fun and laughter from his grandparents. My parents live about 45 minutes south of us, so the boys often had sleepovers there, and Grandpa Mitchell loved to get them laughing by telling them stories about *his buddies*, Lewis and Clark. David especially loved the one about Lewis breaking a tooth on one of grandma's chocolate chip cookies. I'm not sure they even knew about Lewis and Clark, but they knew Grandpa was pulling their legs. When visiting Grandpa and Grandma Rozga in Wisconsin, the boys spent hours playing cards with them and laughing at stories about their dad as a kid.

Best little Packer fans on the planet.

Then there is Mike, perhaps the truest professor of sarcasm and David's greatest teacher. When David was eight, he and Daniel went to the neighbor's house to shoot hoops, and David came home a Bears fan. What?! Apparently, our neighbor and die–hard Bears fan used the time to convince the boys that they should abandon the Packers, so David came home and boldly announced his change–of–heart to Mike. Without missing a beat, Mike said, "You can be a Bears fan if you want but you are not sleeping in my house." The boys laughed it off but after baths that night, when it was time for bed, Mike told David to grab his blanket and head to the deck.

David smiled, expecting his dad to laugh. He didn't. As his eight-year-old-smile turned to fear, Mom stepped-in. "Mike! Tell David you're kidding. David, Dad's joking."

"No, I'm not," Mike said with a serious face, "In this house, we're Packer fans. Grab your sleeping bag. And it's cold out, so you might want an extra blanket." At this point, Daniel started crying and begged his dad not to make David sleep outside. He loved his big brother and hated seeing him sad, so he tried desperately to save him from the deck. After waiting longer than I would have liked, Mike smiled and told the boys he was kidding. Geez! Of course, this became a favorite memory as the years went on, and the boys loved telling the story to our friends during their teenage years.

David and Daniel at a Packer game.

David especially loved teasing me . . . probably because he knew I loved it too. One of his routine pranks was sneaking up behind me in the kitchen and flicking the flab on the back of my arms. Then he'd run away like lightning before I could catch him. He'd stand on the opposite side of the island, taunting me. I moved left, he moved right . . . a fun, mother-son *dance* that still makes me smile. All the while, he laughed as I told him that I didn't need to be reminded of my arm fat, thank you very much! As time went on, I began greeting him in the kitchen with a Jackie Chan pose. Hiyah!

One afternoon, as I shopped for groceries, my phone started ringing from my purse, only it wasn't the usual ringtone. David had changed it to a song from some screamo band, of all things, and then waited until he knew I'd be in public to call me. Everyone around me was staring as I frantically searched my purse, my oversized purse! It took a while, and in the meantime, the phone kept getting louder and louder. "David!" was all I said when I finally answered and, of course, he was laughing wildly. He brought so much joy to ordinary days.

A few months before David's high school graduation, Mike and I decided to surprise him with a Chevy Colorado, so he would have a safer and more dependable vehicle for college. As we left the dealership, the salesman handed Mike the keys to the shiny red truck, and Mike handed them to me so I could follow him home. I was so excited that I could hardly stand it! It would be awesome to see David's face and I couldn't stop smiling. All the way home, Mike kept passing me in the left lane and then slowing down again. The apple didn't fall far from the tree. Suddenly, my phone rang, "Hey, who's the babe in the red truck?" Oh wow. *I'm a mom, not a babe!* It made me blush and I knew David and Daniel would be mortified if they knew. I'll keep this under my hat!

We strategically parked the bright red truck in plain sight. There was no way he could miss it. Knowing he would be home soon, I sat anxiously at the kitchen window, watching the road in the distance. It was a used truck, but so nice and I knew David would go crazy for it. I could hardly wait to see the look on his face. Finally, I saw his green Grand Am accelerating down the hill at a pretty good pace. He fishtailed Vince into the driveway, jumped out, and walked around the truck several times. He was screaming with joy as he picked me up and gave me the biggest bearhug ever. He was ecstatic. So was I.

There was so much to do leading up to David's open house and so little time to get it done. I remember standing in the garden, a few weeks before graduation, trying to get everything planted before the party when I saw him getting ready to jump in his truck. "David!" I hollered, "You need to help me with the mulch today!"

"Can't Mom; I'm busy with graduation stuff."

"Well, it needs to be done for. . ." He was halfway down the driveway before I could finish, ". . . your graduation party!" I was so irritated, but I chalked it up to senioritis and gave him a pass.

Eventually, we got it done but not in the timeframe I planned, which meant Daniel had to help too. He was not thrilled, "Why do *I* have to help? It's not *my* graduation party." Ah, teenagers. Daniel's only consolation was that payback would come in three years, when David would have to help get ready for *his* graduation.

David was a gifted musician, who filled our hearts and home with music. *Loud* music. I miss the sound of it so much. He had great admiration for his high school band directors, a dynamic duo who had their work cut out for them with David. Let's just say, as a young freshman, he didn't take band as seriously as he should have. When you belt out a *wah-wah-waaaaah* on your baritone after one of the directors finishes a serious talk with the band, it may not end well.

David playing with the Pride of Indianola Marching Band.

Dr. D. and Mr. Crandell were incredibly patient and spent many hours mentoring David to become a better musician, both in and out of the classroom. He grew more comfortable in it and in the spring of his freshman year, he received the Most Improved Musician award. Over the next three years, he received several more awards, including Outstanding Soloist and the Semper Fidelis Award for Musical Excellence, given to him just weeks before he died. In addition to these awards, he and five of his classmates were selected to play alongside the United States All American Marine Brass Band during the spring of his senior year. It was such a great experience.

None of this is shared with intent to brag about his accomplishments, only to share that David was passionate about music and worked hard to grow as a musician. In the months following his death, Mr. Crandell and Dr. D. placed a "road sign" outside of their office where David spent countless hours throughout his four years of high school, with the words *Rozga Plaza*. He would have loved it.

Outside of school, David loved worshiping Jesus with our church's youth worship band, led by our youth pastor, Jon. In spite of Jon being a Bears fan, he and David were very close and spent a lot of time playing music together, serving on mission trips, and taking shots at each other's teams. During his senior year, David had the opportunity to play for a local baseball league but turned it down since games would be played on Sunday, at the same time he played guitar in the worship band for church. He loved playing baseball, so this was a decision that really deepened his faith.

In addition to music, David was an avid hunter and loved spending time at our farm with Mike, Daniel, and his friends. He was rarely still, but when he was, it was to sit in his deer stand. It was where he went for tranquility, to hear no other sound but the rustling of leaves. He truly loved spending time in nature and often talked about the moments he enjoyed there, alone with God. One of the first times Mike and I drove around the farm after David died, we stopped so I could sit in his tree stand. Did I mention I don't like heights? But I wanted to sit where David sat. I wanted to see what he saw and to feel the same tranquility he told us about. At that moment, I had an overwhelming sense that David was sharing it with me. It was so meaningful . . . and very emotional.

David also loved hanging out with his little brother, or maybe I should say *annoying* his little brother. Like any siblings, they spent a lot of time bothering each other, but they also had an amazing bond. Some of their best times were spent watching Packer games together, both at home and at Lambeau Field. In case you haven't picked up on it yet, our family is a bit obsessed. In fact, a few months before he died, David demonstrated his obsession by getting a "4" tattooed on his back shoulder, the number Brett Favre had been wearing since before David was born. After Mike reminded him how risky it is to publicly glorify a human being, David mustered up a sarcastic little smirk and calmly replied, "I may have a four tattooed on my shoulder, but I have Jesus tattooed on my heart." Oh, David.

David with Packer Hall of Famer, Fuzzy Thurston.

Like any other kid graduating from high school, life stressed David out at times and he disagreed with his family now and then. The future wasn't always clear and life wasn't always perfect, but he continued to have dreams and make plans. He continued to enjoy life. There were projects and events that he was excited about, and he was making plans for college life. But one decision changed everything. Ended everything. And we were left behind to pick up the pieces.

His energy and passion for life were what made his death so inconceivable, and what motivates me every day to tell his story. Just one week before his death, David walked across the stage to receive his high school diploma; a symbol of great accomplishment, great memories, and great hope for the future. He was an excellent student with a great sense of humor. Most of all, he was loved as a son, brother, grandson and friend.

It may be easy for people to read about David's death in the newspaper or on the internet and make assumptions about his life and about our family, but what happened the evening of June 6, 2010, doesn't even come close to defining who he was. A more accurate snapshot of his life was the constant stream of people standing in line during his six-hour visitation to pay their respects and share stories that celebrated his life.

I'm quite sure that our experience, raising David and Daniel, wasn't extraordinary. We had joys and difficulties, like any other parent. When our babies were born, we prayed for God to watch over them, to help us raise them responsibly, and to show them how much they are loved by God. We are just ordinary people who love our kids and want the best for them. As they grew, we never could have imagined the pain that was ahead–the searing, agonizing loss. And I'm so thankful. I'm so thankful for the memories we made as a family. I'm so blessed to be David and Daniel's mom. I'm so grateful for all of it; every late-night snuggle, every Saturday afternoon baseball game, every (loud) jam session, every birthday, and every laugh we shared.

Our last Wisconsin vacation with David.

The memories I have of David are my most precious possession. They are all I have of him now, and they need to last a lifetime because my identity as his mom is forever changed. In the midst of tragedy, I found myself focused only on what was lost. I was consumed by it. Naturally, grief is ugly, and there will never be a day that I don't miss my son. In fact, not so long ago, I wondered if I would ever be able to really smile again, let alone laugh. If I would ever be able to look at the future with genuine hope in my heart, and find contentment within the gaping hole left in my world. My life will never be the same, but thanks to the living, breathing power of God's Word, I continue to find healing . . . and even hope. I still feel sad. I still cry. But by the power and love of Jesus, I am able to get out of bed every morning, put one foot in front of the other, and walk into the future . . . even though I have no idea what it holds.

RAW JOURNAL ENTRY

October 2010–Five months after burying our son

I find myself in the darkest, most isolated places and asking so many unanswerable questions; to lose a child? In such a horrific way? How will we survive this as a family? Will our son Daniel be okay? What about my marriage? Some marriages don't survive the loss of a child. . .How can I accept this? How can I suddenly stop mothering David? Just like that and poof, I'm not his Mom anymore? He can't be gone. God, where are you?

FIRST AID FOR YOUR GRIEVING HEART

Healing Prayer

Dear Jesus, I'm so thankful for the time I had with my loved one, but my heart aches for more. Help me today, right now, to find comfort in memories and in knowing that clinging to you and your promises is my only hope for survival.

Healing Truth

Visit the following pages to unleash God's healing power over the lies that threaten to defeat you: *My identity is gone* (p. 160); *I will never feel content again*(p. 175); *I'm forgetting my loved one* (p. 230).

Healing Words

Embrace your grieving heart today by writing about the dreams you had for your loved one . . . dreams that were shattered when your loved one died. Over time, as you confront the hardest parts of your loss, you will find relief. Trust me. What did you love most about your loved one? Were there difficult times . . . or not enough time? What dreams are the hardest to let go of?

Chapter 3

Shaking from the Inside Out

Soon after the ambulance took David away, a sea of cars flooded our driveway and spilled into the street. Adults, kids, neighbors, and friends filled the yard in huddles of raw emotions, sharing despair and disbelief. All I could do was shake my head into the shoulders of those who hugged me. There were no words. Or maybe there were too many to choose from. Just days earlier, David was hugging and laughing with these same people, in this same spot, celebrating his graduation. *This is not right!*

As the sun started to set, I dreaded night. Still, darkness came and nobody was leaving. Someone suggested going to the church, so the people who had gathered together on our lawn soon formed a large circle in our youth room. Mike, Daniel, and I listened as parents and students shared special memories of David. While their words were appreciated, there were none as loud as the ones in my head. *This is not real. This can't be happening. He can't be gone.* Nothing made sense. Nothing would ever be the same. And I had no idea what to do about it. I never felt more helpless in all my life.

Although the sharing couldn't last all night, I wished it could've. *We have nowhere to go. I will never sleep.* We couldn't go home because people were there to "take care of things." Those words still make me want to throw-up. Thankfully, our neighbors and sweet friends, Jerry and Lori, insisted we stay with them. We were so fragile and their home became a temporary cocoon for us. They fed us, prayed for us, and loved us through what would be the most devastating days of our lives. They loved David too, and were grasping for ways to help us endure those early hours of grief, even as they dealt with their own. *How would we ever survive this without the kindness and generosity of others?*

We were exhausted in every way. Daniel took the futon and was out as soon as his head hit the pillow. Mike and I took the bed and hoped that our cries wouldn't wake him up. We stared at the ceiling most of the night, holding each other as we endured the waves of tremors and tears that came and went. Disbelief was our haunting companion. Mike prayed that God would get us through the night and then get us through the unknown that loomed in the distance. I sat up every time Daniel stirred, wanting to be there for him. It was the longest night of my life.

In the upstairs bedroom, David's girlfriend Carrie and several girls who graduated together the week before bunked with Jerry and Lori's youngest daughter, Rachel, who had grown up with our boys. On top of everything else, I was so worried about Carrie. I was worried about everyone in the house, really. *Are they all staring at the ceiling, too? Are they crying and shaking, too?* Thankfully, when I snuck up and peeked in their room, all was quiet and they appeared to be sleeping. Rachel is a natural caregiver so I knew Carrie was in good hands, but I still worried.

Carrie and David's senior prom, just weeks earlier.

When morning finally arrived, people began coming to the door with food, flowers, and supplies that would be needed for other visitors; tissues, paper plates, and even toilet paper. They also brought their tears. Most whizzed in and out, not knowing what to say. What *could* they say? Peg, my best friend from college, drove three hours every day for three days, just to sit with me.

Though an assembly line of food poured through the door, I couldn't eat. My friend, DeDe, practically spoon-fed me. I couldn't even drink coffee. Between the day David died and the day of his funeral, I lost a noticeable amount of weight and the sensation of being physically sick was relentless. *Will I ever be able to eat again? Do I even care?*

The days with our neighbors are a bit of a blur. Daniel spent some time downstairs with his friends, playing video games to escape reality, at least for a little while. Mike and I spent our time in Lori and Jerry's sunroom. It's where visitors came to offer support and where we planned David's funeral with our pastor. One of my most vivid memories is how much I dreaded the night. But it came anyway. And it always brought anxiety and sleeplessness.

The only times we ventured out were when we had to meet with the funeral director. Jeff drove us around the winding roads of the cemetery in a big white van, to pick out David's plot. Eventually, we decided on a place near a tree line, thinking deer might graze there. David would like that. Talk about surreal. Three days ago, life was . . . well, life. We were anxious to pick out his bedding and everything else he would need away at college. And now we were picking out a cemetery plot. Jeff gently took us through all the details and decisions. It was gut-wrenching. When it came time to discuss the casket, I had to speak up. I didn't want David in a casket. And I didn't want to explain why. I knew the casket would be closed, but it still made me sick to think about what would lie inside. But I didn't want him cremated either. Mike kept asking me questions. I had no answers. *I don't want to be doing any of this! I can't do it.* The horrific reality of losing our son was becoming more and more real.

When we returned to the neighbor's house, I cringed at the sight of the van still parked next door in our driveway. AFTERMATH was printed in bold letters across its side, shouting to every passerby that the experts were there to clean things up. In hindsight, I realize that they performed a very necessary service at a difficult time. Still, in the grief of those first days, I hated that van! And hated that name! It was the reason we couldn't go home. And even though I dreaded going home, their presence irritated me. It was a mocking reminder that David took his life . . . in our basement . . . when I was *home.*

It prompted the questions all over again. *How can this be happening? David didn't intentionally take his life. Did he? I know my son! It doesn't add up. He knew I would be the one to find him. He wouldn't do that to me. Would he? The stack of half-written thank you notes, ready to be mailed, still lay on the table. Would a person intent on taking his life start writing thank you notes? Never. And why would he have purchased parts the day before, to make a potato gun with his dad? Why would he spend the energy to go to Missouri and meet Carrie's family if he didn't care about living? Or am I fooling myself? Am I in denial?* There were so many unanswered questions, haunting questions, and they were just the tip of the iceberg.

Mike knew I felt sick about going home and he tried to help me focus on the many good memories our family experienced inside those walls. Easier said than done. Though we never discussed it, I suppose he was reminding himself of the same thing. Two days after David died, we finalized plans at the funeral home and headed back toward our neighbor's house.

But that's not where we were going. Just like ripping off a bandaid, Mike told me it was time to return home. *Oh, God. Please NO.* He hadn't told me earlier because he wanted to minimize the amount of time I had to dwell on it. He explained that while we were away our friends had cleaned the house, finished the laundry, and filled our kitchen with food. My heart raced. *How am I going to do this? How can I possibly think of the good times, when just two days ago I found my son? Oh God, help me.*

I learned very quickly that all I could do was pray three simple words: *God, help me.* There wasn't anything else. When I felt paralyzed by fear. . .*God, help me.* When I feared losing Mike and Daniel. . .*God, help me.* When I couldn't stop thinking about the moment David died. . .*God, help me.* When I was angry and doubted everything that I thought I knew about God. . .*Please help me.* When the future terrified me and my heart tore at the thought of life without David. . .*God, help me!* I was completely powerless over every single emotion . . . every single moment. All I could do was cry out to God, and beg him to help me. There was nothing else I could do. Nothing.

I feel like I should pause here, for just a minute. Those were dark days; the darkest of my life. And this part of our story is not uplifting. It's raw and probably hard to read. I get that, but thanks to Jesus it is not the end of our journey or the end of joy. For many days, months, and even to this day, there is heartache. I will grieve the loss of my son as long as I live, but the overwhelming darkness no longer holds me captive like it once did. I am able to function–and even thrive–because I choose to cling to the truth of God's Word. His promises bring healing. They give hope. If you or someone you love is experiencing the darkest days of loss, I pray that you find the strength to keep reading and that the story of my raw survival helps you to discover your own version of God's peace that passes understanding. Even when it doesn't feel like it, you are precious to Jesus. You are loved and you will get through this. Hang in there with me.

Being back in that house, just days after losing David, was more dif-ficult than I even imagined, and more difficult than I showed. It wasn't home anymore. I desperately wanted to leave, but there was no place I could go to escape my emotions or my fear. It was a bit like the dark rain clouds that hover over cartoon characters, following them wherever they go. The doctor prescribed Xanax for times when my anxiety was out of control, like any time I thought about the basement. I couldn't even look at that door, let alone go down there. I took the Xanax only when I was absolutely over the top because I didn't want to get into the habit of popping them like candy, then have to deal with addiction issues on top of everything else. I had to be realistic, but cautious.

I couldn't look at the family pictures on our bookcase or go upstairs to David's room. I couldn't read anything. I didn't even enjoy hearing the birds chirping outside anymore. Absolutely nothing was normal or right. *AFTERMATH.* That's what we were left with. Just like the words printed on that van, this was the reality we were left to claw our way through in order to survive. But how, when there were so many unanswered questions?

RAW JOURNAL ENTRY

I continue to rack my brain. I put on my Mom investigator hat, and what I discovered is a long list of things David cared deeply about. Here's what I know; He was living in the moment and planning for the future. Just hours before his death, David met with Carrie's mom about taking care of her lawn and doing some household chores for her while she was away from home. He was planning for college and excited to attend a concert in Tennessee that summer with friends. He wrote out a detailed itinerary for the trip so we'd know his schedule. I still have that piece of paper. If that weren't enough, he left a message for my parents on their answering machine about getting together for dinner. Why? Why would he bother putting any effort into anything if he didn't care about life?

Two days before David's funeral, a few of our questions were answered. And new ones surfaced. Without our knowing, the police had been investigating the circumstances surrounding his death by interviewing his friends, trying to determine if he was under the influence of drugs or alcohol and if he had been suicidal. At the same time, Carrie was doing her own investigation. She and David returned from Missouri just hours before his death, having had a great time together with her family. She knew something wasn't right, so she set out to get answers.

She learned that while she and David were in Missouri a couple of his friends purchased something called K2 from a store at the mall. This was a synthetic cannabinoid, sold legally at the time, that they learned about from some college friends. They wanted to try it out, and if they liked it, they would take it on their Tennessee trip. This information was later confirmed by David's texts. He knew what was going on. He planned on smoking it, too.

The K2 they purchased was sold as incense but, when smoked, is intended to mimic the effects of marijuana. Because they bought it at the mall, they had no reason to believe it was unsafe. None of them suspected it could be a powerful hallucinogen or that it was coated with mind-altering, poisonous, and even deadly chemicals. And none of them would have imagined that it had the power to end a life. If they had, they never would have smoked it. The police investigation into David's death determined that he was not suicidal or depressed. It only showed that he had smoked K2, which left them baffled because they'd never heard of it. It wasn't until 18 months later that testing done in Pennsylvania confirmed the presence of synthetic cannabinoids in David's system.

Mike and I had no idea any of this was going on at the time. We were focused on making funeral arrangements and simply trying to breathe, so when Carrie said she wanted to talk with us, I was scared. *What if she and David had a fight? What if a break-up drove him to this? What if he really had been depressed? What if . . . ? What if . . . ? What if . . . ?* My mind was racing.

Carrie, Mike, and I sat under the walnut tree in our yard as she told us that the boys had smoked K2 the day David died. *What on earth is K2?* She had no clue. All she knew was that they smoked it and David was dead. She also knew that right after smoking it, David told his friends that he felt like he was in hell and described it as *the worst place imaginable.* As a Christian, he knew hell to be the very opposite of God . . . the epitome of darkness. He didn't say, "I don't feel right." He didn't say, "I feel like crap." He said, "I feel like I'm in hell." This was true terror. His friends, none of whom were as affected by the drug as David was, took him outside, hoping the fresh air would help him feel better. Obviously, it didn't.

Our conversation with Carrie was just the beginning of a growing whirlwind. Mike immediately called the police to share what we had learned, only to find out that they were learning the same thing. This began a journey to understand and educate. Just like other parents, Mike and I talked to our kids about sex, drugs, texting while driving . . . all the conversations parents are supposed to have with their kids. But we couldn't talk to them about what we didn't know. If David and his friends had known then what we know now, there's no way they would have smoked the stuff. That evening, we met with David's friends and their parents, seeking to learn more about what happened. We sat on our neighbor's sun porch and told them that we love them and that we don't blame them for the decision they made that day; a choice David made as well. He was gone and no amount of blame or regret would bring him back. It was a tragic lesson in the power of one bad decision, and we simply asked them to make wise choices in the future.

The week David died, he had started an online order for his college laptop and put a bow on hold at Bass Pro for fall hunting trips with his dad. The day he died, he planned to play video games with his brother and go to graduation parties with friends. David had plans to live . . . plans that were destroyed by smoking K2, and ended with a 4x8 piece of land along a tree-line. If *what–ifs* and *why–nots* had the power to change the past, then David would still be here. But they don't. And my long journey to survive the loss of our son hadn't even left the starting gate.

FIRST AID FOR YOUR GRIEVING HEART

Healing Prayer

Dear Jesus, my body is exhausted and my mind is frail. Day and night, I try to grasp what has happened and I have so many questions. I'm afraid. I'm angry and I feel powerless. All I can do is cry out to you for help, God. Please help me to get through this.

Healing Truth

Visit the following pages to unleash God's healing power over the lies that threaten to defeat you: *I will never sleep well again*(p. 166); *Fear controls me*(p. 169); *I could have stopped this* (p. 163).

Healing Words

What thoughts keep you up at night? What fears fill your mind? Embrace your grieving heart today by writing your thoughts and fears, however irrational they may seem. Get them out and then commit them into the hands of God and ask him to fill your mind with peace.

Chapter 4

Saying Goodbye

It was a warm and windy Wednesday, just three days after David died. Visitation. I was on autopilot as I stood in the back of the church with Mike and Daniel, in my pink Brett Favre jersey. The same memorabilia displayed at our home for David's graduation party one week earlier now lined the path into the sanctuary; photo boards, the life-sized Brett Favre cutout, and the family photos Dawn took after graduation. There was a sense of Deja vu. Many of the people waiting to give us hugs were the same as well, but today was different. Today, instead of laughter and pranks, there were tears on tired faces.

Four more hours, then we can be done. Three more hours, then we can be done. Only thing is, people just kept coming. We couldn't see it from where we stood, but the line wound around the walls of the church and through the parking lot. . .so many people waiting to honor David's life. We were overwhelmed and it still chokes me up when I think about it. There were people from all over; people from church, people we knew from when the boys were little, people who drove long distances, and many friends and family. Some shared memories. Some could barely talk. Sometimes we couldn't either. We just hugged them, thanked them for coming, and moved on to the next. It was especially difficult seeing David and Daniel's friends. I think I hugged them the tightest. I know I did. I pleaded with them to ask for help . . . to tackle their pain and fear head-on. I promised to do the same.

We didn't recognize everyone that came. Re-introductions had to be made, but that was okay. One unfamiliar face belonged to a young man about David's age. "You may not remember me," he said, "My name is Josh, and I used to live down the street from you." *Wow!*

"Of course, I remember you, Josh!" Joyful tears rolled down my face as we hugged. He and David were buddies back in the day. Eventually, Josh and his family moved away but David never forgot him. He hadn't forgotten David either. He handed us a couple of pictures of the two of them together, playing in the sandbox. Oh, how I'd love to go back in time. It was a bittersweet reunion . . . and an emotional one.

The funeral director suggested I bring several pairs of shoes, so I could change when my feet started to hurt. Of course, I never would have thought of that, but I trusted his expertise and was so thankful I did. A four-hour visitation quickly turned into six. Throughout the evening, Jeff would walk by and whisper, "It's time to change shoes, Jan." Later, I thanked him for taking such good care of me and suggested that we may know each other well enough now to go shoe shopping together someday. We both smiled.

As the conveyor belt of people kept coming, Mike and I stayed busy doing what you do at a visitation, until all at once, we looked at each other. *Where's Daniel?* We looked around and didn't see him anywhere. I was worried. *Was he okay? Was this all too much? Does he need me?* Then someone pointed to him. He was greeting people waiting in line! *What?* He later told us he felt bad that they were waiting so long, so he decided to go to them. It was incredible to see.

God's Word promises to give us grace at the exact time we need it most (Hebrews 4:16). As I look back, I see how this promise was evident throughout the evening. I think we all remained on autopilot, but by God's grace, through the enormity of our loss, we were still able to hug and listen and even smile from beginning to end. Daniel was able to recognize the needs of others and engage with friends, family, and people he didn't even know. Though we had few words to pray in those first days, God knew our hearts and he gave us what we needed. His love is amazing.

The next day was the most surreal of my life. The funeral. The day we buried our son. The day we said goodbye. *How can I say goodbye? How can he be gone? Oh God, please, I don't want to do this!* But I *had* to move. I *had* to get myself ready for the day. I *had* no choice. *Oh God, please, I don't want to do this!*

So, what do you wear to your son's funeral? There isn't a Pinterest page for that. I didn't want to search my closet, and I sure as heck didn't want to go shopping. I didn't want to think about it, period! Thankfully, my friend

DeDe picked up a few things from a local boutique and brought them over for me to try. It was a huge help. One less thing to worry about.

Thursday morning was gloomy, inside and out. I stood in front of the bathroom mirror and just stared at the reflection. I was so sad. My hands shook uncontrollably, too much to put on make-up or style my hair. They were useless.

I've attended many funeral services over the years and heard many pastors speak of peace, comfort, and eternal life in heaven. But now, it would be about our David. God's promises would intersect with our pain today. . .with the harsh reality of our life. This time, we won't walk away saying, "What a great message of hope. . .blah, blah, blah," and carry on with our day believing the message was for someone else. No. This message *was* for us, and there was nowhere to hide.

Looming questions consumed me. Mike and I had recently started watching a series of DVDs called *The Truth Project* and the question it asks was never more haunting than it was the week we lost David. "Do I really believe that what I believe is really real?" *Is Heaven really real? Can I trust any of it anymore?*

David and I were together when he prayed and placed his faith in Jesus. He was nine. God heard his prayer, and I believe from that moment on, David's eternity was certain. He understood that nothing could undo it. *Right?*

My head was spinning. I grew up in the church. I've heard God's Word for years. I already knew the answers. Or, so I thought. But if I knew the answers, then why was I being hounded by doubt? Had I simply been *reading* the Bible but not *relying* on it? I felt like a rookie, but surely I should be a veteran by now.

This was just the beginning of the onslaught of questions and doubts that threatened to break me. The struggle was real. Everything I knew about God's Word became vital in the battle against doubt. Every day I had to decide if I would recommit to what I knew to be true or let suffering undermine everything. Either way, the future would be with or without faith, with or without God. There were life-changing decisions to make. But first, there was a funeral.

With all of this swimming around my mind, my head was throbbing. *God, please get me through this day.* As I prayed that simple prayer, staring at my defeated reflection in the mirror, the Holy Spirit broke through the paralyzing agony and spoke to my soul, *David is in Heaven. He knew Jesus. He had Jesus in his heart. The Jesus that David is walking with right now is the same Jesus that lives in me. Same guy! We're in different places, yes, but because we share a Savior, we walk simultaneously with him.* Boy did I need this! Amazing.

Those words provided a sudden glimmer of hope, and an eternal perspective which gave me the energy I needed to face the day. David and I remain closer than I could ever imagine. Jesus and my Heavenly Father are closer than I can comprehend. Simple, yet incredibly profound. I remind myself of this often because it breathes life into my soul. Life that I so desperately needed then, and continue to need every day.

I am a worrier. Maybe you can relate? Honestly, it is my Mom default mode, and it's terrifying at times. Mike and I enjoyed taking our boys to my parents' house over the July 4th weekend because there were rides, games, and food vendors on their town square. Every year, the boys begged to go on the rides. I pushed them toward the boats or cars, but they loved those big swings. You know the ones; they start out going around slowly and then rise into the air as they go faster and faster. Good grief. It made me dizzy just watching them. It didn't help that I could easily imagine one of those swings flying off the rusty, unstable crossbars, sending the boys sailing onto the concrete. Am I the only mother with an overactive imagination? My heart raced every time. I prayed every time, too, but if I *really believe that what I believe is really real*, then what good was worrying? Worry doesn't change anything. Ever. David is in Heaven with Jesus. He is safer than Mike, Daniel, me. . .any of us. And one day, I will go there too. One day, I will see David again. Okay, focus Jan. I needed to reel myself back in.

Most people at the church were already seated by the time we arrived. Our family met privately before the service so our pastors could talk and pray with us. As we bowed our heads and closed our eyes, it felt like I might pass out. Between the lack of sleep, lack of food, and buckets of tears, I did not feel well. *Oh God, what if I can't make it through my own son's funeral?* I looked around at my family surrounding us. It was too much. I just prayed God would get me through. It's all I could do.

We made our way into the sanctuary as a small brass band played a traditional New Orleans funeral song. Odd? Maybe. But there was nothing normal about our last three days and today was about David. His life was full of music and he would have been so proud to have his band directors and fellow student-musicians play at his service. It was meaningful for us, too, and an honor for those who played. It was beautiful. The music continued throughout the service, as our youth group worship band played the same songs that they had played together with David. He would have loved it. Celebrating David's life by listening to people he admired, playing music he loved, was emotional for all of us.

Having just learned about K2, Mike spoke with our pastor and decided it had to be addressed at the funeral, especially with so many kids and parents in attendance. We didn't know much about it at the time, but we knew it could be deadly. It's what brought us together. Look how it affected David! It had to be talked about. Parents needed to be aware and kids needed to be smart, so none of them would ever have to suffer such horrific loss.

More than a thousand people filled chairs, sat on the floor in the aisles, and spilled into the foyer as Mike pleaded with parents to talk to their kids about synthetic drugs, using David's death as an example of how one bad decision can change everything. I was so proud of him. And his words turned out to be the first of many, educating others about synthetic drugs.

Daniel also spoke. At just fifteen years old, he was completely determined to do this on his own, to honor his brother. Despite being visibly shaken, he shared the most amazing message of hope with the overflowing crowd. It was his first sermon, really . . . at his brother's funeral. And when I say "sermon," I'm not just whistlin' Dixie. His outline was more than two pages long.

From the moment he learned that David died, Daniel ran to the only place where lasting hope could be found . . . into the arms of Jesus, and he was able to share that hope with others. It was the start of his own, powerful ministry and his brother would be so proud. Mike and I are proud, too. In fact, I keep a copy of Daniel's outline from that day and will treasure it always, as a reminder of God's faithfulness and of the way he used Daniel to minister.

Pastor Mitcham urged those in attendance not to let what happened to David define who he was. While it's true he took his own life, he also loved Jesus. He is a child of God, who is now with God. And even though circumstances can make us question a person's eternal destiny, God's Word makes us confident that David is living out the promise of John 3:16, "For God so loved the world that he gave his one and only son, that whoever believes in him should not perish, but have everlasting life."

David's youth pastor also spoke and we learned something new that day about David. Jon shared how David had talked to him about the urgency he felt to talk to his friends about Jesus. I had no idea. He loved being with friends, we knew that, but he also cared about their eternal destiny. The profound spiritual impact that Jon's leadership had in David's life–in so many lives–is beautiful, and learning how much David had grown in his walk with God and personal relationship with Jesus, comforted our aching hearts.

As the service ended, a deluge of rain pounded the roof. *Really?* It was a quick return to reality. So, instead of going to the cemetery, lunch was served while we waited for the rain to pass. "Have you had anything to eat, Jan?" Jeff was at it again, going above and beyond. *No, I haven't. And I'd thank you to mind your own stomach.* He was being kind so I smiled politely, but I could feel myself slipping back into a daze.

Our final goodbye was said at the burial service . . . publicly, anyway. David's former youth pastor spoke, referencing verses from Revelation, but it's a bit blurry. It's terrible not remembering, but I do remember being glad Pastor Dave was part of the day. Part of me wishes we would have recorded all of it; the visitation, the funeral, the burial. I know. It's weird, maybe even morbid, but I don't want to forget *anything* about my son. I remember every detail of the day he was born. I want to remember the day we celebrated his eternal life. I want to remember all of the *good* stuff we experienced and heard that day.

Reliving those darkest days is hard. Really hard, but I write about them as a record of God's unfailing love and a testimony to his faithfulness. David is never coming home. He isn't going to college, or getting married, or having kids. We can't change that. In just four days my world turned upside down and inside out, and I wasn't sure I would survive. But I did. I am. And so can you. Breath by breath, day by day, I learn that God is my strength and that contentment is found only in him. The only hope for survival, in the midst of blistering loss, is clinging to these Truths with all my heart and all my soul . . . even when I don't feel like it. Especially when I don't feel like it.

RAW JOURNAL ENTRY

June 6, 2011–One year after our son died

The cemetery was soggy the day we buried David. Why did it have to rain? After the pastor spoke, Mike, Daniel and I hugged each other through tears of disbelief, hearing only the sound of the light rain as it hit the tent above us. There was no other sound. Everyone was motionless. So many hearts were breaking. You could feel it. I remember wrapping my shaky hands around the urn. I kissed it lightly and whispered, "I love you, David."
    . . . Now what? My God, now what?

FIRST AID FOR YOUR GRIEVING HEART

Healing Prayer

Lord, thank you for small victories. Thank you for your promise to be with me through grief. I need your help to believe that I will experience joy again one day. By the power of your Holy Spirit, I can experience contentment again.

Healing Truth

Visit the following pages to unleash God's healing power over the lies that threaten to defeat you: *I will never feel content again* (p. 175); *If I worry enough something will change* (p. 190); *My loved one may not be in heaven* (p. 172).

Healing Words

Do you have any fears about walking into the future without your loved one? What does that look like? What can you do now to be better prepared for that? Embrace your grieving heart today by writing about the things you have already survived and about any fears you have about walking into the future without your loved one.

PART II

SURVIVNG THE FIRST YEAR

Chapter 5

Now What?

Funeral. Done. Flowers divided up. Done. Out-of-town family leaving for home. Done. Adjusting to life without David. Not even close. Is it even possible?

We were on our own now. No distractions. No people. No David. All that was left was our revolting reality . . . and silence. Deafening silence. We had been on an adventure of shifting emotions–from excitement and anticipation to horror and anguish. Now, just one emotion remained. Pain.

Will this ever feel different? Do I even want it to? How can I possibly laugh or shop or have casual conversation? I can't do it. I won't do it. My friend Lori worried I would never be able to smile again, or make jokes like I had so many times before. To be honest, I was worried too. When your whole world crashes in, the uncertainties are like grains of sand in the ocean, thrashing about by the changing tide. There's no hope of an orderly process to healing. No Google search that leads to full-proof steps for how to overcome loss. Grief isn't linear. It's haphazard and immensely messy. I wish I could have seen at the time, that haphazard and messy were okay . . . necessary even. I wish I could have believed that someday it would hurt a little less and that I would laugh again; and that it wouldn't mean I was forgetting David.

Funeral flowers lined the base of our fireplace and it hurt to look at them. Each one was a constant reminder that my son was gone. I realize now that they were also a heartwarming reminder of how much he was loved, but in the early days of grief, the bad stuff usually shouts the loudest. It was difficult having them in the house, but I also hated throwing them away when they began to wither. It's not logical, I know. In fact, few of my thoughts during those early days were logical, which is why it became crucial for me to focus on God's truths. And this did not come easy. It had to be a daily, purposeful decision to read the Word and claim it as truth.

This would be our year of "firsts" and it started with Father's Day. Exactly two weeks after David died we went through the motions. Watching Mike open his gifts was more than awkward and I couldn't imagine what he was feeling . . . or what Daniel was feeling. It would be the first of many *Hallmark-card* days to come, reminding us that someone we love is missing. We would celebrate because that's just what you do, I guess, but I dreaded it. What a downer.

[If you picked up this book hoping for pages filled with simple solutions and smiles, you might be disappointed. But if you're looking for someone to share your grief journey with, who is real and raw, then I'm so glad you're here! I pray that you will be encouraged as you read God's promises and that they will give you authentic hope for your future, just as they have for me. Read on my friend!]

It was clear from the start that our family would need professional help, together and individually, so we contacted our church for a credible, faith-based counselor. We were fooling ourselves if we believed we could shrug-off the enormity of this and trudge through it on our own. It was David, after all . . . our son, brother, friend . . . and our future was fragile. Even so, it's a frightening thing, walking into an office to talk to an outsider about your loss, or about anything for that matter. *What do I even say? Where do I start? Talking to him isn't going to change anything.* Maybe I was trying to talk myself out of it. *Surely I can handle this on my own.*

Enter the words of Dr. Phil, "How's that workin' for ya?" To be completely honest, I was a mess. The last thing in the world I could do was handle this on my own and yet I couldn't imagine anyone being able to help either. If you feel the same, I urge you from my grieving heart to yours, ask for help. Don't over-analyze it. Just do it. If you don't know where to go, start by reaching out to your pastor or to the counseling department at Focus on the Family (1–800-A-FAMILY) to request a reference to someone in your area. Next, visit the GriefShare website (*www.griefshare.org*) to find a group that meets near you. I know it may sound as awful to you as it did to me, but please trust my experience. When we are drowning in the pain of loss, we need someone to help us find hope through God's Word and to provide practical guidance for our daily struggles through grief. I understand that the notion of attending specific grief support sessions may add to your nerves and emotions at this fragile time, but I think you might be pleasantly surprised at how they're able to help. I pray that you will be refreshed and comforted by the wisdom and experiences of others, and that you will be an encouragement to them as well, simply by sharing your heart.

One ongoing struggle that I discussed with my counselor was my fragility at night. Fear was always present in the dark and it intensified every night when I got up to use the bathroom, only to hear an almost-audible voice, *your son is dead*. Again and again. Every single time. *Your son is dead*. It was haunting. My shoulders would instantly droop in defeat, fighting back tears and shaking my head, as if I could force it not to be true. Night after night I crawled back into bed thinking, *I hate my life*. (There may have been an added expletive that wasn't very ladylike, and certainly not Christlike, but very human nonetheless.)

I wasn't suicidal; just angry. I hated my current reality and was completely frail emotionally . . . so frail, that I didn't have the strength to protect myself from the lie that my life was over. I couldn't fight back. I was defenseless. *How can I live life without mothering David?* It tormented me. And I really did hate my life.

When I shared these thoughts with my husband Mike, he gave me a needed reminder. I still have a son who needs me, a husband who loves me, and (even though it was impossible to believe at the time) a purpose for the future. In no uncertain terms, Mike never wanted to hear those words again. He was right. It was time to stop giving power to lies and start focusing on the hope that is only found in the eternal God. He has plans for me. He has plans for you. Whether we *feel* like it or not, as long as there is breath in our lungs, we have hope for the future.

In the early days of grief, I had blinders on and being reminded of this truth brought no joy. At least not at first. The arrows of lies being hurled at me were more powerful than the Lord himself. Of course, I knew it was wrong to feel that way and eventually it was time to throw this nightly voice into the pit where it belonged. As Christians, we're told to put on the full armor of God so that he can fight for us. He is the one that's strong enough to be strong when we aren't. His armor ricochets each and every fiery lie that comes our way. And it was time to reject the lie that I was alone in the darkness. God was with me.

I started asking God to help me fight against any evil thoughts invading my soul and from that point on, when I heard *your son is dead*, I responded swiftly by claiming, *David had eternal hope. He is in Heaven. He is safe with God*. It may sound cliché, but these words were my battle cry and I repeated them often. My fight for survival was just beginning and I began gathering spiritual weapons, not only for this battle but for future ones as well. Suit me up Lord, I want to be ready.

Some of my hardest battles came in the form of emotional ambushes; brief but intense reminders of David that came without warning and left a path of debris in their wake. It might be a song on the radio, a smell in the air, or a familiar sight.

Ambushes are brutal and can instantly ruin your day. They may take you back to the way your loved one died or where they died. Your heart races at the sound of a siren or the sight of a car accident. You begin to sweat when the phone rings or when driving by the hospital.

After we lost David, I developed an issue with guns–the sound of gun shots to be exact. Do you know how many television shows and movies have the sounds of gunshots? I had no idea. Until now. Finding shows we can safely watch has been challenging. Mike has an app that gives detailed information about the violence contained in shows and movies, so this has become a valued tool in our home, to prevent ambush.

However, not everything is preventable. As we ran into Sam's Club one day, about a month after David died, there was a series of booms in the distance. I hadn't been out of the house much. Now, all of a sudden, I was hearing sounds that invaded my mind with vivid memories of that awful day. *What is that? Oh God, it's gunshots. We have to get out of here, NOW!* What hadn't occurred to me is that it was July 4th weekend and the booms we heard were fireworks going off in the corner of the parking lot. By the time we realized what it was, it was too late. My heart hammered in my chest as we started toward the car. Then, the smell of smoke hit my nose. Total ambush.

Over the months and years, I've learned to handle these situations with less panic. I've learned that it's okay to excuse myself from the situation and allow myself a few tears. Mostly, I've learned to instantly ask God to fill my mind with his truth and to wrap his loving arms around my shaking soul. He is faithful and he listens. Everyone grieves differently, so it was difficult at times for Mike and Daniel to understand my reactions to things. This is why it is so important for all family members to seek professional help.

In contrast to sudden ambushes, worry was my constant companion. There wasn't anything unpredictable about it. While I avoided our basement altogether, Daniel frequently went down to play video games with friends and Mike went down occasionally as well. Every step they took down the stairs pulled the breath from my lungs and made my heart race. *When will you be back up? What are you doing down there?* I'm certain it frustrated Mike at times. Would these questions change anything? Would they ever stop? I was scared and even embarrassed.

I sat upstairs, worried I would hear a gunshot. It was crazy, I know, but tell that to my imagination. It made no sense. Yet, it made perfect sense. I worried constantly about losing other people I love. It terrified me and I tried to control my fear with information. I needed to know where Daniel was . . . all . . . the . . . time. It annoyed him, but I couldn't seem to stop. When I finally opened up to him about my intense fear of losing another son, he understood and was very sweet about it, but to be completely honest . . . it didn't stop me from worrying.

Symptoms of PTSD first began when we moved back into our house. They could be brought on by a simple memory of David's graduation party–seeing a certain serving dish or photo, remembering the smile on his face or things we laughed about that day. Sometimes the memories were much older–thinking about holding him for the first time, or his first home run in little league. No matter what I thought about, it always led back to finding him, lifeless in our basement.

Worry led to panic, often without warning. Out of nowhere, my body would start physically twitching, like bolts of lightning shooting through me, and there wasn't a damn thing I could do about it. It was an involuntary journey to a terrifying abyss. I had to consciously avoid thinking about anything that might provoke it, but then worried that suppressing it may cause more harm than good in the long run. I learned to just take it like a punch in the gut: cry, pray, and wait for the next one. There was always a next one. *Will this ever stop? Am I slowly going crazy?*

After returning from one of my frequent (and perhaps less effective) "anger walks," I stormed into the house and announced, "I want to break something!" Mike had this, *"Are you serious?"* look on his face. But I *meant* it. As I walked that day, it felt like people were looking right through me: "Oh, there's the mother of the boy who. . ." It was probably my imagination, but maybe it wasn't. I needed to break something.

"Just don't break anything expensive," Mike said casually, which forced me to smile a little. Thank God for his sweet sense of humor!

"I want a punching bag, Mike."

"Jan, you'd break your hands. Do you have any idea how hard those are?"

"Don't care. Want one."

Not long after, Mike took me to a popular sporting goods store in Des Moines. We headed straight to the punching bags, "Go on, hit it." I put on my best Rocky Balboa face, and *OUCH!* Needless to say, we didn't get one.

All of this . . . the ambushes, the worry, the PTSD, the crazy notions . . . all of it became regular topics of discussion during counseling sessions. Truly, I wouldn't be where I am today without them. My counselor taught me how to talk with others about my fears and struggles, helped me understand the root of what I was dealing with, and gave me the necessary tools for fighting back . . . without having to break my fingers. I wasn't going crazy. I was learning to cope with the effects of trauma.

One of the greatest challenges Mike, Daniel, and I have had to face together since losing David is learning to live with a completely different family dynamic. Each of us mourns the unique relationship we shared with him, and we all mourn the loss of family meals, trips, and holidays with all four of us. Mostly, we are intensely burdened by the list of things we will never get to experience with David. Mike and I won't ever go to David's wedding, love his wife, or spoil his kids. Daniel will never be the best man at his brother's wedding. We'll never go on the traditional family vacations that we imagined, in a Northwoods home with Daniel and David's families. Everything is different now. And it's doubtful that we will ever be on the same emotional page as we deal with the change.

It sounds a bit odd, but I find so much comfort in accepting the fact that our grief will never be over. It's not a destination to which we must arrive. There is freedom in allowing ourselves to move through life, one day at a time and sometimes moment-by-moment, knowing that it is going to be messy. Tempers will run high. Hurtful things will be said. I will be misunderstood and I will misunderstand. We all hurt. We all need time to heal and each of us needs a pass from time to time. God gives us so much grace and it's important that we allow Him to work through us, giving us the strength and wisdom to offer grace to each other. Truth is, this was our new reality. None of us felt brave, so it didn't do any good to pretend otherwise. I don't recommend it.

I couldn't presume to know what Mike or Daniel were thinking. It was a destructive guessing game. Instead, I had to ask questions and then allow them the courtesy of opening up in their own timeframe . . . not mine. Surviving grief with others is an exercise in prayer and patience, and peace only comes when I stop trying to figure out the future and start resting in God's best for this moment, and for the ones I love.

Not only did we have each other to think about, we are blessed with so many people who knew and loved David, who were also grieving and wanted to help. Oh boy. That isn't something I was up to. *I've got this, remember? Okay, I really don't, but nobody needs to see me like this.*

After deleting at least three of their messages from our answering machine, I reluctantly accepted an invitation to have coffee with a few of my closest friends. I didn't want to go. I couldn't eat. I couldn't talk . . . not really. And I wasn't interested in listening to their in-depth prayers for me or for our family, hearing my own groans of grief coming out through theirs. It sounds awful, I'm sure, but I didn't want to stir up any more hurt than I was already feeling.

Mike encouraged me to go, "Let them love, encourage, and pray for you, Jan. You need this." He was right. I did need it. They were so happy I agreed to go and they promised to keep it simple; coffee and homemade rolls, with no pressure for me to have any of it. That was freeing.

I forced my feet to walk through the front door of the house and saw four women who love me sitting at the kitchen table. *How can I possibly explain what I need them to pray for when I don't even know it myself?* All I really knew was that I desperately wanted my son back and no one could help me with that.

A flood of emotions rushed in and tears streamed down my face as words began pouring from my mouth, "Why did this happen? How can I live without David? I miss him so much! Mike and Daniel are hurting. Why did God allow this? Can we survive it? Will my marriage survive? I don't care about cooking, laundry or cleaning. I have no energy to do anything. I'm not even sure I'll ever want to eat again. I don't care to wash my hair, brush my teeth or paint my nails. Nothing matters right now." They took over from there. My heart was overwhelmed as each one prayed for me . . . for Mike . . . for Daniel. The words washed over me and were like medicine to my soul.

In the weeks that followed, these beautiful women organized meals so I wouldn't have to cook. They turned my heart's cry into action to meet a physical need. Honestly, though, it was awkward. I'm much more comfortable being on the giving side, taking meals to others, but when I put pride aside and allowed people to serve us, we were profoundly blessed. I'm so thankful that my friends didn't give up on reaching out to me and equally thankful that God gave me the strength to be transparent and show them my grief.

People who see your grief genuinely want to help. If what they offer is truly not helpful, it's okay to say "no thank you" or "I'm not ready for that." But if what they offer is helpful, let them help. They know you are hurting and they are probably hurting, too. They feel helpless because they can't take away your pain, but they can cook a meal, scrub your toilets, and do the laundry. Truth is, you would be doing the same thing for them if they were in your shoes, so give yourself (and them) the blessing of saying *yes*. Whether it's your pastor, counselor, closest friends, or even strangers, let people love you . . . mess and all.

Surviving loss is not an individual sport. It may feel safer to retreat into your own thoughts and *let the world pass by*, but you simply can't do it alone.

God created us to have fellowship with others. It's his purpose for us, even when it hurts. Especially when it hurts.

RAW JOURNAL ENTRY

November 2010–17 months after our son died

Lord, I'm a mess! Please help me to focus and rely on you. There are many worldly options for me to choose from, to help me cope, but ultimately, I know they would leave me empty. My emotions are off the charts, and they change from moment to moment, but your promises remain the same. They never change . . . Only you can mend my broken heart and wavering faith. Only you can help me to move forward, even if it feels like I'm moving at a snail's pace.

FIRST AID FOR YOUR GRIEVING HEART

Healing Prayer

Dear Jesus, thank you that I can always trust you. Please help me to be vulnerable and to seek help when I need it. Help me to be gracious to others in my life who are grieving and to keep the lines of communication open.

Healing Truth

Visit the following pages to unleash God's healing power over the lies that threaten to defeat you: *My identity is gone* (p. 160); *I am alone in the darkness* (p. 181); *I can get through this on my own* (p. 184); *If I worry enough something will change* (p. 190); *If I don't say yes to everything then I'm failing to heal* (p. 200).

Healing Words

What has it been like to be around your family and friends since your loss? When have you experienced an emotional ambush? How did you respond? Are you connected with a counselor or grief group? If so, how has it helped you? If not, is it time? Embrace your grieving heart today by writing about how you are dealing with the emotions of your grief while interacting with family/friends. And who have you reached out to for help?

Chapter 6

Fighting for Control

As the weeks passed, I became more and more aware of two things. First, I had no control over the timetable of my own grief. Second, I had no control over anyone else's either. Let's be honest, I had no control over anything. Still, I felt like it was my responsibility to fix everything for everyone; Daniel, Mike, David's friends, our friends, even strangers . . . you name it. Our marriage was statistically in danger and my family needed me to hold things together. Daniel would be returning to high school as an only child. Surely he needed me to help him navigate this new reality. People in the community needed to see me grieving appropriately. (Sounds ridiculous, right? But so real.) And David still had friends who needed to know Jesus.

Even as I write this, it's exhausting. Maybe it's a mom thing, to feel so burdened by the needs of others. Maybe obsessing about helping others took a little of the focus off my own pain. Or maybe I was simply desperate to make David's life (and death) matter. Whatever the reason, I worried day and night about the health and healing of others, wanting to ease their pain and wondering how many people were hurting that I didn't even know about. I couldn't stand it. Looking back, I realize that this compulsion was counterproductive to my own healing process, and not from God. There's nothing wrong with wanting to help others, of course, it's what we're supposed to do. Right? But when it is driven by fear and worry, it is not healthy.

Each year, when David and Daniel headed off for the first day of school and Mike was at work, I danced. Yep, right there in the living room, I did a short, but very enthusiastic, happy dance. The house was my own . . . all day . . . for nine months! I took the necessary precautions by closing blinds and locking doors. Nobody needed to see that. Unfortunately, there was no escape for the poor dogs. The only human who even knew about it was my friend, Lori. Every year, she'd call during the first day of school and ask, *"Did you dance today?"* A little silly, I know, but a fun tradition and she always knew the answer.

There would be no dance this year. I was still thankful for the time alone, but this was painfully different. I was sad. Our world was upside down and this would be a time for me to release all of the emotions that had piled up over the summer; a time to cry out loud to God. I didn't want anyone to see that, either. The dogs remained my only witnesses and they weren't talking! They sheepishly came to the couch where I sat. *Why are you so sad?* Truth is, they knew David was gone and they missed him too. Lori didn't ask me if I danced that year. She knew.

I desperately worried about Daniel. He was a sophomore now and, aside from the occasional illness, this was the first time in his life he went to school without his brother. David would have been away at college by now, but still . . . I can't imagine. Before he left each day, I offered an emotional escape route, reminding him that he could come home if he was having a bad *David day*. I never intended to suggest that Daniel couldn't handle school, but at the same time, he'd just lost his brother! I couldn't stand the thought of him becoming overwrought, surrounded by his peers in crowded class-rooms, with nowhere to go. I couldn't take a chance so I gave the attendance office a heads-up and knew that Daniel wouldn't abuse it. He didn't.

One of my greatest fears was that he wouldn't have anyone to talk to about all of this . . . or that he wouldn't talk at all. I wanted to make sure he could express his feelings of grief with friends, his pastor, Mike, me . . . anyone. He couldn't bottle it up.

"You can talk to us anytime, Daniel."

"Okay, mom."

"If you need to come and sleep on our bedroom floor, you absolutely can."

"I know, mom."

One time, after repeating this conversation for the millionth time, Daniel paused and said, "I'll tell you what, if *you* need me to come and sleep on your bedroom floor, you can let me know and I will." It was an insightful response from a fifteen-year-old. He was right; there were times I needed him close.

As moms, we want to protect our children, but my mom superpowers couldn't take away his pain. They couldn't fix his grief. All I could do–all any of us can do–is to let our kids know we're there for them when they need us. And they *will* need us. The most difficult part of being there for Daniel was that I really didn't know *how* to help him. One thing is certain; worrying day and night was not the answer. Trying to impose my expectations for what he should need, was not the answer.

I was actually overwhelmed by apprehension when he became distraught with grief. I'm sure that sounds bad. I wanted to be there for him. I needed to be there for him. *But how? I'm not strong enough.* I've mothered him for years and comforted him a thousand times, but not like this . . . not when I was weak and scared too. I feared he would see right through to my inadequacies, leaving him worse off than before. In the moment, the only thing I could do was to listen to his heart while mine broke, and tell him that I love him and that God would get us through this. I had no idea how, but we would just have to be weak together and rely on his promises. I wanted to do so much more, but that's all I had. And honestly, I think it's all he needed.

The lie that threatened to defeat me in those moments was that I was failing to meet the needs of my son, but the truth in Scripture is that God is the *only* one able to meet our deepest emotional and spiritual needs. It wasn't up to me then and isn't up to me now. We are called to encourage others and help them experience God's love, but nobody will find authentic, lasting healing in another human being. Mike can't provide that for me and I can't provide it for Daniel. It was useless . . . pretending to be strong because I simply wasn't. None of us were. So, the best thing I could do for Daniel was to grieve with him. [Who do you need to grieve with? Trust me, they don't need you to be strong. They just need you to be there; to hug them, cry with them, and cling to the promise that God will get you through, somehow.]

As fall came closer, there was a certain awkwardness that hovered over our home; like David ran to the store for some milk and would be back home any minute. Like he was going to walk down the stairs from his bedroom and we'd realize the whole thing had been an awful dream. In our heads, we knew David was gone but it took some time for our hearts to catch up and to process it all. Through counseling, each of us was working to grasp this new reality, but we were out of sync as a family emotionally and physically, and we had to reinvent our lives together . . . even though we all hated the idea.

We needed to eat, clothes needed to be washed, and bathrooms needed to be cleaned, but I lacked motivation for even the simplest of tasks. Folding laundry was a drudge and I had given up baths altogether; something I enjoyed so much before losing David. And I didn't want to eat . . . let alone cook! In my head, I wanted to be a good wife and mother, to be there for Mike and Daniel, but I was so fragile. And instead of giving myself permission to heal in my own time, I guilted myself relentlessly. *What kind of mother am I? What kind of wife am I? I'm failing them!* Yes, they did need me, but not to be perfect . . . just to be present. It was also okay to let some things go now and then, and it was okay to accept (and even ask for) the help of friends. The reality was, the waves of strength came and went, just like the weak ones, and my prayers remained the same either way: *Help me!* I wonder if God ever tires of hearing those two words.

I think we all felt like we were walking on eggshells around each other, not wanting to stir up any unnecessary emotions, but the truth is that there was an ocean of emotions constantly lurking under the surface anyway, whether they got "stirred up" or not. We each needed the freedom to have bad moments . . . to cry, to yell, to stare off into space. Once I was able to give up my fight to control my own emotions and the emotions of others and embrace them as a natural part of the grief journey, I experienced far more strength and peace. Of course, this is an ongoing exercise in surrender, even now.

August 29th. My birthday . . . and another *first*. Another dreaded *Hallmark-card* day. It had only been two months since David died, and I couldn't have cared less about celebrating. In fact, *who cares that I'm 49! I don't!* Bad attitude? Yeah. The awful reality is that I would have to perform. I'd have to pretend to care . . . to be happy. Mike and Daniel needed me to feel special and to have a good day, so I needed to let them. But wow, it took a lot of effort. I know I was being selfish, but I was also being real. There is a fine line between putting on an act with a bad attitude and making a willful decision to have a good attitude because you know it's the right thing to do. I've walked this line a lot since losing David.

There were many times like this during our first year. Who am I kidding? There are still times when I have to tell myself, "Just put a smile on your face, Jan, and get through it. You can cry your eyes out later." And that's usually what happens. Celebrating special occasions without David is an emotional, messy fight that begins several weeks ahead with psyching myself up to get through it, and ending in utter exhaustion. And I'm sorry to say that nothing magical happens after the first year. Though the pain is less piercing, I will struggle with special occasions for . . . well . . . forever.

Thankfully, I can claim the promise that God still has good plans for me; not to harm me, but to give me hope for the future (Jeremiah 29:11). It's the same promise he gave to the Israelites, right before they were taken into slavery for generations. Dear friend, hope for the future is ours, even in really hard times . . . even when all we can see is struggle and all we can feel is pain. God is here. He is actively at work for our good and for his glory. No matter how much we ache inside, we are not alone. God tells us not to fear because he is always with us; not to be dismayed because he is our God. He promises to give us strength and to hold us up with his strong hand (Isaiah 41:10).

These are such powerful truths, but to be shamefully honest, scriptures like this used to irritate me. My circumstances didn't feel good or hopeful and I certainly didn't feel strong. This is why it is so critical to avoid the lie that emotions define us. They don't. They're important and we cannot ignore them, but if we allow them to define us, they'll quickly take over our lives. We don't want that. God doesn't want that.

While emotions are like a sail that catches the wind and tosses us from side to side, Truth is the rudder. It gives us purpose and stability, and it guides us through waves of emotion . . . getting us safely to shore. Too often we are all sail and no rudder, but we are children of the one true God and his Word is true. Choosing to claim God's promises is absolutely essential to surviving grief. He understands. He knows when our smiles are fake and our hearts are weak, and he loves us anyway. And the more we claim his truth, clinging to his promise to get us through, the less grief will control us.

Hearing Jon's words at David's funeral, about how much David wanted his friends to know Jesus, has never left my mind. David's burden instantly became my own; like he passed me the baton and it was my responsibility to finish the job. I worried about his friends. A lot. My heart ached for them because I knew they would soon be leaving for college with hearts packed full of loss and memories of David. *How would they cope? How can I help?* I prayed for them often but somehow it didn't seem like enough. I had to do more.

Whenever I would see them, I reminded them that my heart had room for them and that I was ready to help if they wanted or needed it. I wanted so desperately to fix things for them and my motherly instincts were on overload, so I needed to be careful. These kids already had mothers and it wasn't my job to interfere. Still, I couldn't mother David and the idea of *mothering* his friends felt good.

Throughout the summer I sent text messages of support, sharing the hope of Jesus and letting them know I was praying for them. Mike and I enjoyed it so much when they would stop by to just hang out, share how they were feeling, and tell a funny memory or two about David that we hadn't heard before. It was bittersweet, for sure, and tears rushed in when they left. *David is gone. It really happened. He's not coming back.* The painful reality is that they were going back home; to their lives, to their moms.

Summer was almost over, so Mike and I decided to have some of David's friends over for a BBQ. It would be a little sendoff party before they left for college. *Push through Jan. Just push through.* A few of the guys decided to get commemorative "4" tattoos, similar to David's, so we lined them up on our deck, one in front of the other, to snap a photo of the row of shoulders. They certainly didn't need to get tattoos to remember David, or even to honor him, but I must admit that it's nice knowing they have such tangible reminders of him . . . something that will prompt stories about David for the rest of their lives.

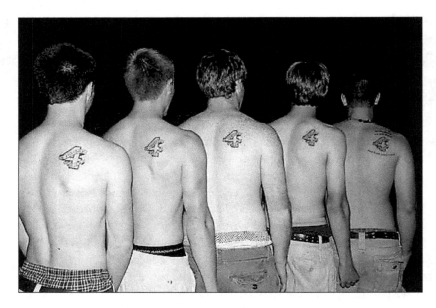

David's friends revealing their "4" tattoos in his memory.

Within a week, all of these kids would leave for college. *Oh God, this is hard. Will they continue to keep in touch? Will it be too hard for them? Will life just . . . go on?* I had written letters to several of the kids, which was a struggle, but I simply decided to write the same words I would have written to David, if he were leaving for college. Some received a Bible with their letter and they all received kisses on the cheek and bear hugs. Tight ones. I didn't want to let them go. I had a job, remember? It was up to me to make sure they knew Jesus and my job wasn't done yet.

As they drove off, I went back into the house and cried like a baby, not knowing if we'd ever see any of them again. We were saying good-bye to a piece of David all over again, and entering the beginning of *"things David won't experience."* First on the list: college.

I made a promise to God and to David, under the stars on the same day he died, to help others find hope in Jesus. It was simple really. I would proclaim the saving power of Jesus to those who don't yet believe. For those who already placed their faith in Jesus, I would encourage them to see Him in a fresh new way and to recommit themselves to Him. I had to share the only hope I knew for navigating life through stormy waters. This is still my promise and I think it always will be. However, I'm learning to accept that I am only responsible for speaking the truth about Jesus. The rest is up to Him. If the truth is rejected, it doesn't mean I've failed.

God reminds me that this work is for his Holy Spirit, not for me. It is my responsibility to share my heart and my story, to share the hope of Jesus, and to share how I continue to cling to God, as He gets me through the horrific devastation of losing my son. But everyone has their own journey to experience and their response to God is not in my hands. It is in God's hands . . . and in his time. Again, I found myself letting go of my desire for control, but I fully admit, this was challenging.

Working through grief with my family and friends, and David's friends, was emotional. Dealing with people in public was downright awful. I found myself dodging behind displays at Walmart and doing U-turns in the middle of grocery store aisles. I've driven in circles in parking lots, waiting for someone I know to drive away. All of this, to avoid potentially awkward conversations. Who am I kidding? They were always awkward. *What do they think of me? Of David? What do they expect me to say? Are they judging me for buying wine?* Good grief! It almost wasn't worth leaving the house.

Then there were the "looks." You know the ones. It was like people were looking right through me. *Oh, there's the mother of the boy who committed suicide. That poor family. I've seen them on the news.* I automatically wanted to explain what we were learning about K2 and how it affected David. I wanted to justify what happened by explaining the truth, that this synthetic drug altered and tormented his mind. I was so protective when it came to David. *But maybe they won't believe me. Maybe they'll think I'm in denial.* I felt so judged. I felt like David was being judged, too. Whether it was true or not, I felt it. I believed that the opinions of others mattered; that I had to act a certain way or say certain things to redeem myself. To redeem David.

But the truth is, I had bigger fish to fry. Being anxious about the thoughts of others, many of whom were strangers, was only dragging me down and causing me to expend energy that I didn't have in the first place. Fear of what others thought of me and about how to handle grief threatened to overtake me. But focusing on the truth that God knew my heart–even the ugliest parts–and loved me anyway, kept me safe and helped me to breathe (Proverbs 29:25). I found myself in the cereal aisle whispering truth: *You love me, God. You love David. You will get me through this. It doesn't matter what they think. I'm okay.*

One way I dealt with the pressure and pain was to journal. It was my safe place; a private exercise in saying what couldn't be said out loud. The first time I wrote was just a few months after David died, with shaking hands on the keyboard, typing words for my eyes only; raw streams of emotional emptiness, helplessness, and hopelessness. Period. Sounds pleasant, doesn't it? But I never meant for it to serve any other purpose. It was simply another way to release pain. Maybe, if I could release the angry, scared, desperate things I was experiencing, the anguish would slowly dissipate. Then I could get back to normal. Not so.

While journaling didn't make anything normal again, something else happened; something completely unexpected. As I poured out my soul, ranting and raving, the entries almost always ended on a positive note . . . a Godly note, to be exact. Scripture would come to mind that I had heard in Bible studies or church, from years earlier. I would grab my Bible, look them up, and claim the promises for myself. They spoke to the depths of my hurting soul and brought glimmers of hope for the first time like nothing else could.

My journal entries shifted away from rants and toward promises in Scripture that were relevant to my "struggle of the day." Each time, I was encouraged. Each time, I felt loved by the Lord in ways I never thought possible. I always walked away hungry for more. God was truly walking with me through my pain, spoon-feeding me his Word, and encouraging my heart. For the first time, I began to believe that I really could experience healing and even spiritual renewal. For the first time, I was beginning to experience what it was like to really need God's Word, to rely on it and not just read it. It became my life preserver.

I wrote my very first entry four months after David died, on a blustery day in October, and I continue to journal these many years later. These entries have turned into a six-binder, 500,000-word collection that documents God's precious record of faithfulness. He has never left me alone.

To this day, whenever I'm asked to speak or talk with others who have experienced loss, I refer to the lessons of truth in my journals because they are my story of raw survival, and I don't want to forget any of it. God has sustained and guided me through the worst loss I could ever have imagined, so I rest confident that my future is safe . . . no matter what this unpredictable world throws my way.

Journaling may not be your cup of tea and that's okay! But I promise, God desperately desires to walk with you through your grief. He wants to replace your anguish with his presence. He wants you to feel loved and to have hope. He does! Find a way today, right now even, to intentionally talk to him. Tell him every ugly detail–speak it, cry it, write it, or yell it–and ask him to encourage you with his Word. The Truth Companion (at the end of this book) is a powerful tool for claiming God's promises, right where you are, and I encourage you to use it on your own journey for survival. He will honor your willingness to claim his truth, even when it doesn't feel good. He loves you. And there *is* hope.

Maybe it's a struggle for you to believe that. In the early months, after losing my precious son, I struggled to believe it too. But my "new normal" was uncharted territory so I didn't have a choice but to continue to cling to God as I weaved in and out of the paralysis that grieving brings. As I began to accept my lack of control and surrender to God's promises and his perfect timing, I began to experience the healing and hope that only Jesus can bring. There were even some good and joyful moments sprinkled along the path of that dreaded *first year*. It was impossible to imagine how God would be able to help me survive. But, oh wow. He has.

RAW JOURNAL ENTRY

February 2013–Nearly three years after our son died

Faith, as small as a mustard seed, can move mountains. These "mustard seeds" are available to all of us, especially when bad things happen that shake our world, if we just ask. It's as if God is whispering, "Pick it up. Just pick it up. Let's talk about this. Open your heart and allow me to help you put the pieces of your shattered life back together. I'm here. I want to help! I'M HERE! Please don't ignore me. If you open your heart and listen to what I have to say, you will be encouraged and be given hope to sustain you. I will be your strength during this time and also in the future when trouble comes your way. Pick up the tiny mustard seed of faith, even if you think it's too small to make any difference right now, and I will give you what you need. Have faith. Remember that it was FAITH that brought you to Christ to begin with. By faith, surviving loss is possible."

The Bible tells me, "I tell you the truth, if you have faith as small as a mustard seed, you can say to this mountain, 'Move from here to there' and it will move. Nothing will be impossible for you." Matthew 17:20

FIRST AID FOR YOUR GRIEVING HEART

Healing Prayer

Dear God, I try so desperately to control my grief, to control what other people think, and to fix what I have no power to fix. Help me to rest in you today, Jesus, and to surrender to the truth of your perfect timing and the healing that can only be found in you.

Healing Truth

Visit the following pages to unleash God's healing power over the lies that threaten to defeat you: *My faith is too weak* (p. 178); *I'm failing to meet the needs of my family* (p. 187); *If I worry enough something will change* (p. 190); *What others think of my grief matters* (p. 193).

Healing Words

What daily tasks cause you stress? What causes awkwardness in your home or with others? What are you fighting to control? Embrace your grieving heart today by writing a letter to God, telling him how you feel and explaining how you wish for things to be different.

Chapter 7

Checkmarks

When I had no interest in celebrating anything, a feeling that threatened to become permanent, a dear friend taught me the importance of acknowledging victories . . . however small they may have seemed at the time. In addition to sending brief, encouraging texts, Dawn had a unique way of helping me through things I didn't want to do; things I didn't feel capable of doing, and things that required me to be more courageous publicly . . . and sometimes privately. She celebrated all of it on my behalf, with one simple word: *Checkmark.*

First trip to the grocery store? *Checkmark.* First attempt to read a book? *Checkmark.* Finally getting my hair colored and cut? *Checkmark.* Sending David's friends off to college? Surviving his birthday? Thanksgiving? Christmas? (The list is long) *Checkmark!*

Dawn has been my champion, making a big deal of every attempt to conform to my new normal. During that first year, she knew that every new step I took and every "old thing" I muddled through was a huge accomplishment for my hurting heart and each one was necessary for my survival. Having her in my corner, cheering me on in this *simple* way, was priceless and I pay this kindness forward when working with others who are grieving. In fact, just six years after losing David, Dawn lost her husband and I was privileged to become her champion as she walked through grief also.

If you're reading this to better understand the needs of a grieving friend, please don't underestimate the power of your emotional presence.

It is often the "small" things that mean the most. Those of us faced with heartbreaking loss need to know that we're not alone, even when (especially when) we don't feel like socializing, and your support doesn't have to be complicated. Our burden is lighter when others are willing to share the weight of our grief.

If you're reading this because you are the one who has lost a loved one . . . *checkmark!* I'm so proud of you for fighting for survival and pray that you find hope in these pages. Allow me to be your champion. I may not know your name, but God does. I don't know what *checkmarks* you're adding to your list, but God does. You have the strength, through Jesus, to endure your new reality. You do! Celebrate every milestone, however big or small, and soon you will have a record of how God's faithfulness is getting you through.

One such milestone came when I turned the calendar to November, just months after losing David. There, looming in the distance like a dark basement in a horror movie, was a trifecta of holidays that we'd have to face without him. *Focus on the checkmarks, Jan.* I would earn a virtual check-mark for making it through Thanksgiving, another one for Christmas, and wrap the whole mess up with a checkmark on New Year's Day. Right? Not even close. It seemed logical, but the reality of it was quite different.

I always assumed that people grieved each of these holidays separately; each one independent of the other. But that's not what happens. At least, that's not how it was for me. My first holiday season without David became more like a two-month chain of falling dominoes. Relief never came and from one calendar square to the next I found myself in a continual stream of sadness, whether the day was decorated with a holiday icon or not. It tested my endurance level, one day after another, after another, after another, after another. Period. It was a part of the new normal I didn't care for.

The holiday *festivities* began when the "Cut Your Own Christmas Tree" sign popped-up across the road from our house, at the tree farm where David had worked for several years. He trimmed trees and mowed during the summer months and sold Christmas trees during November and December. Though he enjoyed the work, his favorite part of the job was definitely Cindy's home cooked meals on weekends, during the busy holiday season. After he died and on behalf of our neighbors, Cindy asked to plant a tree in our yard, to honor his memory, and assured us that whichever tree we chose, David would have touched it. Maybe *that* tree would be enough this year. *I mean, do we really need to go through the motions? Drag home a Christmas tree and decorate it? Hang lights? Bake cookies? Ugh.* It was supposed to be a joyful, happy season. But the only thing I wanted for Christmas, I could never have.

First, I had to survive Thanksgiving, my first chance to earn a holiday checkmark. *Great.* I dreaded it, but it came anyway. Our neighbors invited us over for a traditional Thanksgiving feast, but we didn't accept. Nope. Not this year. I had no desire to socialize, even with friends I loved. I had no desire to cook either, but went through the motions anyway. A turkey breast replaced the traditional Butterball, along with potatoes, stuffing, rolls, and vegetables.

There we sat. Three of us, not four. The oak table in our formal dining room seemed four times bigger than any previous year. With the food on the table, we just sort of stared at each other and David's voice echoed in my ear, "Dibs on the gizzard!" Gross. But he loved the stuff that came in the white plastic bag, stuffed in the bird's cavity.

We held hands as Mike prayed, his voice cracking as he thanked God for all we are thankful for, including David, and tears filled our eyes. No heart ached less than the other. *Stuffing anyone? Give me a break.* To be honest, it felt disloyal to continue such a special tradition without David. So weird. So surreal. *Can we just not do any of this, God?!*

One of the most challenging things, when grieving during the holidays, is the pressure we put on ourselves. *I should be doing better by now. I should be crying less. I should maintain traditions. . . I should. . . I should. . . I should. . .* What we *should* do is give ourselves permission to avoid the things that are simply too hard. Everyone healing from loss experiences the holidays differently, and sometimes it's difficult to understand why another person needs to do a certain thing, or not do a certain thing. Putting expectations on grief, our own or others, is incredibly counterproductive. At the same time, we sometimes need a gentle push to move past unhealthy barriers to healing. This is why it is vital to keep lines of communication open . . . especially during the holidays, and to ask God for the wisdom to discern between things we need to skip and things we need to walk through, even when we don't want to. We didn't go to our neighbor's for Thanksgiving because my heart wasn't ready for it. It's okay. They still love us.

After watching some mindless TV, the three of us drove to the cemetery. The only official thing that marked David's grave, at that time, was a small sign with his name, date of birth, and date of death. The unofficial marker was a large, green "4" made of styrofoam and decorated with bright yellow, plastic flowers. It was a gift from a few of David's closest friends and it was perfect.

I wrestled, during those early months, about how often to visit the cemetery. Was it too much? Not enough? Sometimes I went to pray and sometimes I just wanted to talk to David, sharing what was going on in our lives and how much I missed him. Mike occasionally ate lunch there, and once the stone was set, we went often to swap out the seasonal flowers in the Packer vases. Regardless of how much or little we visited, it was always sobering and surreal. Still, we wanted to be there, especially on that first Thanksgiving and were reminded that this patch of ground was merely a memorial to the life David lived; a reminder that he is in heaven with Jesus. Like so many times before, I tearfully brushed away the grass clippings that covered his name and thanked God for him.

I coasted the rest of the day, just wanting it to be over. That's how it was most days; just wanting to go to bed, knowing I'd survived another day. At least when I slept, it was a break from the pain. As my head hit the pillow that night, knowing our first Thanksgiving was in the books, I thanked God for helping me through the day and for the peace of knowing he would get me through the next one. Then, I thanked God for David, over and over. The first Thanksgiving without David. *Checkmark.*

The closer we came to December, the more my heart engaged in a tug of war between sadness, fear, anger and guilt . . . each one fighting for control. The sadness and anger I felt always seemed to lead to a desperate sense of guilt, shaming me for not being able to focus on the joy of the birth of Jesus. The pain was so all-consuming that it suffocated any glimmer of holiday spirit, and I beat myself up for it. Daily. *Real productive, Jan.* Christmas would come whether David was here or not, and I wasn't sure if that thought was more comforting or infuriating.

Thankfully, our Heavenly Father is patient and kind and merciful. In the midst of growing anxiety and roaring pain, he gently whispered to my soul, "You can mourn the loss of your son, Jan, and still celebrate the birth of mine. You can mourn the loss of *your* son and STILL celebrate the birth of *mine.*" And for the first time in way too long, I was able to exhale; exhale guilt and breathe in peace.

The lie I'd been wrestling with is that my grief was wrong. It was dishonoring God and I should be ashamed of myself. But God's truth is that it's okay to be sad. It's okay to cry. It's okay to miss David. It's okay to wish he was still with us on Christmas morning. It's okay. But it's also okay (necessary even) to embrace the eternal perspective that brings hope. As big as this life seems, it is a single heartbeat on an eternal screen. Jesus was born, lived a perfect life, died, and was raised to life again, to abolish sin and suffering. Faith in Him is the only path to real healing, and his birth and sacrifice on the cross brings life, hope, mercy, and peace.

> *"For God loved the world so much that he gave his one and only Son, so that everyone who believes in him will not perish but*

have eternal life. God sent his Son into the world, not to judge the
world, but to save the world through Him." John 3:16–17

God continues to love David more than I ever could and he cares deeply about my loss. He understands my grief and knows that I need to be reminded to focus on *his* son, now more than ever. Because of Jesus, I know that I will see David again. Because of Jesus, my pain is not permanent. Because of Jesus, I can do this. The same Jesus that walks with David in Heaven, walks with me right now, and there is comfort knowing that we share a Savior. That *is* something to celebrate . . . even in the midst of pain. Especially in the midst of pain.

But what if you're not confident of the eternal condition of your loved one? Or even your own eternal destiny? Death is certain, but where we go after death is a matter of faith. As Jesus hung on the cross, suffering and dying to pay for the sins of all people, the criminal next to him used his dying breath to profess belief in Him. He'd witnessed the insults and brutal torture that Jesus suffered. He'd also witnessed Jesus' response to it all . . . responses of humility, love, and even forgiveness. In the short time they spent side by side, the criminal knew enough about Jesus to trust him as the Messiah, and he wanted to go where Jesus was going. The thief simply said, "Jesus, remember me when you come into your kingdom."

Without hesitation, Jesus assured him, "Truly I say to you, today you shall be with Me in Paradise." (Luke 23:43) God is merciful, anxious to save anyone who does the same. We cannot presume a person is eternally lost, and fearing that they are doesn't change a thing. In the end, our eternal destiny is determined between our hearts and God's. So, if not knowing the eternal condition of your loved one causes fear and anxiety, focus on the truth that God is merciful and he desires for every person to come to him. (See Appendix A on page 251 to learn more about God's gift of eternal life.)

I continued to meditate on the words whispered to my soul–*You can mourn the loss of your son and still celebrate the birth of mine*. It wasn't a one-and-done revelation that magically replaced pain with joy, but it did remind me that joy is not lost. Even years later, it is so important for me to make time during the holidays to simply rest in God's presence and meditate on the precious gift of Jesus.

This meditation on Jesus turned my thoughts to Christmas cards. We sent them every year and it's something I had always enjoyed. Not this year. No . . . desire . . . at . . . all. Writing so many thank you notes in response to expressions of sympathy, just a few months earlier, about did me in, so I had no interest in putting myself through it again. *People will understand. Right?* But God began to change my mind, prompting me to send photo cards with one of the last family pictures taken with David, on the day of his high school graduation. I had so little energy already and spending it on preparing and sending Christmas cards would hurt. Not to mention, I would have to sign three names on each one, instead of four. (Why didn't I think to add pre-printed names on the cards!) Still, God continued to nudge, and it was a chance for me to share the message with others that he had shared with me: *Although this will be our first Christmas without David, it is comforting to know that we can still find joy in celebrating the birth of our Savior Jesus Christ.*

Of course, everyone really would have understood if no card arrived from us that year. It would have been okay. Anguish and joy are often intertwined on this road of grief, and it is important for me to embrace each moment as it comes; to let the voice of God speak to my heart, knowing that he is faithful to give me the strength I need to do difficult things. Christmas cards? *Checkmark.*

December finally arrived and, as if the holiday trifecta weren't enough, I turned the calendar page to see the square announcing Mike's birthday. It was a big one that year. Fifty. *Should I plan a party? Would he even want one?* Normally, this wouldn't even be a question. Of course I'd plan a party! But nothing was normal anymore and the thought of it was overwhelming. If I did nothing, Mike might feel unloved or unimportant. If I did, he might be overwhelmed, too. To be honest, I was still a bit of a zombie at that point and it was an awkward predicament. But David and Daniel always loved a good birthday party, so I decided that planning a celebration of this milestone was an important "yes" to give.

Life doesn't wait for us to heal. It pushes us forward, even when we don't feel up for the challenge, and sometimes we have to force ourselves to break free from the pain and engage with others . . . *whether we feel like it or not.* (These seven little words became an important mantra.) Even when something feels impossible, if it is a leap that we know we need to take, God is able to provide the emotional and mental strength we need to get through it. And we can trust him to bring us to the other side stronger and better prepared for our next challenge.

As the crowd of smiling faces sang Happy Birthday to Mike in the upstairs party room of a restaurant on our town square, we both felt loved. It wasn't the traditional belly-laughing, rip-roaring party it might have been. We hurt, but God got us through . . . again.

The December 25th square on the calendar was fast approaching. *Was this really it? Christmas? Joy to the World? Feels more like Oh, Horrible Night.* I know, I know. I was supposed to be celebrating God's Son. And I really was trying. While I had definitely been given a beautiful reminder to hold on to, one that encouraged my heart and kept me from falling completely apart, I still felt empty much of the time.

Instead of staying home for Christmas that year, we decided to drive to Wisconsin and spend it with Mike's family. We wouldn't stay with his parents this time because we were walking through unknown emotional territory and would need some privacy, so they arranged for us to stay in a condo, with a beautiful view of the lake, where we could go to collapse and unwind after an emotional day or escape if we needed time alone. It was perfect.

The days were spent waltzing around grief; the proverbial elephant in the room. I tried hard to focus on the family that surrounded us, but pictures of David were everywhere at Grandpa and Grandma's (as they should be) and I found myself distracted. Grandpa went all out with Christmas decorations, as he always did (think Clark Griswold!) so the house was bright and festive, to say the least. But I didn't feel bright or festive. I wanted to, really, but I didn't. I couldn't.

One thing that is especially hard when enduring profound loss, is small talk. In fact, it can be completely unbearable. *David is gone. He should be here. And we're talking about football? Hunting? Food?* I love Mike's family and they were certainly not doing anything wrong. On the contrary, they were trying so hard to be supportive and they were doing exactly what we needed the most, carrying on with special family traditions. Even though it didn't *feel* right. It was a part of our new normal that we would need to adjust to.

All I could think about was how much David would have loved being with us. *How can I feel happy when he is missing this? When I am missing him?* I found myself obsessed with what he would be doing if he were there: doting on his cousins, playing cards with Grandpa, and laughing at lengthy family discussions, with everyone talking at the same time and disagreeing loudly about what each one remembers about any given subject. He loved sitting back, enjoying the show with a big smile on his face. Before the day was over, he would be schmoozing his Auntie Laura, convincing her to make him some sort of apple dessert. I smiled at the thought of it.

One of the last photos of David and Daniel with their Wisconsin cousins.

We all attended Christmas Eve service together at a small church in the north woods. As the Pastor shared the Christmas story–the same one I had heard a hundred times before–I listened more intently than ever. Tears filled my eyes and streamed down my face; tears of anguish, missing David, and tears of joy, so thankful for the birth of Jesus who died for me and lives in me. I don't know if it was difficult for Mike's family to see my tears or not. I imagine it may have been, but I've learned two things about crying. First, our grief is *our* grief. It may be hard for others to witness because they don't know how to respond to it, but the truth is that we need to allow ourselves to grieve and not worry about the comfort of others. Second, God made our tears with such a specific and wonderful purpose.

While every mammal produces tears to keep eyes irrigated and clean, human beings are the only mammals to produce tears in response to emotion. And tears resulting from emotion are chemically different than tears meant to protect the eye.[1] They are natural stress-relievers that lower blood pressure, remove toxins from the body, and reduce manganese; a chemical that increases anxiety and irritability. In short, when we cry tears in response to grief, our bodies and minds experience healing. Wow God! So, embrace the unique mammal he created you to be and cry those tears! They will literally help you survive the emotional storm of grief. Believe me, I cried

1. Griffith et al., *Crying that Heals*, 167–179.

enough tears that Christmas to relieve plenty of stress, but it didn't mean I had any more energy to face the new year. Maybe next Christmas will be easier? Anyway . . . *checkmark*. Two holidays down, one to go.

One evening in late December, Mike flipped through the TV channels to find a movie for us to watch, something we did often. It was a mindless escape. Wine was another *escape* for me. Yes, wine. So, as Mike flipped the channels, I sipped away at my second glass of Pinot Grigio. He finally chose a western. Most people like westerns. I used to. But within minutes, the gunshots began. In true western style, the shootout lasted for what seemed like forever. *Will this ever end!* I tried to ignore it, looking away and continuing to sip. *Will I ever be able to hear even imaginary gunshots without my heart beating out of my chest?*

I raised my glass to Mike, "Will there ever be a time when I don't need to numb myself with wine or beer at nighttime?" He really didn't know what to say and I left the room before tears took over. There I stood, in front of the bathroom mirror, sobbing because I missed David, because I was afraid of being afraid, and because I was so angry that grief continued to control my life. Then I saw my hand in the mirror, clinging to my empty glass. *Am I too dependent on alcohol? Could this habit become an addiction?* It would be so easy to allow external "fixes" to overtake me; trying to fill voids with retail therapy, alcohol, busyness, or just hiding away from any form of reality. Not only were external "fixes" counterproductive to my own healing, but Daniel also needed to know that they were not the answer to coping with the loss of his brother. Ultimately, the only productive way to deal with my pain was to continue dealing with my pain. This was a significant revelation and from that moment on, I refused to let alcohol be an escape. I still enjoy a glass now and then, but I keep it in check.

With just one calendar square standing between me and the new year, all I could do was replay the past 12 months, like a movie; over, and over, and over, and over. I mean, isn't that what New Year's Eve is all about? Celebrating the past and anticipating the future? Honestly. I didn't want to do either. 2010 was a cruel year and I wondered if 2011 would be any better. *I hope so. God, I sure hope so.* Few things have been harder than turning the calendar page to that first new year; a year that David would never know. New Years. *Checkmark*.

Into the new year I went, journeying to a destination I may never reach. It was becoming more and more clear all the time that I would never stop grieving the loss of my son. It will change, of course. I will cry less and smile more. I will feel less pain and even look forward to things again. But I will never stop missing David and wondering how his life would have turned out. I will never be done with grief.

Sitting alone with God, writing about our first holiday season, I surrendered myself completely to him . . . again. I was a mess, with nowhere to go except into the strong and merciful arms of my Savior. I was desperately trying to trust him; trying to be strong and to move forward. *Do you see me trying, God? Do Mike or Daniel? Does there have to be a tragedy for you to get my attention? You have my attention! Help me, God. I'm scared and I feel alone.*

Remember that tree Cindy planted in our yard, to honor David's memory? Well, full disclosure, we killed it. Can you believe it!? We weren't physically or emotionally equipped to keep up with the necessary maintenance that a new tree requires, but thankfully Cindy understood and made arrangements to replace it with another tree. That one is thriving and Mike decorates *David's evergreen* every year with Christmas lights. It shines so bright from the top of our hill. I love that tree and here's what it's taught me: we failed and the tree died, but the story didn't. A new and beautiful tree lives on because we didn't give up.

My story will not end in failure either, and neither will yours. As long as we refuse to surrender to the lies that threaten to defeat us. . .as long as we take refuge in the arms of God and embrace his promise to get us through, we will survive this. Those first holidays were grueling. The days in between were just as grueling. But Christ who lives in me continued to give me the strength I needed to take another step . . . and then another . . . and another, until one day I realized that there really were days when it didn't hurt quite so bad. And I began to really believe that there is hope for the future. *Checkmark.*

RAW JOURNAL ENTRY

December 2010–Our first Christmas without our son

I feel weak and angry tonight. God, help me to move even closer to you through this traumatic time in my life. This world and life as I know it seems foreign to me. I feel like a stranger here, surrounded by people who are indifferent and callous. Life continues, but I can't seem to catch up to life. Help us, Lord, we need you so much. We are all hurting and fighting to push through, trying with all that we have to keep our eyes fixed on you. Give us your Spirit, Lord. Let us feel your presence. We need you to survive. Literally. We need you to survive.

Lord, hold us as we continue to work through the grieving process this Christmas. Please remind us, when the sadness is overwhelming, that you know what it feels like to lose a Son, and that you sent yours to the world for us. . .to save, forgive, restore, redeem and set forth a home in Heaven for us when it's our time. I can't imagine what our lives would be like if we didn't have a personal relationship with Jesus! Thank you for the gift that he is to us, not just at Christmastime but every day of the year. We would be lost without You! Comfort me and fill me with Your truth. I have to continue to choose truth.

FIRST AID FOR YOUR GRIEVING HEART

Healing Prayer

Dear Jesus, help me to celebrate my "checkmarks" as proof of your love and faithfulness. Thank you for understanding my grieving heart and for giving me the gift of tears. Please give me wisdom to know when I need to say "no" and courage when I need to step out in faith to engage with others, knowing it will be hard.

Healing Truth

Visit the following pages to unleash God's healing power over the lies that threaten to defeat you: *My loved one may not be in Heaven* (p. 172); *Grieving during the Christmas season dishonors God* (p. 196); *If I don't say yes to everything then I'm failing to heal* (p. 200).

Healing Words

What difficulties have you faced–or do you fear facing–during holidays or special events? What do you wish others understood about your grief? What external "fixes" do you turn to at times and how is that impeding your progress? Embrace your grieving heart today by writing your own story of holiday struggles and victories.

Chapter 8

The Same Power

Iowa winters are long and can be filled with snow, ice, bitter winds, and below-zero temperatures . . . for months. The brown hues take over the Iowa landscape and the acres of farmland, as far as the eye can see, are desolate, brown and scattered with the dried remnants left behind from the previous year's harvest. By March, we long to feel the warm sun on our faces again and look forward to emerging shades of green, which are among the most brilliant. Always Stunning. Ten months after David died, spring was on the horizon but it still felt like winter in my heart; as colorless and barren as the fields outside our window. *Will I ever feel safe and warm again? Will I ever experience the hope of new growth?* I really didn't know.

It was April now. Easter baskets and giant bunnies filled the aisles of every store, along with the fresh scent of white Easter lilies and big signs announcing, "Congratulations Graduates!" Farmers prepared their fields to accept new crops, turning dingy brown soil into black gold. Brightly colored flowers of pink, purple, yellow and blue would soon begin to replace the shades of evergreen, and even the air smelled different . . . better. But all these signs of spring–of new life and fresh starts–took me back to the weeks before David died. Instead of feeling excited about warmer weather and pots full of flowers, I was replaying the year before. Instead of celebrating life with the rest of the world, I was stuck on death.

When the boys were little, Easter mornings were the best. "Come on Daniel!" David's feet dashed down the stairs, followed quickly by Daniel's.

"The Easter bunny came!"

"Look at these crazy boxers!"

"Did you get peanut butter eggs, too?"

As I prepared for our first Easter without David, so many fun memories swirled in my heart, which lifted my spirits. But as usual, my fond reflections were quickly replaced with heartache. This Easter morning, there would be no dashing feet or laughter. We were sad. Still, we did our best to maintain the spirit of our traditions: candy, church, and family dinner, followed by a trip to the cemetery. There wasn't a gravestone yet. We were working on it, but it had become such a drawn-out, emotional process. *How in the world do we encompass David's life and our love for him on six square feet of granite? It isn't possible.* I felt guilty that it was taking so long, and I gained a whole new appreciation for the immensity of this gut-wrenching task.

There we sat, next to a modest grave marker and a green and gold styrofoam "4" (a reminder of David's obsession for his favorite Packer). It was quiet for a long time and my mind drifted back to the Easter message we heard that morning. It was the same message I had heard repeated since I was a little girl. No surprises. Jesus died on the cross, was buried, and three days later he was resurrected. End of story. Bring on the ham, cheesy potatoes, and chocolate eggs!

In my head, I clearly and redundantly grasped that Easter is all about *life*. Jesus died and rose again to give *life* . . . to give hope. It's the greatest reason for celebration. Just as the spring season brings dormant things back to life, so Jesus gives life to our souls. *So, why am I sitting in a cemetery feeling desperately sad? Why doesn't the truth of the Easter message take away this pain?* The lie that threatens to defeat me is that thoughts and feelings of death will always define my life. Jesus says, "I am the resurrection and the life. He who believes in me will live, even though he dies; and whoever lives and believes in me will never die" (John 11:25–26). Powerful. Jesus has power over death and his free gift of eternal life is for anyone who places their trust in him. *I know this, God, so why don't I feel it?*

Jesus answers with a challenge, "Will you choose death . . . or life? Which will you focus on?" David died. I can't change that. It's awful and painful and it's part of my story forever. But the truth is that Jesus *lives* in heaven, he *lives* in me, and he is preparing a place for me to *live* in heaven with him someday. Hope is found in *life*, not death. The Easter message can only ease my pain if I choose to focus on the life he gives . . . as I focus on Jesus.

Everything in my life comes back to David, and everything comes back to Jesus. It just does. The reality of the latter always follows the heartache of the former. Always. And truth tells me that healing will only come as I hold tight to the knowledge that Jesus loves me, strengthens me, and will never give up on me. Eventually, my broken heart will catch-up to what my mind already knows. I just need to be as persistent as my pain.

Matthew 14:22–33 tells the story of Jesus and Peter walking on water. Now, what in the world does that have to do with persisting through pain? More than you might imagine! Jesus had been ministering tirelessly from town to town, along with his disciples, when he learned that John the Baptist had been killed. Clearly grieving, Jesus withdraws to be alone in solitude, but he is followed by thousands of people who want to learn more about him. I can't imagine. Even so, he has compassion for them. He heals them, teaches them, and even feeds them. (It's the same thing he does for us!) And that evening, surely exhausted, Jesus retreats to pray on the mountainside while his disciples seek rest together in a boat, far from shore.

Early the next morning, as waves and wind crash against their boat, the disciples notice someone coming toward them, walking across the lake. They are terrified, thinking it is a ghost, until they hear Jesus say, "Take courage. It is I. Don't be afraid." I mean, think of that!

It fascinates Peter and he hollers impulsively, "Lord if it's you, tell me to come to you on the water." Out of the boat he jumps and begins walking toward Jesus, until . . . he notices the wind. He takes his eyes off of Jesus and is instantly overwhelmed by the conditions around him. Fear sinks him. But as he calls out in desperation, asking for help, Jesus *immediately* lifts him from the waves. The two climb into the boat and the disciples worship Jesus, probably with mouths hanging open in awe, proclaiming him to be the Son of God. Powerful.

The power that allowed Jesus to serve thousands of people in the midst of his own grief, the power that allowed him to walk on stormy waters, the power that raised him from the grave, lives in me. It's the same power. It is available to me. And to you. Romans 8:11 says, ". . . if the Spirit of him who raised Jesus from the dead is living in you, he who raised Christ from the dead will also give life to your mortal bodies because of his Spirit who lives in you."

Just like Peter, we have to step out of the boat and seek to be in God's presence; talking with him in prayer, focusing on the truth of Scripture, and choosing to trust him to get us through. When David died, I didn't leap out of the boat in anticipation. I was pushed. In fact, my boat capsized and I was immediately drowning in waves of fear and grief. I didn't ask for it. I didn't like it. And I didn't know if I would survive it. Every time I focus more on my circumstance than on Jesus, I'm sunk. But by God's mercy, as I continually choose to turn my eyes to him and focus on his love and power, my cold heart finds relief. God is my life preserver, and I'm so thankful for that.

Mother's Day brought a new kind of storm, an emotional hurricane, really. I was tearful and moody, and did not want to leave the house. I cried a lot, trying to purge all of the emotions I'd been avoiding or hiding, which felt better for a little while. Until the next time they swirled around. Grieving these special days was becoming a predictable and repetitive battle of emotions that I dreaded. *Will it ever get easier? Jesus, pull me from the waves!* It's something I asked often throughout that first year.

So, Mother's Day. Hallmark at its best. Mother's everywhere share sappy stories of the days their children were born; holding them for the first time, being so in love. I know, because I am one of them. We think about the times when we (moms) were the only ones who could console our kids when life got hard. We think about how our joy has multiplied as we've watched them grow. *Can I love them any more than I do right now? Could I be any more proud?* Potty training, t-ball games, band concerts, first dates . . . and then, in a blink, we're writing checks to order caps and gowns for graduation. We smile, a little sad that time has moved so fast, but we know that the next chapter of motherhood will also bring joy. *Isn't life wonderful?*

At least, that's how it is supposed to be. When Mother's Day arrived for me, I was on autopilot, flying through a wormhole of past celebrations and present-day realities. Hard to smile? Yeah. But I managed somehow and politely thanked Mike and Daniel as they wished me Happy Mother's Day. My gift was an eBook reader. "We thought maybe this would help you get back into reading again, like you used to, Mom." I knew they wanted me back. Of course they did! And so did I.

One of the hardest parts of Mother's Day is the battle it brings between the sadness of missing David and the need to celebrate with Daniel. I love Daniel so much and thank God for him. And he needs me to be fully present. It would break my heart if he ever believed that my grief outweighs my love for him, so I simply had to reel in my emotions and focus on the moment; to adapt to this new normal the best way I could. When I found a moment alone, I picked up the oversized Mother's Day card that David gave me just weeks before he died and read his hand-written words, *I love you Mom, David.* Reading this has become a Mother's Day tradition each year since. What a treasure.

I also treasure text messages from other moms, especially the ones who know what it is like to lose a child. Our hearts are tied together all year long, but especially on Mother's Day. Cheryl's son, Ryne, was a student at Texas Tech when he died after using K2, just like David. He was 21. "I'm lifting you up in prayer this Mother's Day." Cheryl's loss was so fresh, but this is the message she sent me, just six months after losing Ryne. We have an unfortunate bond that allows us to connect in a very meaningful way, about how we're coping and to encourage one another. Though we've only ever talked on the phone, we're forever connected and I hope to meet her one day. Friendships like this, the ones formed through common grief, have been essential to my healing process. It's worth putting yourself out there, to connect with other grieving hearts. It lets you know you're not alone.

Grief is painfully repetitive. But so is God's comfort and mercy. 365 days a year, we cycle in and out of struggles that are hauntingly similar. We fight similar emotions and, just when we think we have a handle on something, it slips through our fingers. In fact, it's easy to question whether or not we've moved at all, from the day our loved one died. When I doubt my progress, James 4:8 holds this promise: "Come near to God and he will come near to you."

Do you feel like you've failed in the midst of grief? Do you struggle with anger? Are you exhausted from painful emotions? Is it difficult to even get out of bed? Draw near to God. I promise . . . he promises . . . that he will draw near to you. Draw near to him on the good days and the bad days. He wants so desperately to breathe life into our aching souls.

I wish I could tell you that drawing near to God will remove the process of grief. It won't. But it *will* give you the strength to move forward. The power of Jesus wants to reign in you and restore your joy. You are priceless. God loves you desperately and he hurts when you hurt. I urge you today, right now, draw near to him. Talk to him. Maybe you don't even know if God is real. Or maybe you're angry with him. Maybe you've never prayed before. Be honest! He is never shocked because he already knows your heart. It might sound something like this:

> *Dear God, I'm angry and don't even know if you're really there. I want to believe it. I want to believe that you have the power to heal my grieving heart and to help me to go on with life. I need you to show me that you love me. Amen.*

By the end of May, David's stone was finally ready to be set and we were thankful that it would be in place before June 6th, the one year anniversary of his death. We wanted it to be life-giving to those who would visit and to serve as a reminder of our eternal hope found in Jesus. The black granite stone stands close to the tree line and holds two stone vases on either side, which are etched with a letter "G" and frequently restocked with yellow flowers. We had to. He loved the Packers. The best part is that his grave doesn't look lonely anymore. There is a picture of Daniel and him, taken on graduation day, as well as one of David's favorite senior pictures. On the back is a large etching of our farm, including his tree stand with some wildlife and his guitar leaning against the bottom of the same tree. There is also a paragraph, sharing a description of David. Of course, this had to be condensed to fit the stone. I joked with the monument people that we would need to etch "To be continued" at the bottom so we could continue the paragraph on another stone! What can I say? I'm wordy. And then there's the huge caps etched across the front: DAVID MITCHELL ROZGA. It looks very nice and it honors David, but nobody can fully understand the agony of seeing your child's name across a tombstone, unless they've experienced it themselves. It's just not right.

It will always be surreal.

Sitting by his stone for the first time, my mind raced through memories of one year earlier; seeing him in his purple cap and gown, watching him walk across the stage to get his diploma, taking photos at his party, and seeing his face lit up with a wider grin than I'd ever seen on him before. It was such a special time . . . so full of joy and hope for his future. A week later, he was gone. No more joy. No more future.

Reliving every moment leading up to that horrific day was unavoidable. *Has it really been a year since I was scrambling to get the house ready for his graduation party? A year since I stood in the aisle of the party store, crying over what napkins to buy?* I know now, many years later, that seasonal reminiscing is part of my new normal. It just is. It still makes me cry, but it also makes me smile. Some people call it *bittersweet*. Good name for it.

With David only gone a year, and so many of our memories wrapped around graduation, Mike and I decided we would only attend selected graduation parties. That's all our hearts would allow. And even then, I wasn't looking forward to any of them. It sounds terrible, doesn't it? But my pain was preventing me from seeing the obvious. These kids were feeling the same joy and anticipation that David felt the year before. Their parents were feeling the same sense of pride and happiness that I had felt. With each step, up each driveway, I asked God to lessen my pain and to help me remember that this was not about me . . . or David. I needed his power to guide my heart to celebrate because it was about these kids now. It's about their families. #recalculating.

I decided to post a picture of David on Facebook, on the anniversary of his death, a tradition I still continue. He's not here, but he is still my son. He always will be and I will always be proud of him. Many people respond with words of encouragement and things they remember about David. I love knowing that people haven't forgotten him and that they still love him, too. It's comforting. It's also comforting to reflect on that first year and realize that the force of my repeated pain was continually met by God lovingly, relentlessly, and repeatedly giving hope. Thank you, Jesus, for giving hope. Year two begins tomorrow.

RAW JOURNAL ENTRY

June 2017–Seven years after our son died

So, each spring as the brilliant greens begin to take over the Iowa landscape, I find hope. As the perfect rows of tiny green shoots start to peek up through the rich soil below, the farmer knows that a time for harvest will follow. All in due time.

And so it is with grief. I long for any signs of growth, recovery, and renewal. That's what I want. I had no idea that my grief would ebb and flow in a way that would jumpstart my pain over and over again. I've never experienced anything like it, ever! But my heart keeps track of everything. Sporadic seasons of grief invade my life–out of nowhere–and I can't shake it off. It clings to me.

But it's so comforting to trust that God knows just the right time to slowly bring the dormant grass and flowers back to life after a long Iowa winter. Surely, he loves me enough to do the same. I know he does.

FIRST AID FOR YOUR GRIEVING HEART

Healing Prayer

Dear Jesus, I want to draw near to you; to stay focused on you and your promises. I believe what you say in your Word, that the Spirit who raised you from the dead is able to give me the strength I need for today, tomorrow . . . every day.

Healing Truth

Visit the following pages to unleash God's healing power over the lies that threaten to defeat you: *I could have stopped this* (p. 163); *Death will always define my life* (p. 204); *Grief has power over me* (p. 207).
**To understand more about God's free gift of eternal life, see Appendix A on page 251.

Healing Words

Do you ever feel like Peter, sinking from fear or sadness? Have you felt God sustain you above the crashing emotional waves in your life? Do you still need to feel rescued? Embrace your grieving heart by writing to God about your fears, struggles, and past victories . . . draw near to him by reflecting on (or searching for) his faithfulness.

PART III

SURVIVAL AS A WAY OF LIFE

Chapter 9

Simmering Pots: *Grief and Marriage*

I burst into tears the minute he walked out the door. He was upset. I know. But I was upset, too. *He shouldn't have said those things! I shouldn't have said those things. But . . . he . . . I . . .* As I sat in our living room, I had the overwhelming feeling that we'd reached our breaking point; in marriage, in grief, in everything. *I lost David and now I'm losing Mike.* Imagination took the wheel and I was off on a terrifying ride . . .

Through decades of marriage, we endured and even grew closer through a range of difficult issues but none prepared us for the day our son shot himself or the unthinkable years to follow. How could anything have prepared us for that? Our marriage was strong, but was it strong enough to survive this? Were we strong enough to grieve *together*? I hoped so, but I honestly wasn't sure. Not only were Mike and I fighting to survive our own pain, but we were also fighting to understand the pain of the other. Future uncertainties were infinite and potential scenarios played in my mind over and over. Not only was it exhausting, but totally counter-productive. It led to the overwhelming fear that we were defeated . . . maybe not now, but eventually.

There's no sugar-coating it. Grieving *together* doesn't always make things easier. Not only do you have your personal fears and emotions to process, but the fears and emotions of your spouse and the complexity of being on different pages nearly every day. The only hope for survival is to walk the path of loss together, guided by the light of God's truth. Nice soundbite, right? But trust me, there isn't anything *nice* about it. It's a day-to-day, minute-by-minute exercise in emergency preparedness. No experienced hiker would venture into the wilderness without a compass and a flashlight, and no married couple should venture into grief without the light of God's truth. It's the only way through.

The words in this chapter are some of the hardest for me to write because I love my husband and want to honor the work God continues to do in our marriage, while being uncomfortably honest about some of our most painful struggles in the wake of our son's death. It's my prayer that sharing our story brings hope and healing to yours.

You've heard of having an elephant in the room? Well, we had a herd. I believe one of the most tragic misconceptions about successful marriage is that the two people involved are simply more compatible . . . nicer . . . wealthier . . . stronger . . . more spiritual . . . fill-in-the-blank . . . than *we are*. Surely there is some "*thing*" that makes it easier for them, and if we only had that "*thing*" our marriage would be easier too. But easy marriages only exist in our imagination. Weakness. Short fuses. Anger. Anguish. Outbursts. Pride. Disappointment. Selfishness. Avoidance. Emotional disconnect. Lack of grace. Lack of intimacy. It's all part of the human condition and the marriage relationship. We put two broken people together and expect bliss. Thousands of books have been written about falling in love and staying in love. This isn't one of them. This story–our story–is about two weak people, fighting for survival as we cling to God's grace for ourselves and each other, and learn to live life without our son. Spoiler Alert: There will be no magic before-and-after "reveal" of the Rozgas.

Mike and I are still a work in progress. Truth is, the marriage issues we faced prior to losing David would have to lie in wait as we turned our attention to our survival and not much else. Grief demands this, but it isn't an excuse for any of us to ignore that which will eventually crop up again. Of course, grieving together would be easier if we had the whole marriage puzzle figured out before losing a loved one, but this is unrealistic. Marriage is a living breathing thing, and just when the last piece of the puzzle is placed, somebody changes the picture. Boy, does the loss of a loved one change the picture! Before David died, even though we loved each other and were committed to growing our relationship, we had disagreements about our differing communication needs, social interactions, and even sex. Losing David didn't change any of that. It simply put all of our "pots" on the back burner as we focused on putting one foot in front of the other. During the earliest and most traumatic days, Mike and I clung to each other. We were more vulnerable, prayerful, and tender than ever. Things that seemed like a big deal in our marriage just days prior, were instantly irrelevant as we only worked to get ourselves, each other, and Daniel through the days. Grief certainly has a way of imposing perspective.

In the 22 years before David died, Mike and I endured miscarriage and tubal pregnancy. We had disagreements about disciplining the boys, our finances, personal health issues, and various other life decisions. Through all of it, we were still standing. But burying a child is different. It's *the unthinkable.* As persistent thoughts of David took up residence in my heart in the days following his death, I didn't have room for much else. Let's face it, I had a hard-enough time just getting out of bed and maybe brushing my teeth. But eventually, as the days turned into months and months into years, the issues we faced prior to losing David came back like a boomerang. The pots we'd moved to the back burner slowly began to simmer. Gosh, I thought we'd be able to pick up where we left off and simply tackle the issues. This shouldn't be hard, right? Think again. We had no idea the toll it would take to dive back into our normal marriage routine.

The emotional, social, and physical aspects of our marriage were neglected as we grieved. We paid attention to each other a lot, but it was almost always about helping each other through grief rather than concentrating on each other as husband and wife. Of course, this is all very natural, but there was a morning when I just sort of woke up and realized that life was moving on and previous marital issues were still lurking beneath the surface. Who am I kidding? Sometimes the issues didn't lurk, they jumped out and screamed! But sometimes in the midst of grief, we inadvertently end up placing painful issues on the back burner, which adds even more hurt to grief that already consumes us. It ultimately becomes impossible to juggle everything.

One simmering pot that threatened to destroy our marriage was emotional distance. If we failed to connect emotionally, it could potentially divide us, and maybe even end us. I'm an overthinker and Mike tends to be pretty black-and-white. Neither of which changed after David died. Still, Mike became very intentional about asking me open-ended questions and showing genuine concern for how I was doing and what I needed from him. This had to be difficult for him. In fact, I didn't realize until much later how much these questions cost him emotionally. For him to dig into my emotional world meant that he had to risk exposing his own. Talk about vulnerability! He chose to walk directly into my pain, knowing that there wasn't anything black-and-white about it. Engaging in conversations about our pain and fears meant that we both had to be honest about the thoughts and feelings that were more natural and comfortable to suppress, and we both had to listen with a sincere desire to understand. Looking back, I wish I'd been more transparent. But every time I tried to be open and honest, I would over-analyze everything: *Did I say too much? Should I have said more? What did he mean by that? What isn't he telling me? Am I the only one who is afraid? Is he going to think I've lost my mind? Have I?*

Grief by nature is a builder of emotional barriers. Even though Mike was great about asking questions, I sometimes had a hard time experiencing peace in our conversations. I may be the one who overthinks everything, but surely Mike was wondering the same things, *wasn't he?* It was exhausting and it created fertile soil for superficial and stressful conversations. We both knew that a high percentage of marriages fail after losing a child and, because of this, we became more guarded about what we shared instead of less. Honestly, I didn't even want to think about most of what swarmed around in my mind, so why in the world would I want to say it out loud and bring him down? We weren't fighting, but I often felt as though the emotional distance between us was growing, or at least that's what my paranoia told me. It was difficult for me to understand why Mike didn't seem concerned. *Or is he concerned and just doesn't want to talk about it?* So much futile speculation.

What took me too long to acknowledge is that my husband is not a mind reader. Neither of us is. So, each time we make assumptions or overlook something, instead of talking honestly about it . . . we harm our relationship and stumble on our path to healing. If I need to be held, I have to *tell* him. If I need to talk about David, I have to *tell* him. If I wonder why he is having a hard time with something, I have to *ask*. When the clouds of grief create painful perceptions, I need to go to Mike. Every. Single. Time. And the same is true for him. It is only through honest, vulnerable conversation that we grow to understand how differently we grieve from one another. No matter how obvious it may seem to us at the moment, it is an unfair practice to assume that our spouse knows what we're thinking or what we need.

Deciding how we would deal with our first Christmas without David created two opposing scenarios. It was very important for Mike to maintain tradition by having a Christmas tree with all the trimmings. I really couldn't relate. In fact, it irritated me. *Why in the world would we put up a Christmas tree and act like everything is normal!* I assumed that he would never understand why I *wouldn't* want a tree. I know my apathy irritated him, but he *did* understand. Through honest conversation, I realized that he understood but that he also embraced the idea that Christmas was coming whether we celebrated it or not. . .whether David was here or not. We were going to hurt and cry whether we had a tree or not. The heart of the issue is that neither of us was wrong. Just different. And discussing "different," in the light of God's truth, diffuses the darkness . . . every single time. All of a sudden, the issue of having a tree or not having a tree became secondary as I realized it had nothing to do with material traditions or whose grief was better or worse. It had to do with communicating and seeking to understand. And remembering the reason for celebrating Christmas in the first place.

The not-so-simple truth is that Mike's grief for David is different than mine. He experiences different challenges because he had a different and distinct father-son relationship with David. However, as much as I try, I will never fully understand his grief any more than he can fully understand mine. When we try, it often leads to unintended hurt feelings. Constantly reminding ourselves of this not only increases the grace we have for each other, it also helps us to grieve *together*, instead of without each other.

One topic that Mike and I struggled to see eye to eye on is hunting. He and the boys love hunting together. It's a Rozga family tradition. Mike grew up hunting with his Dad and it is a passion he passed on to David and Daniel as soon as they were old enough. But after David died, I didn't want guns in our house (for obvious reasons) so Mike packed them up and took them to our neighbor's house. Deep down, I hoped they never came back. *Surely, they won't want to hunt anymore. Right?* I hoped that they would understand why a gun of any kind would spark anxiety in me, knowing that it was what David used to end his life. Still, the day came when Mike told me a gun safe had been ordered and the guns were coming back, to be safely stored in our basement. My heart raced. After days of anxiety and anger, we sat at the table and I prepared to make things clear to Mike. He needed to know just how strongly I felt and how insensitive he was being. Turns out, the same could have been said of me.

I sat stunned as he explained two things. First, the reason he took the guns out of the house was that he didn't want Daniel or me to have access to them during a time of unbearable pain. Second, he shared how close he feels to David each time he watches a sunrise before a turkey hunt or hears the rustle of leaves as he sits in the tree stand, watching for that 10-point buck. Hunting isn't the same for Mike without David, but continuing to hunt is an important way for him to stay connected with some of the best memories he and David shared. Sigh. I got it. No matter how difficult it was for me, I couldn't take that away from him. Mike showed respect for my feelings by purchasing a gun safe and protecting me from conversations and television shows involving guns and hunting. He continues to remind me that synthetic drugs are the reason our son isn't here today. . .not firearms.

As I have prayed for God to lessen my fear and protect Mike and Daniel, as they continue to hunt, it has become easier for me each time they go–so much easier than it would have been had Mike and I dug our heels in, judging each other's actions before seeking to understand the deeper issues caused by grief. There are usually deeper issues lurking under the surface. We've learned that it's far better to struggle through the hard realities than to live in the darkness of what might be. Let's be honest, all of us are master builders of emotional barriers that protect our innermost thoughts and most intimate struggles. It's natural to be afraid of laying our hearts open and letting our spouses see every gory detail. But God is not the author of fear. Fear promotes a litany of disconnect that is destructive, especially when our marriage is under fire. God gives us the tools we need to experience healing as we surrender emotional barriers and learn to exercise grace, even when we disagree.

As we allow each other to grieve uniquely and listen to each other with a sincere and prayerful desire to understand, we find light for our path. Intentional, honest conversations aren't always comfortable but they are necessary for the survival of your marriage. With communication comes knowledge. With knowledge comes understanding. And with understanding comes the destruction of false assumptions and damaging preconceptions. There's only one way to move forward, broken together with Jesus: Just talk. Pray together. Agree to focus on one issue at a time and not to bounce back and forth between subjects that hurt. You're on the same team, remember? So, actively ask God for the wisdom to recognize your own emotional barriers, the strength to be transparent, and the humility to respond to your spouse with grace. Patience, transparency, and grace. All day. Every day.

Another simmering pot threatening to destroy our relationship was our social life. Mike is a social guy. He loves going out and having people over. He serves at church and in the community on various committees, and he loves getting together with friends to hunt, fish, golf, and play cards. While losing David certainly resulted in a period of time when he didn't feel like he could have fun or laugh, it didn't fundamentally change his desire to be social. Me, on the other hand? I love staying home and loved it even more after David died. Back then, I didn't even want to leave the room to use the bathroom, let alone go out in public. Any thought of re-introducing myself to the public and interacting socially, flooded me with anxiety. I was comfortable staying home. Period. End of discussion. The most I could bare was to venture out with Mike for a quick, anonymous dinner in a nearby town, or to grab an ice cream cone and eat it while driving around to nowhere. Avoiding people in our town meant we could avoid "the looks." Oh, *there's that poor family.* It really did feel like all eyes were on us, whether it was true or not. And to be honest, it didn't feel right to be out and about when David wasn't here.

As time passed, Mike believed it would be good for us to begin socializing again. I wanted more time. How could I possibly get excited about walking right into what I perceived as the *normal* lives of others, with families fully intact, when ours was not? The very idea made my heart feel as if it were being slammed into a brick wall. It wasn't that I resented them for it, I just wanted it for myself again.

Even though I consider myself to be a people person, my default reaction to social invitations is usually the desire to decline. I know this annoys Mike at times. I get it. *But surely now, just weeks after losing our son, he will cut me some slack.* I was in constant fear that we'd have to leave the house and he was increasingly convinced that we needed to. Simmering pot! Needless to say, it took more and more patience on his part and more and more courage on mine, and we finally reached a compromise . . . dinner on our deck with friends.

The evening came and it was awkward. Mike knew I didn't want to do it, and I was irritated that he even asked me to. But there we were, adult beverages in hand, eating chips and salsa, and making small talk with two of our closest friends. As the hours passed, there were glimpses of normal conversation and even a laugh or two, which cut like a knife even more than I expected them to. It seemed disloyal somehow, as though we'd already forgotten that our son was dead. *This is so ridiculous. I just want to be alone, with Mike and Daniel.* Only recently I've accepted that this feeling wasn't wrong . . . just misleading. When we struggle to engage in situations that would have been normal prior to the death of our loved one, we simply have to treat ourselves with compassion and without judgment.

Looking back, I realize that "normal conversation" was exactly what I needed, even though I didn't feel like it, and it was the beginning of a healing process that I continue to walk through today. We have precious friends who I am so thankful for, but having a full social calendar continues to be a struggle for me. The point is, Mike and I have had to find a way to meet each other in the middle and bring balance to the social aspect of our marriage, even as we continue to grieve. When Mike encourages me to get together with friends or go out to a restaurant in our town, he isn't being mean or insensitive. When I don't want to go, I'm not trying to drag him down. It's not a *personal* attack. Together, with God's help, we are finding balance. It's good for us to be still and experience solitude at home, and it is also good for us to be among friends and engage with our community. It's important for us to provide each other with loving nudges in the right direction. Baby steps are not only possible, they're essential to the survival of our marriage, especially when we're on different ends of the same spectrum.

Now for the most awkward simmering pot. Correction, boiling pot. Sex. You're probably wondering how I can possibly write about such a topic in a book about grief. But if we're honest, it's impossible to ignore. Sexual intimacy is part of the God-given formula for becoming one flesh and it is part of every marriage, either by its presence or its absence . . . even during unthinkable times. Grief rocked our world when David died and we both needed time to process the shock of it. I was utterly depressed. Nothingness encompassed me and sexual intimacy was the last thing on my mind. I thought about David . . . all the time. I worried about how I could live without him, all the time. I had blinders on to anything else. In fact, it made me angry when other things demanded my time or attention because all I wanted to do was grieve. It's all I *could* do. On the flip side, I knew I couldn't ignore the topic of intimacy in our relationship for long, without it becoming a destructive cycle. Even though I felt completely empty, I asked God to help me trust that his design for marriage hasn't changed just because our son is gone. He created our bodies purposefully, to be physically intimate, safely within the confines of a loving marriage relationship. In my grief I need to be reminded that emotional connectedness through intimacy brings healing to body, mind, and soul. This is a powerful truth. Our world dramatically changed, but we found stability in knowing that God never does. His truth and purpose for marriage doesn't change with our circumstances. It is timeless and eternal. He gives us his best so we can be our best . . . together. We need to trust that, even in the midst of our pain . . . especially in the midst of our pain.

For women, sexual intimacy requires emotional energy, which is something we have so little of when grieving. For men, sexual intimacy delivers deep feelings of reassurance and comfort, which is something we need so much of when grieving. Maybe the feelings are reversed in your relationship, but honestly, why would God create us to be in opposition? Well, he doesn't. The truth is, he creates us to need one another . . . uniquely. To be *one* flesh. Especially when we're grieving.

Ladies, let me say this as delicately as possible. No matter how empty you feel, no matter how *not in the mood* you are, pray for wisdom in this area of your marriage and for the strength to love your husband fully. Men, pray for the strength to be attentive to your wife's emotional needs and love her tenderly. Physical and emotional intimacy work powerfully together in marriage. You can't have one without the other. Both release hormones that reduce stress, lower blood pressure, and aid sleep. Both are designed by God to grow a deeper bond between you, enabling you to face life's ups and downs together.

The enemy loves nothing more than to destroy the sexual intimacy of grieving couples. Do you hear his lies? *How can he possibly think about sex right now? How can she ignore my sexual needs at a time like this? I barely have enough energy to make coffee . . . there's no way I have the energy for intimacy. It's shameful that he'd want to do something enjoyable when we just lost our loved one.* These are powerful, destructive lies that can only be crushed by God's truth.

There is healing power in marital intimacy when it's within a loving and safe relationship. The truth is that we honor God when we honor our vows to love each other completely–for better or worse–to love and to cherish, even in the most tragic times. Remember that you are one flesh in every sense and in every situation. As you work together, you will grow stronger as a couple. That's the way marriage should be anyway, right? Praise God for that.

Just as our grief continues to ebb and flow, so does our relationship. I love Mike desperately. He loves me. We are two imperfect, selfish, broken people who love Jesus and we thank him daily for giving us to each other. The biggest challenge is resisting the temptation to blame every struggle on our grief, and to fight against each other instead of fighting with each other. Grief certainly winds itself around every issue, but we refuse to give it navigational control. It's there. In fact, I never realized just how invasive grief would be in our marriage. But we remind each other frequently that we are on the same bus . . . the same team. We pray together every night, thanking God for getting us through another day and surrendering our grief to him. It's something we didn't do before losing David, and it has become our greatest weapon in our fight against lies.

Mike and I have absolutely no power or control to change what has already happened, and we have no way of knowing what the future holds. Our only source of light, showing us a way through the darkness, is from the Lord. No exaggeration. I'm still not sure how we will do it at times, but I know we will because we've chosen to find a way through together. We need to do things differently at times. It's okay. We're broken together. And we'll find healing together.

Our farm is a place to find peace and quiet, and I knew Mike drove there after storming out. As I sat in our living room alone, crying and overwhelmed, I feared that we had reached our breaking point and wondered if Mike would even *want* to come back home. He was so angry and, as the hours passed, I felt more and more defeated. More frightened. I just desperately wanted to feel safe in his arms again. To forgive and forget.

I thought back to the day, soon after losing David, that Mike and I were on our deck, watching the sun fade in the sky and talking about our fears and concerns for the future. I bluntly asked him if he thought we were going to be okay and told him that if he couldn't handle the strain of our loss and wanted to leave, to please respect me enough to tell me to my face. He quickly reassured me that he wasn't going anywhere. We *would* be okay. We would get through this together. His quick response really struck a chord within me. He had no idea what was ahead for us, yet he spoke expectantly. Faith the size of a mustard seed was enough for him to trust that God would get us through, and I felt a glimmer of hope.

I reached for that hope as I waited for him to return. When he finally walked through the door, I could tell he had something to say. Sitting in his truck at the farm, among the broken rows of harvested corn, he'd had an epiphany. "We're being lied to, Jan, and we can't fall prey to it." He was absolutely right. If we allowed the enemy to have control over us by convincing us that our marriage couldn't survive, then we would fall into a pit of deceit so deep that we might never climb out. I know that our marriage will survive because we made an intentional decision to grieve *together* by focusing on the truth of God's Word.

Satan wants our marriage to fail. He wants your marriage to fail. He wants us to argue and see our spouse as the enemy. More than that, he will do anything to stop us from trusting God for restoration. Be alert. We are in battle! 1 Peter 5:8 says, "Be alert and of sober mind. Your enemy the devil prowls around like a roaring lion looking for someone to devour." Recognize the lies as just that . . . lies. Claim the power of Joshua 1:9, "Have I not commanded you? Be strong and courageous. Do not be afraid; do not be discouraged, for the Lord your God will be with you wherever you go."

When you call on his name and recommit yourself to one another, the Lord will fight for you, just like he fights for us. Mike and I aren't anything special, but our story of survival is special because it's the one God has given us to tell; the one He's walked through with us. We may not know your name, but we pray for you. We pray that God is actively working in grief-filled marriages, crushing the lies that are meant to destroy. And we pray that you will seek professional help if and when the struggle becomes too great. It made all the difference for us.

Grief tests your faith. Big time! Emotional and spiritual healing takes time and effort. In the midst of your pain, spend time with Jesus. This is the time for you to cling to him, not to become stagnate or run in the opposite direction. God is our refuge in times of trouble. Lean into him as you lean into your grief and mind your own spiritual business. While it's important to seek God together, it is not your job to judge what your spouse may or may not be experiencing spiritually. You can't force change in their relationship with the Lord, so be patient with one another and never stop lifting the other up in prayer.

Every step you take today impacts the direction of your marriage. It's a sense of urgency not meant to put additional pressure on you to perform, or to fix, or to be perfect. In fact, it's quite the opposite. It's a sense of urgency meant to provoke surrender and authenticity . . . maybe for the first time. If you are grieving, then your marriage has entered a totally new dimension. One side of your proverbial scale is buried by grief while everything else seems like nothing. But "everything else" doesn't go away. Make a decision today–right now–to deal with your simmering pots together; in truth and as one flesh. Patience, transparency, and grace. All day. Every day. Wash, rinse, repeat.

Will you choose to pick up your tiny mustard seed of faith and trust God or will you run in the opposite direction? By now you know what I would suggest. This is a big deal and it will change the course of your marriage . . . not just now, but when future trials come. And they will come, but God will walk the road with you. You are not alone in the fight for your marriage.

RAW JOURNAL ENTRY

September 2011–Fifteen months after our son died

Rough weekend. . .Mike and I had an argument. I spent most of the afternoon at the cemetery with David. I thought about going away for the night. I was packed and ready. Past problems are creeping back into our marriage, and they all come back right where they left off before David died. It's hard because you can't ignore them, but they are even harder to tackle.

So I sat at the cemetery and prayed, cried, and thought about where life has taken us. The enemy is no doubt working his way into our thoughts. It's not bad to have some of the issues we struggled with come to the surface again, but we should know, now more than ever, to handle each other gently, in his love. We failed to do that. And when Mike and I are not connected, everything else unravels. That's my reality anyway. I can't focus on our marriage and suffer with grief and not have it affect our relationship. Lord, I just need to keep my focus on you and to hold on tight to what I know to be true. You are at work in our lives, and you continue to have a plan.

FIRST AID FOR YOUR GRIEVING HEART

Healing Prayer

Dear Jesus, the waves are crashing hard against my marriage as we struggle to preserve it amid the tragedy we now face. It's so hard not to feel defeated, and yet I know you want us to trust and rely on you fully. Please help us to listen only to your truth and not to be discouraged. I know that you are with us and you are for us. We will get through this with your help!

Healing Truth

Visit the following pages to unleash God's healing power over the lies that threaten to defeat you: *My faith is too weak* (p. 178); *Our marriage is never going to make it* (p. 210); *We shouldn't desire sex when we're grieving* (p. 213).

Healing Words

What pots are simmering on the back burner of your marriage? Which ones are boiling? Be specific. What truths do you and your spouse need to cling to during this time? Are you behaving like you're on the same team? Embrace your grieving heart today by writing about what you can begin doing to rectify any challenges that threaten to destroy your marriage. If you have already experienced areas of healing in your marriage, write God a letter thanking him for specific ways he is guiding you through grief.

Chapter 10

Repeat Mourning

Burns heal from the inside out. For this reason, when the infant son of our friends suffered a third degree burn to the back of his hand, it had to be gently scrubbed and redressed daily. Can you imagine the pain and tears? Every day for several weeks, Mom and Dad held their crying son tightly, whispering calming words that he couldn't possibly understand at such a young age. As the tissue covering the burn was removed, the wound was covered with antibiotic cream and his hand rewrapped with protective gauze. He would have been so much more comfortable if they had just left the wound alone, hidden in its protective wrap, but they knew that the pain was necessary for healing.

This process of caring for burns is eerily similar to the process of caring for our grieving hearts. As much as we might love to wrap ourselves up and tuck ourselves away from the world, the wounds left by loss cannot be ignored. Instead, they must be repeatedly dealt with through a daily confrontation of emotions, and every time we scrub the surface it hurts . . . really hurts. Thankfully, we have a loving Heavenly Father who holds us tight in the process and whispers words of hope and healing into our souls. Can you hear him?

Truth is, every time I feel like I'm healing, something or someone comes along and rips away the hypothetical scab. I've always believed God loves me but sometimes I feel like that little baby, confused by pain. *Why do you let this hurt so much, God? Don't you care? Don't you see that I'm suffering? Will this ever stop?* All the while, God is beside me, holding me close and walking with me through the relentless process, over and over and over and over again . . . not because he wants me to hurt, but because he wants me to heal.

The movie *Groundhog Day* is a classic. It follows a pessimistic weatherman who finds himself reliving the same day repeatedly, for years. He wakes to a "rise-n-shine" message from the radio . . . again. He reports on Punxsutawney Phil . . . again. He and his fellow reporters are stranded by a blizzard . . . again. Every morning at 6 a.m. his alarm clock plays the same song and everything that happened the day before begins again. Can you imagine waking up every single day and reliving the same thing over and over again? Oh, wait. You already do. And so do I.

When we lose someone we love, the months and years that follow can seem like we're stuck in our own *Groundhog Day* movie. For me, even many years after losing David, every day still holds grief. It may be different for some, but for me, the only real variable is whether my level of emotional intensity will be low, medium, or off the charts. I never really know what to expect, but yet I do. It's important to note that daily grief doesn't mean there isn't hope or healing. It doesn't mean I should give up. Knowing that I will miss David until the day I die doesn't make me feel hopeless; it reminds me how much I love him. In fact, I'm thankful for the monotonous days because they allow me to catch my breath and to realize that I really am healing. Inevitably though, there are influencing factors that reopen my wounds and send me into repeat mourning.

Repeat mourning often comes in the form of social invitations: graduations, weddings, babies, outings with friends, birthday parties . . . events that require me to engage with others in their normal world while I struggle to find mine. Repeat mourning transports me back to my earliest days of grief. It's a byproduct of each event we attend and even the ones we don't; an in-your-face reminder that life is marching on, without David. Seriously, it's easier to stay at home. It's easier to pretend that none of this is happening . . . to stay wrapped in the gauze of denial. But life does go on. It will go on, with or without me, and even when grief takes me two steps forward and one step back, my wounds are still healing, even though it may not feel like it.

Several years after David died, I returned home from the grocery store to see a wedding invitation laying on the kitchen island and the tug-of-war began. *Crap. We should probably go. If David hadn't died, we would go. But he did die. Sean was one of his best friends. We have to go! But I can't. Will our presence cause them pain? Won't we just be a spectacle anyway? And what if they felt obligated to invite us? It's such a special day for them, but I'm so weak. I'm not sure if I'm strong enough to go. This is too much!*

In a matter of seconds, my seemingly safe, uneventful day was hijacked by feelings of desperation, sadness, and even anger. And my heart began to burn. The reality of my loss rose to the surface once again and default mode kicked-in. Protection mode. *You're not ready for this, Jan. Decline the invite so you won't hurt.*

Losing someone we love affects every aspect of our lives and it always will. I really don't mean to paint a hopeless picture. It's not hopeless. It's just hard. And while it's natural to focus on self-preservation, it can be a dangerous place to get stuck. Keeping emotional pain tightly wrapped up does not prevent us from hurting, it prevents us from healing. It is absolutely okay, necessary even, to say "no" sometimes . . . but not every time. Sometimes, we need to push out of our grief bubble and trust that saying "yes" is what's best for our healing.

In Ecclesiastes, God tells us, "There is a time for everything and a season for every activity . . . a time to weep and a time to laugh, a time to mourn and a time to dance. . ." A time to stay home and a time to go to the wedding, even when I know it will hurt. Sometimes we simply have to *put our game face on* and guide our hearts in the right direction. There are definitely times when I've felt God nudging me to take a leap of faith and accept various invitations, but I chose to ignore him. And then, there are times when I listen and I'm blessed . . . and emerge stronger. As hard as it is to understand, facing our pain promotes healing.

Well, before I knew it, Sean and Shelby's wedding day was here. Mike and I took our seats among the rows of beautifully-dressed, smiling guests and browsed the program: Maid of Honor, Bridesmaids, Best Man, Groomsmen. Groomsmen. David and Sean were going to be roommates at college just five years earlier. I swear I could actually see his name listed on the program. He would have been so excited for Sean. All I could do was sigh and try to hold myself together. Soon, all eyes were on the flower girl, as she carefully dropped each petal from her basket. Bridesmaids and groomsmen followed; step, pause, step, pause. Cue the music for the bride. Tears pushed against the back of my eyes as Shelby made her way to the front.

I wanted so much to feel happy for them. *I am happy, really! But I am also unbearably sad and I'm worried about what others will think of my tears. Will they suspect they are only for David? Are they?* After the *"I Do's,"* the bride and groom welcomed everyone into the reception hall. It was one of the most memorable days of their lives. Let the party begin! It was the oddest damn thing (#rawtalk) to attend such a wonderful occasion while feeling such grief. Celebration, excitement for the future, hope for a growing family. All of this joy, all of this hope, was shouting to the void in my heart; a glimpse of what my son would never get to experience. File it under "planned ambush." I walked right into it. And it was absolutely the right thing to do.

This is the reality of life after losing someone we love. As we celebrate the new beginnings and milestones of others, our sadness fights for equal time, and we're left with the pain of missed opportunities for our loved ones. It's not that we don't feel genuine joy for others. We do. We just may need to remind ourselves to smile in the moment. Sounds terrible, doesn't it? But it's true. We have to remind ourselves to smile . . . a lot. Hello repeat mourning.

Attending the wedding was a huge stretch for me emotionally, especially when it came time for the mother-son dance. *This is going to be one heck of a checkmark, Jan! You can do this!* And I did, but when it was over, it was time to leave. As Mike and I made our way out and into the parking lot, a tear fell with each step I took. Mike took my hand as soon as we were settled in the car, "It was a nice wedding, huh?"

"Yesssss. And David should have been here!" It didn't matter that five years had passed. It still felt fresh. Heaviness clung well into the night. That's just the way it is. It's emotional work committing to attend events like this, participating in them, and recovering from them afterward. Hard work, high emotions, raw grief. But I'm so thankful we didn't miss it! The voice that initially shouted to my soul, telling me I couldn't do it, was replaced with a check mark. YOU DID IT!

As time goes by, I am learning to accept and adapt to this part of my new normal. I wish I could tell you that it gets easier, but I can tell you that over time I bleed a little less and heal a bit more.

Our mission is to embrace the life we have, grief and all, and to re-engage with the rest of the world. Period. There is no sugar-coating it. Re-engaging in the *normal* lives of others will hurt, but it will also help us to find a *normal* for ourselves. And doesn't every grieving heart long to feel normal again? My battle continues and so will yours, but I pray that you find the strength to embrace the bitter with the sweet, knowing that the two will collide and co-exist for the rest of your life. It's the reality of grief, and it's the only way to overcome the heartache of repeat mourning.

The summer we lost David, my mom repeatedly asked me to join her for manicures and shopping, things I never used to pass up. But at the time, I couldn't have cared less about having trimmed and polished nails or window shopping at the mall. I–did–not–care. Aware of my persistent resistance, Mike added his two cents. "You should go with your mom, Jan. She is hurting, too, and maybe she needs to spend time with her daughter." Wow. That was a reality check, for sure. I had been strictly focused on myself and it never occurred to me that Mom may need to spend time with me, for *her* healing.

I was so absorbed in my own loss that I didn't even consider that my mom needed me! She needed to spend time with me, perhaps for her own healing. Truth is, she probably didn't care about her nails either, but we ventured out together and we ended up having a really nice day, twisted hearts and all.

Each time you receive a wedding or graduation invitation, or text to go to lunch with friends, you have an opportunity to engage in someone else's special occasion. They think enough of you to share their news and celebrate with you. There are needs beyond our own. Engaging with people who care about us may reopen our wounds, but it will also nudge us out of our self-appointed solitary confinement and provide unique opportunities for healing. Theirs too. I promise. The truth is, we need to experience community, even when we don't feel like it.

A lot has happened over the past nine years. Our family and friends have reached many milestones. Daniel is adulting and thriving, our nieces and nephews are growing up, and many of David's friends are experiencing the things we had dreamed of for him. The momentum in their lives is just as it should be and we continue to pray for them. Still, it's beyond difficult to experience the same joy we would have, had we not lost David. When others talk about weddings or grandkids, it can sting. When going to Bible study or lunch with my girlfriends, it involves seeing photos of grandbabies, hearing about the milestones of their adult children, and listening to stories about family celebrations. Ouch. Going on our annual summer trip to Wisconsin, where memories of David are everywhere, leaves a void. Meeting the children of David's friends, Jake and Holly, and seeing the photos of their baby girl holding the Packer Beanie Babies we gave her . . . the ones that belonged to David . . . is bittersweet.

Baby Lettington with David's Favre bear.

Along with the pain, there is something *good* in each of these situations. I'm sure you have a similar list. Each time we relive aspects of our loss, we so vividly see what we will never have, and we experience raw grief all over again. Let's choose to allow it to bring healing; to bring the what-never-will-be into the light of God's truth, that as long as there is breath in our bodies, we have hope for the future. It isn't the future we thought we would have and it is surely not easy, but it is still good.

Let's vow to embrace repeat mourning as a path to healing and to live our lives courageously in spite of our loss. Our loved ones would want this for us. Cliché? Not for me. I know David would want me to live life abundantly. You have some spots open on your social calendar, don't you? Starting today, fight against the negative pull that grief brings and start embracing your new life. As you venture out to celebrations, social events, public gatherings, or even dinner with friends, consider setting the following ground rules for yourself.

DON'T BE SHOCKED OR SURPRISED THAT IT'S HARD.

It is hard! And it's difficult to turn your sadness on and off like a light switch, so don't beat yourself up for it. It truly is a test of patience, practice, and prayer as we step out from the safety of our house and into the lives of others . . . even when it reminds us of what we're missing.

PRAY BEFOREHAND.

Who is better to go to for strength than God? He knows this is a big deal for you. Tell him that you're stepping out in faith and trusting Him to give you what you need to conquer your fears. Prepare your heart to enter into the battlefield of "repeat mourning." It truly makes a difference.

ALLOW FOR AN ESCAPE ROUTE.

Consider driving separately if possible, so you can choose the best time to leave. If this is not a good option, then ask your driving friends for permission to keep the timeframe flexible. They will understand.

GIVE YOURSELF A PEP TALK . . . AND PRAY.

It's okay. I'm doing fine. I swear there were times when it seemed I was talking to a toddler. Who says you can't talk to yourself or pray during your event? I've done this during many social gatherings. It's okay to be fragile. Take care of yourself unapologetically.

REMIND YOURSELF TO SMILE.

Because we can be so deep in thought, it's easy to have a stone-face while engaging in social situations. You know, the one you had when you were in grade school working on cursive writing? Yeah, that look. It takes more effort to smile when we are in an emotionally difficult situation, so give yourself a reminder. Like everything he created, God has a good purpose for our smiles. Nerd alert: the simple act of smiling instantly releases chemicals in our brains that reduce stress, relax our bodies, lower heart rate, lower blood pressure, and lift our mood.[1] Why not give it a try!

---

1. Stevens, *"There's Magic in Your Smile,"* para. 11.

LISTEN.

The more recent your loss, the more difficult this will be. Listening requires mega focus to avoid zoning out when people are telling you their story, about a recent promotion at work, or how sorry they are for your loss. Do your best so you can participate in the conversation. Getting your mind focused on someone else, even for five minutes, is a good exercise!

DON'T BE LIKE POOH'S FRIEND, EEYORE.

Fight proactively against the woe-is-me mentality. Engaging with the masses takes some getting used to, but over time it will become more natural, and you may even become energized by it. Cut yourself some slack as you walk through each new social situation, and try your best to focus on something positive. Baby steps.

YOU WON'T ALWAYS GET IT RIGHT.

Did you have to leave earlier than expected? Did you give 'em the old "smile and nod" routine and then get totally distracted by grief during the conversation? Did you break down when they asked you to pass the salt, or when they wanted to know how you're doing? Look, perfection is not the goal! It's okay. Dust yourself off and try it again another day.

GIVE YOURSELF A CHECKMARK . . . EVERY TIME.

Don't underestimate the checkmark. Each one is a powerful, emotional reminder of your efforts to grow, heal, and move forward in your loss. Push aside any sense of failure and give yourself a checkmark for trying!

EMBRACE THEIR JOY, WHILE LIVING WITH THE REALITY OF YOUR LOSS.

Grief pains are part of the journey. Regardless of whether it's in public, on social media, or one on one, the response should always be, "I am so happy for you." Practice, if you have to. Will it be heartfelt? Yes, I think so. The fact that they are important enough to you is reason enough to try. The tears shed in the process are inconsequential, as we put our world on temporary hold so that we can engage in theirs. There are no easy ways to get around this. It only happens through perseverance. You can be sure that it stings a little less over time. Just keep at it.

NEWSFLASH. SOMEBODY'S GOING TO SAY SOMETHING STUPID OR INSENSITIVE.

You've already experienced this, haven't you? And if you allow it to, it will ruin your day. Don't stew about it. Don't fume about it. Your family and friends don't intentionally want to hurt you, but sometimes hurtful things spill out. Believe me, half the time they walk away angry at themselves for saying something they shouldn't have. Haven't we all said things to a grieving person, wishing we could take it back? I know I have. Forgive them and let it go. Seriously, channel your inner-Elsa, and let it go!

IT'S NOT YOUR PARTY, BUT YOU CAN CRY LATER IF YOU WANT TO.

You can fall apart later, Jan. Just a little while longer. I told myself this all . . . the . . . time. It has helped to pacify me during a lot of social events over the years. Tears are cleansing and necessary. You need to be able to release all of the emotions that build up, so don't ever feel guilt or weakness when the dam gives way. Grab the Kleenex box and let it go.

DON'T LISTEN TO LIES. EVER.

The voice that says, "You can't do this!" is a lie. Period. With the support of people who love you and the power of God's Spirit fighting for you, you absolutely can do this. It will be difficult. But "difficult" only makes it more rewarding once you've done it. You. Can. Do. This.

I am a work in progress and so are you. Our hearts ache when memories enter our minds but we push through, until it happens again, and then the drill starts all over. I'm not going to say that practice makes perfect, but I will tell you that as time goes by you will adapt, as I have, to this aspect of your survival journey. There is hope because we are not alone! God is in this! Persevere my friend. Persevere.

RAW JOURNAL ENTRY

September 2013–Three years after our son died

I woke up sad today. Big surprise huh? But today all of the emotions and excitement of the weddings this weekend came to an abrupt halt as reality takes over. Yes, there were two! All I can think about is that David will never experience the same joy his friends are experiencing.

I couldn't help but envision David at his own wedding, taking Grandma Rozga and Grandma Mitchell down the aisle, arm in arm smiling and glowing with so much love. Watching my friend, DeDe dance with her son was so beautiful, but so painful, knowing it will never happen for David and me. Watching David's friend, Sean, dance with his mom felt the same.

I guess this pain is normal, grieving the memories we will never have. I've been anticipating David's upcoming birthday on October 4th. He would be 22. I know it will be difficult to walk through. I can feel my heart ache sometimes, literally ache. All I can do is pray for God to help me and give me peace. That's all we can ever do, pray and believe God will hear us and have mercy on us as we hurt.

FIRST AID FOR YOUR GRIEVING HEART

Healing Prayer

Dear Jesus, give me the courage to engage in the lives and celebrations of others, trusting that you will heal my grieving heart as I begin to embrace my new reality. Hold me close and show me that you love me as I discover that sometimes healing comes through the pain.

Healing Truth

Visit the following pages to unleash God's healing power over the lies that threaten to defeat you: *If I don't say yes to everything then I'm failing to heal* (p. 200); *I can't celebrate something that my loved one will never get to experience* (p. 217); *I don't need to socialize with others* (p. 220).

Healing Words

What opportunities and invitations have you received lately? How are you responding emotionally? Will you go? How did it go? How has it caused you to experience repeat mourning? Write a letter to the person who invited you; a letter you will never send. Tell them how you feel and try to explain how the event could be painful. Then give the letter to God, step out in faith, and ask him to help you make a decision that will promote healing.

Chapter 11

The Tide of Ministry

During the lean days and months following David's death, I focused only on myself. *How on earth will I survive losing David . . . or will I? How will I ever live without him? How can I possibly stop mothering him?* Beyond this, nothing else mattered. I couldn't see past the burning forest of anguish consuming my heart. And the last thing I thought about was reaching out to anyone else experiencing loss, especially someone who never knew David. Really, my only priority was getting through each minute and desperately, urgently, trying to survive.

In God's mercy, he began showing me that, not only did I have the ability to reach out to others (even during the weakest parts of my journey), but that he purposefully designed me to do so. It's because of our mutual weaknesses and common experiences that we can be real and we can be weak *together.* I had no idea, until I myself was thrust into opportunities that I had never experienced or pursued.

Over the years, I have received calls from mothers who have lost children to synthetic drugs, car accidents or illness. I've talked with children who have lost parents and adults who have lost spouses. Incredibly, each time I share pieces of my story, wanting to offer comfort, I find healing for my own heart. Every time. In the middle of my pain, God's promise in 2 Corinthians 1:3–5 provides supernatural relief, "Praise be to the God and Father of our Lord Jesus Christ, the Father of compassion and the God of all comfort, who comforts us in all our troubles, so that we can comfort those in any trouble with the comfort we ourselves receive from God. For just as we share abundantly in the sufferings of Christ, so also our comfort abounds through Christ."

Think about it. The most profitable form of advertising is "word of mouth" in the form of testimonials and referrals. We seek-out the positive experiences of others so that we can have the same experience ourselves; whether it's where to go for a great steak dinner, which mattress is the most comfortable, or which doctor has the best bedside manner. We are masters of giving and receiving information about experiences with superficial stuff, but God desires us to share our experience with the hard stuff, too, and to show others how to find hope in him. Each of us has a survival story, and every survival story has life-giving potential. Pretty awesome.

Three months after her son took his life, I received a call from Cheryl from Texas. Just like David, her son had smoked K2 prior to his death. She talked. I listened and it absolutely broke my heart, but something incredible happened; our brokenness connected us immediately and we both experienced comfort. We talked about how hard it was to run into people at the grocery store because we both felt the eyes of pity piercing through us, or how losing a child changes your marriage relationship. We talked about how difficult it was to go back to church or to work or go anywhere in public because (as much as we appreciated the sentiment) we dreaded answering the question, "How are you doing?" The list goes on.

Cheryl's heartache made me reflect on my own and because of this, I was able to specifically relate to her pain during our conversation. Yes, it was as simple as sharing similar experiences. Insecurities invaded my mind throughout the call. *What if I say the wrong thing? What if I can't help her? What if I make things worse?* But God continually teaches me that hurting people simply want to talk through their emotions and the most comforting thing we can do is to listen. Through more and more conversations with a variety of hurting people, I began to find the answer to the question everyone asks, "How have you been able to survive?" It's definitely not easy but it's very simple . . . I put one foot in front of the other, one moment at a time, fully trusting God to get me through. Period. You may feel as though you have nothing to give. Trust me, I get it. But I also know that when you're ready and when opportunities come, you will be able to encourage others as you trust God's promises in 2 Corinthians, and your heart will be encouraged in return.

Cabo San Lucas, Mexico is a dream destination to be sure. My parents have vacationed there for years and always speak highly of it, but Mike and I never fully understood the beauty until we joined them there a few years after David died. The instant we stepped onto the white sand and looked out at the crashing waves of the Sea of Cortez, I knew exactly why my parents love it so much. There is something so breathtaking about water. Whether watching the forceful waves of the ocean or the glass–like waters of northern Wisconsin reflecting the sunset, my heart is always pointed to God as our perfect Creator. God didn't give waves a mind. They simply move in response to the call of gravity and do what he created them to do; move as one body of water, crashing to the shore and roaring back to sea in beautiful rhythm. Just like waves, we are called to respond to the gravitational pull of life; sometimes withdrawing to receive comfort and sometimes pushing ourselves forward to comfort others. This giving and receiving of ministry is the beautiful rhythm of God's perpetual mercy, and it's a process he uses to bring healing.

The lessons I learn, as I cling to God's truths, give me the courage to lean into ministry without even realizing it. Even on the days when I have no emotional or physical strength for it, the gravity of God's design gently pushes me into conversations with other hurting people that results in mutual comfort. It's absolutely incredible. I am nothing more than a desperate mother who lost her son to a horrible death, trying to keep my head above water. And God's design for ministry is continually turning my broken pieces into beautiful moments of encouragement and bringing hope to hurting people.

Whether we're experiencing loss or not, the word "ministry" often causes us to run for the hills. Perhaps it's because it sounds *churchy* or it conjures up images of professionally trained pastors, missionaries, and church leaders. But true ministry–and often the most meaningful–is not about spiritual IQ. It's simply about our willingness and availability to share our hearts. No perfection required. One of the enemy's biggest lies is that ministry should only be done by people who have mastered some spiritual domain. *I can't possibly help anyone else when I'm such a big mess myself.* Sound familiar?

While *doing ministry* may be intimidating, the idea of letting others minister to us can be equally paralyzing. *Yes, my son just died, but I don't need you to bring a casserole or do my laundry or sit with me and cry. I've got this. It will be easier to figure it out on my own than to let you see the ugly places of . . . well, of me.* It is uncomfortable to let people care for me because it requires vulnerability. Sometimes–many times–it is simply easier to retreat into a protective ball of isolation. The enemy loves telling us that we are better off alone because nobody else can possibly understand our situation or make us feel better about it. What a lie! Pride isn't something we associate with brokenness. In fact, it's a total contradiction. Right? Not exactly. Even when my heart was shattered, the desire to protect myself was often stronger than my ability to be vulnerable, and it wasn't easy to allow others to serve me. In the earliest days of grief, I needed hugs and mutual tears and, yes, even food for my family. It was critical to put pride aside and allow others to help. At the same time, and in the middle of my own weakness and grief, I desperately wanted to do something to ease the horrific pain of family and friends who were also grieving David's death. Without realizing it, I was riding the tide of ministry, giving and receiving comfort as God was comforting me. And in his mercy, God continues to show me that he created us to be in community with one another, especially in brokenness. If we refuse to humbly receive the kindness of others, then we will never fully experience healing. Even more, we will never be able to effectively reciprocate and encourage others.

Just four months after David died, I was asked to do my first public talk. It was an invitation to speak at our church's annual Women's Christmas Brunch the following year, which would be 18 months after losing our son. At the time, it was difficult to string together a coherent sentence in casual conversation, so the idea of presenting a prepared 45-minute talk was daunting, to say the least. *And anyway, what if I don't survive the next year? What if I have no hope to give? Maybe they won't want to hear what I have to say!* Not having any idea how I was going to make it through the day, let alone the year, made the commitment difficult. Still, I trusted God to get me through somehow. He'd better! To quote Princess Leia's plea to Obi-Wan Kenobi, "Help me, Jesus. You are my only hope!" Wobbly faith was all I had, but it was better than none. I agreed to do the talk and it was that commitment which prompted me to begin recording my story of raw survival, as it unfolded in the form of a daily journal. Today, it is one of my greatest personal treasures and a powerful tool for relating to others.

Every journal entry is a record of God's faithfulness, reminding me of every time he has kept my head above water by encouraging me through scripture, song lyrics and even difficult conversations with others who are grieving. In the beginning, journaling was a survival mechanism . . . a safe place to store the pieces of my heart while I simply tried to survive, clinging to God's truth to get me through life without David. Little did I know those *pieces* would become precious tools for ministry. Without them, it would be nearly impossible for me to remember the blur of our first days after David died, including the feelings I had as our family endured each new "first," even the feelings I experienced during ordinary days. Keeping a daily record of the ups and downs provides a tangible testimony of how God has helped me survive moments of hopelessness by whispering truth, perspective, and hope. Little-by-little, I've become stronger because of Christ in me. And rereading my journals, from the darkest moments to the sweetest victories, reminds me that God wants to use my story to share his love and grace with others.

What I've lost will never be replaced, but he restores my soul and equips me to use my painful experiences to show others that there is always hope. Honestly, how could I *not* want to share the same hope I've been given? It's too precious to keep it to myself . . . too life-changing. My journals are not meant to gather dust in my closet. And your story, whether written on paper or recorded only in your heart, is also meant to be shared.

RAW JOURNAL ENTRY

Yesterday was the annual Women's Christmas Brunch. There were roughly 470 women in attendance. As I walked up the stairs of the stage, the Holy Spirit took over. I got through all 45 minutes with a steady heartbeat. My breath never became labored. My hands did not shake as I thought they would. There were moments of stumbling over words, but thankfully it only happened a few times. I did not have the urgency to clear my throat as I often do in the morning, and I did not have any hot flashes!

I wasn't striving for perfection and perfection it was not. It was simply an outpouring of tragic loss, mixed with God's amazing strength, his promises, and of course the saving faith we can grasp onto through a personal relationship with Jesus Christ.

One of the brunch coordinators told me that many people reported making a decision to know Christ after hearing my story, and I am so excited I can hardly stand it. Something good from something tragic. But now what? Now that the brunch is over, what do I focus on? My counselor prepared me for the emotional letdown that may happen after. While I'm exhausted and feeling a bit "lost," I have not found myself spiraling into an all-familiar hurricane . . . at least not yet. And if I do find myself there, it will be okay. God will get me through like he always does.

Though totally nerve-wracking and utterly exhausting, my first public speaking experience ended up being a wonderful opportunity to chat about the glimpses of good that have come from my broken pieces. Over time, I have had many opportunities to share my story of raw survival at women's luncheons, church gatherings, a women's correctional facility, and writing for a nonprofit magazine. I also became a speaker for Stonecroft, an extraordinary worldwide Christian women's outreach ministry. This often involves travel, giving multiple talks over the course of two or three days. It's never easy, but always a blessing. Every time I accept an invitation to turn private journal entries into public talks, my knees shake and my gut churns, which makes me question whether or not I should be doing it at all. *Why would God give me these opportunities when it just about does me in every time? It makes no sense.* Nerves led to constant prayers for clarity, as I struggled with constant fear and lack of confidence. What God shows me is that he gets me through it every time and women find hope and encouragement every time. That's all I need to know. God doesn't call me to speak about my loss because I'm an awesome speaker who can keep a room of women entertained. Truth is, I'm just an ordinary person with a story that is raw and ugly and real. It's not supposed to feel exciting or self-gratifying. It's supposed to point people to the source of true comfort and true hope . . . in any situation.

Mike joined me on one of my three-day speaking trips to southern Minnesota and I was so grateful to have his presence in the audience and encouragement in the car. At the final event, most of the women in attendance were quite elderly and, being November, we were served a traditional Thanksgiving lunch. Just about the time I was introduced to speak, most of the ladies were taking their last bite of pumpkin pie. *If I can keep them awake, it's a victory.* On the way home, Mike joked about some of the ladies who were fighting to keep their eyes open. "I'd like to think they were deep in prayer, Mike!" Aw, the levity!

Thankfully, God doesn't call us to be perfect, he just wants us to be available. It's painful to relive loss, but every time I speak it forces me to focus on the way God continually provides grace and healing. He is so faithful. It never matters what town I'm in or who the audience consists of, the view from my podium shows tears of others who are experiencing loss. I actually wasn't prepared for that. It's easy to forget that we are not grieving in a vacuum and that our feelings aren't unique. The silent hugs and tearful words I receive after sharing my story make it clear that God uses my experiences, as messy as they are, to encourage others. And so often, I see my future self in the faces of women who have been surviving grief much longer than I have, which is both encouraging and scary. *Lord, please let me be a reflection of your grace, even when I'm old and I still miss my David.* I choose to share my story as a way of encouraging others with the hope of Jesus, and I am always encouraged in return. These ladies continue to survive loss and so will I . . . and so will you.

In addition to public speaking, Mike and I experience ministry through GriefShare, a Christ-centered grief support group offered at many churches across the nation. It was only a few months after David's death when we first talked about attending, and I had serious doubts. *What if it only adds to the nightmare? I mean, having to talk about my sadness in a group of distraught strangers? Oh yeah, that sounds like fun. How can it possibly help us to make a dent in our pain? What if I cry the whole time? And what will people think about David . . . about us?* But Mike was right, "Whether we go to GriefShare now or six months from now, we're still going to hurt, and it will still be hard." Okay then. We'll go. I called the church right away, before I could change my mind, and signed us up.

The first meeting was awkward, to say the least. We introduced ourselves, why we were there, and who we lost. Stories ranged from stillbirth to cancer to suicide and more. It was heartbreaking and exhausting, and I wanted to shut my brain off immediately after the meeting. Still, we kept going and I was surprised with something so unexpected: glimmers of hope. They came out of nowhere as if God was saying, "It's going to be okay, Jan. *You* are going to be okay."

There were even times I swore I could hear David's sweet voice whisper to my heart, "It's okay Mom. You're okay, Mom . . . I'm okay, Mom." As quickly as these moments came, they vanished. But they brought the best sense of relief, temporarily interrupting anguish and assuring me that we were moving in the right direction. It was beautifully poignant, knowing that God would supernaturally intervene to give me snippets of hope. It overwhelmed and humbled me every time, and I'll never forget it. I pray continually that you will also experience these snippets of joy as you seek Jesus and allow yourself to engage in the tide of ministry.

As it turns out, going through GriefShare was vital to our healing. The "room full of distraught strangers" became an important part of our grief-family, and it increased our compassion for others. About two years later, we began facilitating GriefShare groups at church. The number of people experiencing loss is astonishing, and we have the opportunity to use our own loss and journey to healing as a means to minister to others. Hello, 2 Corinthians 1:3–5! What a blessing I would have missed had I not allowed myself to be vulnerable.

Even Jesus humbled himself to serve. Yes, Jesus. The Son of God, Wonderful Counselor, Mighty God, Everlasting Father, Prince of Peace. If he can do it, surely we can, too. Philippians 2:4–8 tells us, "In your relationships with one another, have the same mindset as Christ Jesus: Who, being in very nature God, did not consider equality with God something to be used to his own advantage; rather, he made himself nothing by taking the very nature of a servant, being made in human likeness. And being found in appearance as a man, he humbled himself by becoming obedient to death—even death on a cross!"

The idea of facilitating GriefShare was definitely humbling. I worried that we weren't emotionally prepared to deal with the unknown needs of others. Of course, we weren't! I worried that we weren't far enough along in our own grief journey to make any difference in the journeys of others. Of course, we weren't! And I wasn't strong enough to get through our meetings without crying, either. But God's Holy Spirit ministers through us simply because we are willing to be present. It was okay to cry, to be afraid, and to be weak. No perfection required, remember?

In a GriefShare group, you are not alone in your grief or your emotions, regardless of how your loved one died or how long they lived. What matters is that everyone in the group hurts and everyone can relate to the emotional messiness loss brings. No one is crazy. And we all need Jesus. We learn from each other every week and it's incredible to witness how each person has the ability to move through their own pain to engage and encourage others in the group. The perpetual tide of ministry just naturally happens every year as we base our conversation on God's Word and hold tight to God's promises for comfort and hope.

No grieving person ever receives a certificate of completion, as if the journey stops at the end of a session or prayer or conversation. No. This journey is ongoing and requires hard work on our part, well beyond today. Christian or not, Satan works relentlessly to use our foggy state of mind to cloud our knowledge of the truth and to keep us weighed down by pain. It's no wonder we question God. Nothing about losing my son makes earthly sense and nothing about my earthly situation brings hope. The same is probably true for you. Grieving friend, we simply cannot survive without each other or without turning to Jesus for the answer to *every single question* . . . period. We must claim God's promises fiercely and pursue him daily, especially when we don't feel like it. I call it *Jesus 101*. When we've lost someone we love, our lives are complicated enough. We need simple. We need to return to the basics. For me, that means returning to the truth of who Jesus is and what he has done for me. No matter where I turn on this messy journey, I always come back to Jesus, because *everything* comes back to Jesus. It just does. He's the only one that never changes . . . the only one that always brings comfort.

I don't know where you are in your grief journey, but I do know that you have something to give. Grief is awkward, especially for those who haven't experienced it personally. When someone we love dies, God births in us the ability to relate to other broken hearts. In an instant, we know what it means to suffer and we are instantly prepared to comfort others in a way that we've received comfort. Many well-intentioned people try to "help" by filling the silence with words or scriptures that our hearts are not prepared to receive. The scriptures I cherish most and cling to on the extra hard days, are the ones that the Lord has lovingly whispered to my soul . . . at just the right time and in just the right moment. Fellow-grievers understand one another, and we are uniquely equipped to care for each other. If we retreat in unwillingness or fear, then we may miss our greatest blessing.

Anyone can take a ministry course, but God has given us more. He's given us experience. We didn't ask for it and we sure didn't want it, but it's ours. And we can use it to comfort others. Anyone fighting for raw survival is an example of "life goes on." It's messy and painful and exhausting, but *life does go on.* We understand firsthand the unpredictability of grief and the importance of giving our hearts the freedom to mend at their own pace and in their own ways. As we experience God's comfort and hope, we have such an incredible gift to give to others. If we won't allow ourselves to share that gift, then we're burying our treasure in the sand. Yes, I used the word *treasure* to define our grief-experience. The *treasure* in our experience becomes the blessing of our survival story. Just think, embracing grief in this way crushes every lie that tries to defeat our souls and turns our tragedy into an opportunity to share the beautiful truth of eternal hope and eternal perspective.

To be clear, just because we share the hope we've found, doesn't mean every person who hears it will rush to Jesus. In fact, it may reveal unbelief and anger with God for allowing tragedy into their lives. But what does God love more than an honest heart? Those who are angry need a kind ear, willing to listen without judgment. Talking about it opens the door for God to respond . . . to speak life and truth into any situation. When others aren't ready to grasp *Jesus 101*, it doesn't mean we've failed or that we need to push harder. It's just a reminder that God is the source of all healing, not us. Even when a broken person is on the fence with God-stuff, they want to know how others have survived brokenness. My story is my story, and your story is your story. Who can argue with what we experience deep in our hearts? We are called to share our journey to healing, to love them, and to listen. The rest is up to the Lord, in his way and his timing.

Just as ocean waves are a perpetual tide of power and majesty, so is ministry. By serving others, I am served. Embracing this perpetual aspect of ministry gives us the freedom to rise and fall with the tide; pushing forward in some ways and pulling back in others. It's unrealistic to think that we will reach the pinnacle of healing and somehow outgrow the need for the support of others. It's also unrealistic to expect our pain to magically disappear each time we put a checkmark on our ministry list. That is way too much pressure! When we seek Jesus, moment by messy moment, we unleash our potential to encourage others. Not ready? I get it. Simply stay open to the idea that you *do* have something to give, even if it's simply your silent presence. Press on, dear friend, and embrace your ministry journey as a beautiful dance of God's faithfulness and hope. He is writing your survival story, one day at a time, and it has the power to bring hope to a hurting world.

FIRST AID FOR YOUR GRIEVING HEART

Healing Prayer

Dear Jesus, as I struggle with loss, help me to experience your love and truth in ways that bring healing to myself and others. Give me a grateful heart for each person who ministers to me, and show me how my own messy journey to survival can be used to shine light into the darkness of others. Help me to find hope by giving hope.

Healing Truth

Visit the following pages to unleash God's healing power over the lies that threaten to defeat you: *My faith is too weak* (p. 178); *I can get through this on my own* (p. 184); *I am too broken to help others* (p. 223); *Nobody will ever understand or be able to make me feel better about my loss* (p. 227); *Telling my story is futile and/or self-serving* (p. 246).

Healing Words

In the time since you've lost your loved one, have you had opportunities to comfort others? Maybe it's too soon for you. But the time will come when you're able to use your own experience to encourage others. Until you're ready, embrace your grieving heart by recording your survival story, one day at a time. It's not about writing perfectly for all the world to see. Simply write what is in your heart. Are you angry? Sad? Scared? Hopeful? Write about it. Then, ask God for the opportunity and strength to use your story to encourage others.

Chapter 12

When the Bumper Sticker Fades

Next time you drive through town, you'll see them. Memorial bumper stickers. You might even have one of your own. I do. I knew the minute I put it on my rear window that I'd become one of those people who others pity and even gawk at. Admittedly, I've done my share of gawking, too. It takes seconds from start to finish. We try to get as close as possible, straining our eyes to read the name and dates memorialized in vinyl, then leave a haze of exhaust in the rearview mirror as we carry on with our busy day. *I'll leave the sadness in the car behind me, thank you very much.*

Until. Until it's our own vinyl memorial of the one we love, and we're suddenly a member of the club nobody wants to join. It's a way to keep their memory alive, for us anyway, but over time the rain, sleet, snow, and countless trips through the car wash take their toll and the bumper sticker starts to fade. One day we're rushing to put groceries in the trunk and think, "When did this happen?" The day I noticed it, I feared that the fading sticker might be a metaphor for my memories of David. *Are they fading, too?*

As I write this, it's been eleven years since I stood on our deck, unable to move, as ambulance and police lights screamed over the crest of the hill. David was gone and our lives would never be the same . . . will never be the same. And it makes me wonder if there is an expiration date, after losing a loved one, when it becomes socially-incorrect to discuss them. Does ten years mean we should "put our loss behind us" so others won't feel uncomfortable? Are we on our own now, left to hang desperately to the memories that linger as others fade away? These are the questions the enemy uses to taunt me, wanting me to feel sad and fearful and bitter, but God reminds me to give thanks with my whole heart for each precious moment we had with David (Psalm 9:1).

If we allow it to, grief can create a sense of pressure to move into the future in a certain way, so we don't cause awkwardness for others. Uncomfortable comments and fatigued stares send a message to our broken hearts that it's time to just "get over it." Has someone ever said these hurtful words to you? I will never *get over* David. He is my precious son and I will miss him until the day God reunites us. The best way to honor his life and prevent the proverbial bumper sticker from fading, is to continue talking about him, to intentionally remember the details of his life, and to look for ways that his story can impact the lives of others.

TALK ABOUT YOUR LOVED ONE

I don't talk about David to seek pity, to call attention to myself, or make anyone else feel uncomfortable. I talk about him because I love him desperately and I miss him every single day—even many years later—and I don't want anyone to forget about him. I worry that it may be awkward when stories and comments about David become repetitive, but the sad truth is that there will be no new memories to add. Speaking his name in conversations with family, friends, or the cashier at Target, preserves his place of value in my life.

I believe it's normal to feel conflicted about whether or not to mention our loved ones when talking with others. *I want to talk about this-or-that, but what will they think?* Like riding an emotional teeter-totter, I battle between the desire to keep his memory alive and the concern that I will make everybody else feel uncomfortable. *Will they think I have an unhealthy obsession with losing my son? Will they think I'm fishing for sympathy? Am I fishing for sympathy?* Nothing good comes from such an internal debate. In fact, it only leads to greater confusion. But then again, why do I question whether I should or shouldn't talk about my son? There should be no debate! Speaking his name and talking about the precious pieces of his story are as natural as breathing. I need to stop second guessing myself. Maybe you do, too. It's like living on an emotional teeter totter!

Many grieving people *wish* they had memories to talk about, no matter how repetitive, but their children died due to illness, miscarriage, stillbirth, SIDS, or even abortion. And there are only *what-ifs*. Mike and I had the privilege of grieving alongside a young woman who attended GriefShare after experiencing the stillbirth of her son. She was shattered. One way she processes her grief is to periodically post pictures on social media. It is important to her. She wants her family and friends to remember and honor him. He matters. He is missed. Most people respond kindly, but others have been extremely critical. Have you experienced this as well? It's unimaginable to think anyone could be so indifferent and insensitive to the grief of another, and it's even harder not to take it personally. Enter guilt and anger.

Please remember, when others don't understand our grief or how we choose to honor our loved ones, we need to ask God to protect us from the emotions that follow. Grief is one of the most personal emotions we experience and it's so important to give ourselves the freedom to walk through it in our own way and at our own pace, not based on how others will respond. If we put the opinions of others above our own, especially when they are based on judgment, we will be in a constant struggle to heal. How conflicting would that be? If you are supporting a grieving friend or family member, I beg you never to judge their broken heart or tell them it's time to "get over it." Colossians 3:12 says, *"Therefore, as God's chosen people, holy and dearly loved, clothe yourselves with compassion, kindness, humility, gentleness and patience."* Romans 12:15 says to *"mourn with those who mourn."* Grief is cruel enough. Be gentle with your own grief and show compassion for the grief of others.

One of the most compassionate things others can do in response to my loss is to simply stay interested. Even though it's been over a decade since David died, I still need people to ask how I'm doing. Sadly, it's a question that comes less and less often over time. I still need people to say David's name so I know that he isn't forgotten, but people seem to naturally distance themselves from the grief of their grieving friends. They just do. Perhaps you've experienced this also. The only way to keep the memory of our loved ones alive is to boldly begin these conversations. You may be pleasantly surprised to realize that the reason your family and friends don't talk about your loved one is because they fear bringing up something that will hurt you. It's not because they don't care, but because they aren't sure how to show it. When we have the strength to speak the names of our loved ones and engage in conversation about their lives, it gives others the freedom to do the same. Even when others are less than sympathetic, try to extend grace. If you dwell on the negative, you'll get stuck there. Just let it go.

KEEP MEMORIES ALIVE

In recent years, we have started referring to past events in the context of "before David" or "after David" and too many times the years get fuzzy. When my memories become muddled, it feels like an epic fail, and I hate it! It leaves me with the same painful void that I had the day we lost our son; like I'm losing him all over again. *Is my mind playing tricks on me? The details are hazy, but surely I remember him. Of course, I remember him!* Welcome to living through grief. I will never stop fighting to preserve the memories I have of my son. Never. And God won't stop fighting for me, either.

Philippians 4:6–7 promises, when we take our anxious thoughts to him in prayer, "The peace of God, which transcends all understanding, will guard your hearts and minds in Christ Jesus." He absolutely does! In the early months, God guarded my heart and mind by protecting me from remembering some of the details around David's death; details that were especially painful. He has encouraged my heart and mind with surprise glimpses of precious moments that I thought I had forgotten; often when I need them most. When the passing of time causes me to feel insecure about my memories, as though they are fading away, it is not a reflection of my love for David. It's simply a reflection of the temporary world in which we live and I need to commit my anxious thoughts to God in prayer. Truth is, David lives on in my heart and that will never change.

Not every memory fades. In fact, it's easy to remember the big stuff . . . bringing him home from the hospital, his first day of school, the day he got his driver's license, the day he shot his first deer, and the day he revealed his Brett Favre tattoo. I have many vivid memories of important days, but what about the ordinary ones? Too often, these are the ones that get foggy. The distance between that devastating day so many years ago and my world today continues to grow, and so does the gap between memories. I used to recall the smallest details about David, but now? At times, I strain to remember even what his voice sounded like. I can't imagine not remembering that! It's a heartbreaking reality.

One of my favorite brother moments was when Daniel scooped David up after graduation.

I want people to know that I still want to talk about my son. To be completely honest, my thoughts aren't always gracious. *Yeah, it's me again, talking about my David. He's gone, remember? You never bring him up. Do you think it's been long enough that I should be healed by now . . . that I no longer hurt? You're wrong.* Okay, sometimes I'm bitter. And even today, I have to fight against recurring poisonous feelings that surface from time to time. I need to remind myself that it's really not about other people, it's about how I respond in my heart. It's the grief talking. When we're struggling to remember our loved one, it can make us believe that others are as well. It's another depressing reality of grief that can drag us down, if we don't fill our minds with Truth.

When my memories of David feel fuzzy, I have to fight my way through and reclaim the details of life with my son. If I don't, the memories will continue to disappear. So, I fight. And I encourage you to do the same. Take a deep breath, because reigniting memories that we thought were forgotten, takes us directly into the center of our loss. It's okay. Grab some tissues. Grab an old photo album or start a new one. Dig out the family videos and watch them. Ask others to share memories with you. It's not as awkward as you think. You will both be blessed as you reminisce, and chances are, they may have wanted to share with you before but were too afraid of causing you pain. Old memories will bring fresh comfort, and newly-shared details will bring unexpected joy.

This Packer fan always makes me smile through the tears.

David making friends with the food guy at a Packer game.

I don't want to live life without David, but here I am, without him. And if I'm to continue on this path to survival, then I must take time to intentionally remember him. Thinking about his silly jokes, ornery days, and Packer obsession doesn't mean I'm staying stuck in the past, but that I am choosing to walk peacefully into my future while honoring his legacy. David's life is a vital part of our family's history. If my story of raw survival never hits the bookstore shelves, it's okay! It is first and foremost a record of God's faithfulness, one that can be passed on to Daniel's kids and grandkids.

I need to hit the pause button for a moment. It would be wrong to assume that every grieving person has only treasured memories. In fact, many GriefShare attendees struggle with unresolved pain. If you can relate, please know that I pray specifically for you to find something good, something positive, no matter how minuscule. I hope that God will give you the courage to forgive what needs to be forgiven and salvage what can be salvaged. Only Jesus can help you find peace and contentment with what you cannot change. Grieving people need to fight against the "woe is me" mentality every day. It's really hard to do. Bad stuff can always be found, whether it happened before your loved one died or it's happened since, but you must hold tight to anything that brings comfort and let go of the rest.

PAY TRIBUTE TO IMPACT OTHERS

Last spring, when I noticed the shrubs in our yard blooming and the grass just beginning to turn green, I decided to drive by the high school, to see the tree that was planted in David's memory the same summer he died. Surely it would be covered in new leaves this time of year, a tribute to everything good in him. I wasn't prepared to see the dry, brown branches. *It's dead! How long has it been this way?* The memorial tree in our own yard had died and now the one at the high school! My heart broke and tears filled my eyes as I noticed the lone bronze marker which bears his name. *If I would have visited more often, we could have planted a new one in its place by now.* It was such a poignant reminder that time marches on. Within a few weeks, Mike and I made arrangements for a new tree to be planted in a new location, by the new high school football field.

Truth is, few students in our high school today know anything about David. They weren't in marching band with him, and they didn't worship with him at church. To them, it's just a tree. To me, it's David's tree. It's painful when life moves on, but we can make sure that the lives of our loved ones have a positive impact on others, well into the future. It all comes down to the way we honor their memory.

Mothers Against Drunk Drivers, Alex's Lemonade Stand, America's Most Wanted . . . and the list goes on. So many organizations have been formed in response to loss, paying tribute to lost loved ones by striving to improve the future for others. Whether it's a worldwide non-profit or the work of one family, this is a wonderful way to prevent the bumper sticker from fading.

Anne and Dave lost their son, Ryan, in a tragic drowning accident. He was twenty-three. Every year on Ryan's birthday, his parents make it their mission to bless others. What drives them to do this on such an emotionally difficult day? Anne explains that her son was such a blessing to others during his life, so she and Dave want to continue this legacy. It's that *simple*. And it's an all-day event.

First, they head to the bakery department of a local grocery store. Ryan loved cake so they decided to pay for all of the cakes that were ordered on his birthday. When taking their ticket to the check-out lane one year, the cashier assumed they were buying the cakes for themselves and asked, "Did you already pick up your cakes from the bakery?" Anne explained about losing Ryan and their reason for paying for the cakes of other customers. In response, the cashier explained that she had lost three of her four children. They had a brief but powerful moment of encouragement. Wow. We never know how we can bless others . . . even in the checkout line.

On to the next stop. At their favorite drive-up coffee shop, they purchased a couple hundred dollars' worth of gift cards and instructed the cashier to use them to pay for customer orders until the money ran out. Imagine running late for work, but determined to get that much needed coffee. Just as you reach for your wallet, the cashier tells you that your coffee is already paid for. Insert happy dance! Thank you, sweet Ryan.

Next, it's on to Buffalo Wild Wings, Ryan's favorite place to eat, where his entire family meets for dinner. Before they leave, their server comes to the table, thanking them profusely for the hefty tip. He explains that he's homeless and that they have no idea how much the money will help him.

In addition to Ryan's birthday spree, Anne and Dave sponsor children at Christmastime, making sure that they have gifts under the tree. This sweet couple has a special place in our hearts. Anne worked at the boys' elementary school, and they went through our GriefShare group shortly after losing their son. It's such a blessing to share how they purposefully honor Ryan's memory, on an otherwise painful day, by blessing others. And *their* hearts are encouraged as well. It is a living example that pain doesn't have to be paralyzing. How can you make sure that the story of your loved one lives on through a positive impact on others? It might be providing a cup of coffee, a scholarship, a shade tree, or simply a kind word.

Shortly after David died, Mike and I began educating people of the dangers of synthetic drugs. It is a way we pay tribute to David and honor his life. Whether testifying before the U.S. Senate, sharing David's story with youth group students, or impromptu conversations with strangers, it is our desire to prevent others from experiencing devastating tragedy. There is much more about the impact of David's legacy in the next chapters, but suffice it to say that we strive to keep his legacy from fading by continuing to tell his story. His memory lives on and if just one person is positively impacted, one life saved, then it is worth every bit of emotional energy.

RAW JOURNAL ENTRY

August 2011–Fourteen months after our son died

As I prepared for our first Wisconsin vacation without David, I ran upstairs to gather the rest of the laundry and noticed David's bedroom door was closed. A friend had been over the week before to play his guitars and when I opened the door, I saw guitar plugs all around the amplifier. Memories rushed in. I took each strand of plugs, coiled them together, and put everything back in the cubby of the amplifier. David's newest guitar, the one we bought him for graduation, was laying in its case on his bed. I went over and sat it up against the wall where it joined all of the other guitars and a lone banjo that my Dad had given him.

As I put everything in its place, my eyes scanned the room. Nothing was moved or changed since he died. The same pictures were still on the mirror above his dresser. The letter that Mike wrote to him when he turned 18 was on the dresser. I knew I was walking right into a flood of emotions, but I went to his closet, opened the door and cried as I looked at all of his clothes, shoes, hats, school notebooks and books from his senior year, and a bin of graduation cards. Even his graduation gown was there, still hanging where he put it after that special day. Our first vacation without David will be hard. Thankfully, God will be with us, whether we are in Iowa or in Wisconsin, and we will rely on Him to get us through the sadness just the same.

FIRST AID FOR YOUR GRIEVING HEART

Healing Prayer

Dear Jesus, sometimes it's a struggle for me to remember details about my loved one like I used to. I know in my heart I could never forget, but I feel such guilt. Please help me not to feel as though I'm letting my loved one down when memories get fuzzy from time to time. Guard my anxious heart and mind with your peace that transcends understanding.

Healing Truth

Visit the following pages to unleash God's healing power over the lies that threaten to defeat you: *I will never feel content again* (p. 175); *I'm forgetting my loved one* (p. 230); *I just need to "get over it"* (p. 233); *People don't care anymore* (p. 236).

Healing Words

Do you periodically find yourself struggling to remember certain things about your loved one? Do you wish others talked more about him/her? Embrace your grieving heart by drawing near to God today, and writing specifically about the memories you have of your loved one; are they painful, pleasant, a little of both, or are they hard to muster up? Let it all out, then develop a plan to reignite the memories that seem distant.

PART IV

SEEKING A SURVIVING LEGACY

Chapter 13

Beauty from Ashes

And we know that all things work together for good to those who love God, to those who are called according to His purpose.

ROMANS 8:28

Stay with me! I know how this verse can make someone feel after losing a loved one. When I stood in the receiving line at our son's funeral, these words from Romans 8:28 were not comforting. In fact, they were confusing and hurtful. How could anyone possibly use the word "good" when referring to the death of our son? Saying goodbye to him was the most tragic, unfair, and cruel thing we had ever experienced and there was nothing good about it. Let's be honest, nobody uses this verse to intentionally cause pain, but I wish that those who use it to comfort grieving hearts would understand that not every verse is appropriate for every moment. God's Word is true and infallible, of course, but it should always be used with discernment. And sometimes silence is the most Christlike thing we can offer to those who are hurting.

Too many times, the words of Romans 8:28 have caused me pain, like pouring salt in my wounds. Thankfully, in God's mercy and perfect timing, the Holy Spirit shows me that those words don't require me to see David's death as good. They don't even mean that God sees it as good. But they do require me to recognize that God brings beauty from ashes. Isaiah 61:2–3 compassionately displays God's desire to "comfort all who mourn and provide for those who grieve . . . to bestow on them a crown of beauty instead of ashes, the oil of joy instead of mourning, and a garment of praise instead of a spirit of despair." Let that sink in: a crown of beauty instead of ashes, the oil of joy instead of mourning and praise instead of despair. Thank you, Jesus, for this hope!

In his mercy, there is more to our tragic story than suffering. Hindsight proves that good things have happened in the years since David's death; people have accepted Jesus as their Savior, laws have been changed that continue to save lives, and our own story of raw survival is bringing hope to other grieving hearts. It's not the way we wanted our lives to go (believe me!), and we would gladly go back and change everything in an instant, but we can't. Our son is never coming home and the only way for anything good to come from this painful reality is to put our energy into the future, not the past. As we do, God promises to meet us in the middle of our pain and to use the tragedy of David's death to bring positive change. If sharing our story and advocating for change prevents others from suffering, then it is our duty to do so.

Advocacy is defined as "the action of advocating, pleading for, or supporting a cause." Without realizing it, Mike and I abruptly began a journey into advocacy almost immediately after David died. We had to. And putting our energy into the future, instead of the past, never means that we forget David. Quite the contrary, it means that we choose to honor his life and the love we have for him by telling his story and praying that it impacts others for *good*. It's not complicated or formal or perfect. We simply tell the raw, real story of what happened to our family, the lessons we've learned from it, and how God continues to get us through.

One simple truth we plead with others to understand is that what happened to us can happen to anyone. No family is immune; not even yours. From the time David and Daniel were little, we talked with them about the predictable dangers of growing up: drinking, drugs, dating, driving, and a host of other issues. We worked with our boys to create "escape plans" in case they ever ended up in uncomfortable or unsafe situations with peers. We encouraged them to receive mentoring from Christians who are older-and-wiser, showed them how to be responsible hunters and gun owners, took them to church, supported their church missions trips, and taught them about the passionate love of Jesus. We made plenty of mistakes along the way, but we really tried to do everything possible to help our kids make good and safe decisions. For the most part, they have. But in just one moment of poor judgment, our world was shattered.

No parent can assume to know what is or isn't happening with their kids. And the lie that "ignorance is bliss" can be deadly. It's like putting a frog into a pot of cool water and slowly bringing it to a boil. He just hangs out in there, thinking everything is okay and by the time it's too hot, it's too late for the frog! Mike and I knew nothing about K2 or any drug like it, but it shattered our lives anyway. Our story reaffirms that it's not enough to focus on what we think we know, we need to reach beyond to what we don't know. Every parent, grandparent, teacher, youth worker–every adult who lives with or works with kids–needs to keep their eyes wide open to the broad spectrum of ever-changing cultural issues, social media platforms, and family value systems that influence today's kids.

It's necessary for adults to insert themselves into the lives of the kids they love by staying educated about current teen-culture and engaging in honest–and sometimes awkward–conversations. Rampant today is the idea that kids have a right to privacy and that we shouldn't infringe on that right by "poking around" in their business. However, your willingness to poke around could be the very thing that saves your son or daughter from harm. Parents have the responsibility to be informed. We need to do research and educate ourselves about the various social media platforms and electronic communications kids use. We need to talk to youth leaders, teachers, and other parents to learn everything possible about the social culture and jargon flooding school hallways, electronic devices, movies, music, and yes . . . even church youth rooms.

No matter how responsible, mature, or spiritual our kids may be, they are still kids. While older adults are physiologically able to respond rationally, the brains of teens and young adults are wired to respond to emotions with emotion, which often leads to unhealthy decisions that they can't explain later.[1] As adults, it's our duty to come alongside the kids we love and help them recognize the potential consequences of poor decisions. Appendix B on page 257 provides a list of resources to get you started. Turning a blind eye to the ugly details of what our kids see and experience can be fatal. Truth, while often difficult to hear, is always better than ignorance. God's Word says, ". . . everything exposed by the light becomes visible–and everything that is illuminated becomes a light . . . Be very careful, then, how you live –not as unwise but as wise, making the most of every opportunity, because the days are evil." (Ephesians 5:13–16)

---

1. Fetterman et al., *"Understanding the Teen Brain,"* para. 4.

Our family continues to shine light on the fact that legal does not mean safe. Synthetic drugs can be deadly. Vaping can be deadly. Misuse of prescription drugs can be deadly. When speaking to middle school, high school, and even college students, Mike is passionate in telling them not to inject, ingest, or inhale anything that isn't prescribed by their doctor . . . *as prescribed* by their doctor. There are plenty of people in this world who have no moral compass and who are willing to sell anything for a profit, completely unconcerned about the fallout. It might not be K2, but there is always a *substance-next* threatening to destroy our kids. We have to tell them that no promise of excitement or relief is as precious as their lives. I would urge you not to go to sleep tonight before talking to the kids you love about this.

Our urgency to educate the public about K2 and similar substances came quickly because we knew our story had a shelf-life. It sounds harsh, but it's true. If we were going to influence law-makers, then we had to strike while the iron was hot and tell our story before it faded from the headlines. The sad truth of living in a sinful world is that there is always some new thing that comes along and threatens to destroy our kids. And sure enough, before we knew it, headlines about K2 and synthetic drugs were joined by reports of prescription drug and opioid abuse, and eventually the dangers of vaping. It's a perpetual cycle and eventually "older" drugs come back around again. Regardless of what the *substance-next* is, the heart of the issue remains the same: Protect your body from harmful substances, whether they are legal or not.

As you will learn in the next chapter, we have had many opportunities to be in the spotlight, but not one of them has been about calling attention to ourselves. Instead, advocacy is about honoring the legacy of our loved ones by telling our story and praying for positive change. Our work to inform the public of the dangers of synthetic drugs was driven by one question: "How can we stop this from happening to anyone else?" Reliving the tragedy of that night is incredibly difficult for so many reasons, as if we continually rip off the bandage that protects our grieving hearts from a cruel world. No doubt about it, advocacy comes at a high personal cost, but it also comes with lasting, sometimes eternal, rewards. For us, continuing to push through painful emotions for the sake of the cause is necessary. And if one life is saved–one person pointed to Jesus–then it is all worth it.

David loved Jesus. He loved to worship Jesus, and he wanted his friends to love Jesus. Even though his love for Jesus didn't keep him from harm, it made his days meaningful, his legacy purposeful, and his life eternal. Proverbs 31:8 says, "Speak up for those who cannot speak for themselves, for the rights of all who are destitute." David can no longer speak for himself.

If he could, he would be the loudest and most passionate advocate *against* synthetic drugs and *for* finding hope in Jesus. But he can't speak, so we must. His legacy needs a voice. And so does the legacy of your loved one. For thousands of years, God has called broken people to be his voice to a broken world and to advocate for Truth.

Thousands of years ago, a Hebrew boy named Moses was adopted by Egyptian royalty and raised as a prince. But this luxurious life abruptly ended when he was forced to leave Egypt and venture into an unfamiliar land where he lived homeless and alone. He could have stayed there, wallowing in bitter confusion and rebellion. Many would have. But God called Moses to something much greater. He called him to return to Egypt–to the very place that caused him pain–and to advocate for the freedom of God's people who had lived in bondage for generations. Moses was not interested. Over and over, he worked to convince God that he was not the right man for the job:

> "Who am I to go to Pharaoh and bring the Israelites out of Egypt?"
> Exodus 3:11

> "What if they do not believe me or listen to me and say, 'The Lord did not appear to you?'" Exodus 4:1

> "Pardon your servant, Lord. I have never been eloquent, neither in the past nor since you have spoken to your servant. I am slow of speech and tongue." Exodus 4:10

> "Pardon your servant, Lord. Please send someone else."
> Exodus 4:13

Despite his repeated attempts to avoid God's calling, Moses chose to follow God's call by returning to Egypt, because he believed that God would give him the words to speak, the power to perform miracles, and the strength to advocate for positive change. And God did.

So many times, I plead with God not to send me back to my "Egypt"– to June 6, 2010– but instead, to wrap me up tight and protect me from the pain of returning to the story that shattered my heart. And so many times he has worked miracles, as I have stepped out in faith, trusting him to provide the words and strength I needed to advocate for positive change.

When we're called to be the voice for a cause, it requires us to trust that God will not leave us alone and that he will help us to stay focused on the goal. Having passion for a purpose powerfully influences the personal risks we're willing to take. The enemy wants us to stay trapped in the darkness of loss and fear, to feel lonely and afraid, and to believe that telling the story of our loss is futile and self-serving. What lies! Not only is it okay to give testimony of our experiences, but we are called to do just that. Nobody has the power or authority to tell your story as masterfully as you. It has the potential to awaken emotions and help others feel less alone on their journey. Perhaps Jesus chose parables to bring the truth of scripture to life because they go beyond facts and cut to the heart of what others feel, experience, and desire. I believe the reason our story has been effective in changing laws, educating the public, and offering hope is because we have lived it. We aren't just delivering facts about synthetic drugs and telling people to believe in God because it's a good idea. We have authority to affect change because our story tells how our lives have been transformed, how our hearts have ached, and how Jesus continues to sustain us.

Taken days before Mike testified before the U.S. Senate Caucus on International Narcotics Control, just one year after David died.

Mike, Daniel, and I have absolutely been called to fight against the dangers of synthetic drugs and chapter 14 details our journey to advocate for positive change. While I'm eternally grateful for these opportunities, the confession I'm about to make is a difficult one. Brace yourself for some raw honesty. In the midst of talking to state legislators, testifying to the U.S. Judiciary Committee in Washington D.C., and even being interviewed for national television programs, I often struggled with the reality that I am not solely responsible for fighting the battle.

Let me explain. Veronica and Devin Eckhardt are a couple from California who lost their 19-year-old son, Connor, after he took one hit of the synthetic drug called Spice. Connor slipped into a coma and died a few days later. Since this tragedy in 2014, the Eckhardts have had a tremendous social media presence and have been given incredible opportunities to share their story; on a much larger scale than us. As I saw this unfold from afar, I wondered if we could have done more earlier on and why people hadn't believed us when we first started out, the way they believed Veronica and Devin. *Why do they seem to have a stronger voice on this issue?*

They received an outpouring of support from strangers that validated Connor's life and brought them unspeakable encouragement to fight harder for the cause. It was something I craved. *Can I seriously be jealous that they are reaching people and making a difference? Seriously, Jan!* Looking back, I really didn't like the way it made me feel. After all, it wasn't a contest! Once again, I was being lied to by the enemy. My feelings of envy stemmed from wanting people to hear David's story, the way they were hearing about others, but I had to remind myself of the bigger picture. God had been adding boots on the ground since the day we lost David. . .much needed reinforcements for a collective (and very personal) mission.

What the Eckhardts and others are doing to inform the public and influence lawmakers is amazing . . . and it is a team effort. When we venture into advocacy, it really can't be about ourselves. Even though our mission is personal, we have to stay focused on the cause and sometimes we have to set our boots aside and celebrate the successes of others. Veronica reminds me that God's not done yet, even when hope and healing and change get temporarily interrupted. He's not done with the Eckhardt's, and he's not done with us. And he's not done with you, either. What a great truth to hold on to as we wait for "good" to come.

Each story of loss is unique. Even when talking with other parents who have lost children because of synthetic drugs, the details are different. Whether your loss is a result of drugs or alcohol, an accident, complication of pregnancy or childbirth, SIDS, disease, or even old age, nothing about it feels *good*. But God promises to bring something good from it. Who needs to hear your unique story? How can your experience with loss prevent others from experiencing the same? How can your grief be used as a beacon of hope to guide others on the path to healing? What lessons have you learned about life and love? The answers to these questions may reveal a cause that needs your voice. Perhaps you're not ready to answer them just yet. Maybe it's too soon or you hurt too much. But as you draw near to God today and trust him with your story, I pray that you will find new purpose and strength to search for ways that he can use your story for something good. It's not a story you asked for, I get it, but it's uniquely yours, and it has the unique potential to positively impact others and to honor the legacy of your loved one. And maybe, just maybe, you will also be encouraged as you see other hurting people finding peace and healing as you share.

RAW JOURNAL ENTRY

July 2011–Initial passing of K2 legislation, one year after David died

I don't need pomp and circumstance. I realize there are far greater issues to the general public than what my eyes were searching for in that newspaper. Folks probably read through the budget legislation or school aid legislation and think these are at the top of the state's priorities this session. Not me. My eyes scrolled down to the red bold letters that read "DRUGS, the action to be taken by way of Iowa law." It was there I found justice for David. It was there I found protection for our state's youth. It was also there I found joy in the accomplishment, with God leading the battle in Iowa. To God be the glory! No doubt.

Then there is the bittersweet reliving of it all. . .feeling like we've lost our David all over again. And it reminds me why we are fighting in the first place. I am in awe of the way God has worked. Truly in awe! My brother used the word "remarkable" last week in reference to this legislation. . .all within a year and 24 days of losing David as a result of these horrible drugs. We have seen God at work in this, even during the days when the whole situation seemed way too big. But even when I felt so alone knowing the odds were against us, God was in this! And I am overwhelmingly thankful.

FIRST AID FOR YOUR GRIEVING HEART

Healing Prayer

Dear Lord, thank you for the hope of beauty instead of ashes, of joy instead of mourning, and of praise instead of despair. Help me truly believe that something good can come from my loss, even when I feel angry and defeated. Work a miracle by giving me the words and strength to honor my loved one; telling his/her story and trusting it to bring positive change to the world.

Healing Truth

Visit the following pages to unleash God's healing power over the lies that threaten to defeat you: *Nothing good can come from this* (p. 239); *It's easier not to know the dangers that threaten my kids* (p. 242); *Telling my story is futile and self-serving* (p. 246).

Healing Words

What lesson(s) have you learned as a result of your loved one's death? What truth can you share that may prevent others from experiencing similar pain? You may feel that your heart hurts too much to answer these questions. Still, I pray that you find the strength to ask them anyway. If your loved one was still here, what would he/she want others to know? How can you be a voice for his/her cause?

Chapter 14

The David Mitchell Rozga Act

Mike and I ventured into advocacy knowing very little–almost nothing, really–other than the tragic truth that our son smoked a synthetic drug called K2 and 90 minutes later he took his life. Two days after he died, we learned about the K2 and it immediately intensified our search for answers to the question that already haunted us. *Why?* We had no idea what it was, why David had it, or how it may have contributed to his deadly decision that day. So, we began working with others to unlock the mystery of what happened during that 90-minute window.

The local detective assigned to David's case, Brian Sher, began learning about the K2 as he questioned David's friends. It was something they purchased legally, knowing that it was considered "fake pot" and believing that it was harmless since they bought it at the mall. Obviously, just the opposite was true. Over the next few days, we began to learn just how dangerous K2 can be. As Detective Sher continued his investigation, he developed a sense of urgency to warn the public and told us that it is an issue that *"needs a voice."* So, on the morning of our son's visitation and caught up in the hurricane of grief, we agreed to be that voice. We had no idea what that would entail or the emotional toll it would take, let alone where it would lead us, but we had to do something. Very quickly, we realized that the synthetic drug trend was far greater and much darker than we ever imagined, and I couldn't help but wonder what we were getting ourselves into.

SO, WHAT IS K2 ANYWAY?

K2, Spice, and other drugs like them, are primarily marketed and sold as herbal incense, with misleading labels that read, "Not for human consumption," even though that is exactly the intent. The chemicals found in these drugs are meant to mimic marijuana, earning them nicknames like "fake weed" and "synthetic marijuana," but their physical and psychological effects can be far more dangerous and very unpredictable. They're officially called cannabinoids and marketed as a safe and legal alternative, sold in a variety of shiny and colorful packages with designs like smiley faces, images of fruit, and even cartoon characters. At the time of David's death, they were primarily sold as dried plant material that had been sprayed or mixed with chemicals. Today, these drugs are also brewed as tea and even sold as liquids to use when vaping. For far too long, these manmade hallucinogenic-type synthetic drugs were easy to buy at convenience stores and online, making them a legal and inexpensive option. I mean, how bad could it be, right? Kids don't even have to hide it from their parents because packages are clearly labeled as incense. Nobody would suspect a thing. Unreal!

One Drug Enforcement Administration (DEA) agent explained that they witnessed K2 being manufactured by spreading plant material on a flat surface, then mixing one or more chemical compounds (usually purchased from China) into a residential garden sprayer. The chemical is sprayed onto the plant material, allowed to dry, and then packaged for distribution. Batches are sprayed manually, so there is no quality or quantity control. In other words, some packages contain a higher concentration of harmful chemicals than others. This not only helps to explain why the stuff is so dangerous, but also explains why a shared package can affect users so differently. Even legal drugs that are regulated by the Food and Drug Administration (FDA) can affect users differently, so imagine the danger of a drug that's not regulated.

Some of these cannabinoid compounds were initially developed by John Huffman, an organic chemistry professor, while working to find medical treatments for things like inflammation and skin cancer. In an interview with the Los Angeles Times, Huffman warned, "These things (chemicals) are dangerous–anybody who uses them is playing Russian roulette. They have profound psychological effects and we never intended them for human consumption."[1] When people began using and marketing these and other compounds as "incense," to line their pockets with money, our kids became lab rats.

---

1. Zucchino, *"Scientist's Research,"* Para. 23.

IT WAS TIME FOR POSITIVE CHANGE

The task before us was ominous, but we didn't want any other families to experience what we had, so we set out to educate kids, families, and government leaders about the dangers of K2 and other synthetic drugs that were beginning to surface. We believed that our voices (or perhaps I should say David's voice) would lead to positive change that would save lives, and this is what gave us the fuel we needed to press on. Our voices had to be heard. If just one person makes the decision to avoid these drugs, synthetic or otherwise, then it will be worth it. Beginning the day of David's funeral, our family began to share our story and many opportunities quickly followed. We were interviewed by local television, radio, and newspapers, and participated in various Public Service Announcements (PSAs).

One of Mike's first and most public interviews took place on July 8th, just four weeks after David died, when he was interviewed for the Steve Deace program on WHO radio. The live broadcast aired during the evening commute, so we were hopeful that it would reach thousands. As the day approached, I was so thankful that it was Mike and not me. I could never get through it . . . not that soon. In fact, I wasn't sure that I could even listen to it. Steve didn't know David, but he wanted listeners to hear the personal story behind the headlines, so he asked Mike to share stories about what kind of person David was and the role K2 played in his death.

When the day arrived, I sat on the deck with the radio and Daniel sat in his truck by our neighbor's barn. We were both more comfortable listing in our own space. My already broken heart cracked again when I heard David's name spoken over the airwaves. *Are they really talking about my David? Can this possibly be real?* Mike explained that K2 can cause resting heart rates to climb instantly to 160 beats per minute, seizures that last for hours, severe panic attacks, unconsciousness, comas, and even death . . . all of this within minutes of smoking it. There are many types of synthetics offering a variety of highs, none of which considers body composition or age, and none of which are regulated by the FDA. I was so proud of Mike for having the courage to speak out in such a public way.

After sharing what happened to our son and about the dangers of K2, Mike was asked an unexpected question: Are you angry with God? His answer captured my feelings perfectly:

> "Angry at God? I had the honor of being David's dad for 18 years and he's with his eternal Father now, who is a better dad than I could ever be. Things happen for a reason and for God's glory . . . things we will never understand. If David could come back right now, he wouldn't. Why would he? Why would he leave the

Savior . . . a place like heaven? We are only on this earth for a speck of time compared to eternity, and I know that we will be together again someday."

We were both angry that David was gone and neither of us understood anything about it. Still, we both knew that there was a bigger picture; one we may never fully see this side of heaven. Somehow, we had to put one foot in front of the other and use our tragedy to make a positive difference. Mike spoke with such grace, and there is no doubt that God stood with him, as any loving father would do, to give him the strength he needed to speak difficult words as his heart broke all over again. Soon after the interview ended, Daniel drove up and joined me on the deck. "Dad did a great job, didn't he." *He sure did. And I believe David feels the same way.*

Between dealing with the overwhelming pain of loss and being so newly (though profoundly) acquainted with the issue of synthetic drugs, it's fair to say we were flying a bit blind. Thankfully, we were able to surround ourselves with great people who were fully vested in working to prevent even one more tragedy from happening. Little did we know that our efforts would take us from being interviewed in our living room and lobbying at the Iowa State Capitol to testifying before a Senate committee in Washington D.C.

One person who joined us in the battle was local attorney, Mark Schlenker, who first heard Mike's words about K2 at David's funeral. He wrote a letter to Iowa Senator Grassley's office in Washington D.C. stating that, "The unregulated status of this substance is a problem," and urged his staff to look into it further. Within weeks, at Schlenker's request, the German and French Consulates in Chicago sent information to Senator Grassley explaining why synthetic drugs like K2 were already banned in their countries and by the European Union.

In August, Mike and I met with Senator Grassley at a local event and were so thankful for the brief opportunity to tell him about David. We explained our desire to bring national attention to the dangers of K2 and asked him to consider introducing legislation to further protect our nation's youth. It didn't take long for him to respond to that request for help. He offered us the services of his media consultant to help with educational efforts and gave us the name of a staffer, Dave Bleich, who would serve as a contact person through the process. (Poor Dave. He had no idea how persistent I would be!) Senator Grassley was also the co-chair of the Senate Caucus on International Narcotics Control, which was chaired by California Senator Dianne Feinstein. As talk of co-sponsoring a K2/synthetic drug bill surfaced, I tried not to get my hopes too high. But it would be so amazing.

While staying closely connected with developments in D.C., we were also making progress back home. Local leaders in Iowa offered condolences and their willingness to assist with legislation, if needed. Mike and I attended a meeting of the Iowa Board of Pharmacy in July, along with my parents and a few friends. We heard discussions about recent synthetic drug findings, including a presentation by our local police chief. Four days after that, the Board adopted emergency rules to ban the sale or possession of the substance commonly known as synthetic marijuana and sold under names such as K2, Spice, and Red Dragon Smoke. In addition, the Board filed amended rules to classify these products as Imitation Controlled Substances. This was extraordinary because it not only came before the legislature acted on the state level . . . but before the DEA acted on it federally. Typically, it's the other way around.

Iowa's Governor Chet Culver issued a press release that summer, announcing an educational campaign to prevent synthetic marijuana use, stating, "The Rozga family is already suffering a great loss. David's legacy is to help spare other families the same pain, by making them aware of dangers associated with synthetic marijuana." At the same time, we connected with Gary Kendell, the director of the Office of Drug Control Policy (ODCP), who asked us to share David's story as part of the educational campaign. The Iowa Department of Public Health also produced and shared public service announcements to make the public aware, and the Governor's Office of Drug Control Policy issued a statement warning Iowans about the dangers of synthetic drugs and spotlighting David's story. The American Association of Poison Control Centers also issued a press release warning the public. As reports of synthetic cannabinoid toxicity increased, the Iowa Poison Control Center alerted health care providers across Iowa of the serious medical effects caused by these drugs.

Our message was gaining traction, and we were so thankful that these substances were getting national attention. By fall, The Early Show on CBS asked to do a story about David which would reach people across the country, and Senator Grassley addressed his colleagues on the Senate floor in September, informing them of the K2 issue. His remarks were streamed on CSPAN so Mike and I watched from our living room as it unfolded. I shook, even with Mike's strong arm around me, and we both cried when we saw the poster of David's senior picture perched on an easel behind the senator. *This can't be real, can it? Three months ago we celebrated our son's graduation and now he's memorialized on an easel in the U.S. Senate? So surreal.*

Mike spent a great deal of time speaking at schools and churches across Iowa. He also met with first responders, firefighters and law enforcement officers to be sure they understood the severity of the synthetic drug issue. So many doors were being opened and our efforts were making a difference, but reliving that night over and over again, when our wounds were still so fresh, was extremely hard. Many kids, even some in middle school, shared that they or someone they knew had tried K2, increasing our sense of urgency to spread information to a broader audience. A generous coworker of Mike's provided the financial support needed to develop and launch a website which was dedicated to exposing the dangers of synthetic drugs and sharing news of its devastating effects from across the country. At the time, it was the only website dedicated to educating the public on the dangers of synthetic cannabinoids and sharing the unfortunate stories of users. Until then, the only online information about these drugs was focused on how to purchase them.

Two days before Thanksgiving, nearly six months after David died, we received a call from the National Drug Enforcement Agency (DEA). The following day they would be formally announcing a nationwide ban on K2, along with the five chemicals used to make it. This was in response to "increasing reports of seizures, hallucinations and dependency linked to the fake pot [making it] necessary to prevent an imminent threat to public health and safety."[2] Because only congress can make laws, this temporary ban would stay in effect for at least a year, allowing the DEA time to conduct additional research and for congress to work on federal legislation to control these substances permanently. Each time progress was made, it was emotional. When we set out to "be a voice" for this cause, we trusted God to be with us in the fight, and every small victory reminded me of his faithfulness.

RAW JOURNAL ENTRY

Deuteronomy 31:8 "The Lord himself goes before you and will be with you; he will never leave you or forsake you. Do not be afraid; do not be discouraged." Little did I know that this verse would do way more than just bring personal encouragement, it is also proving to be true time and time again in our fight against synthetic drugs. The Lord is absolutely walking before us. He began lining people up for this fight even before we lost David . . . even before I begged him for help. One year ago (four months before David died!), Dr. Anthony J. Scalzo [MD, Director of Toxicology for SSM Health Saint Louis University Hospital and SSM Health Cardinal Glennon Children's Hospital] *had already contacted the U.S. Centers for Disease Control and Prevention to raise awareness of the increasing number of synthetic drug calls to the Missouri*

2. Moisse and Sanchez, *"DEA Bans Sale of K2,"* para. 2.

Poison Control Center. He also raised concern about the alarming number of patients in his emergency room displaying peculiar behavior related to synthetics. Dr. Scalzo began to compile medical papers with his findings because he knew the issue was a "force to be reckoned with" across the country. At the exact same time, we were eagerly planning David's graduation party, having no clue that the subject of Dr. Scalzo's concern would become our worst nightmare. Tony has become a good friend and we're so thankful that he continues to warn others of the dangers of K2 and other synthetic drugs. I wish someone would have warned us.

I began to wonder why there wasn't more communication about this issue among states and individuals who were suffering from the effects of synthetic substances. Why did it take our country so long to notice the problem? It was surprising to learn that synthetic drugs first surfaced in Europe in 2004 and in the U.S. in 2008. By 2009, countries like France and Denmark had already enacted bans in response to them. *So why wasn't this information shared? Or was it?* Honestly, every country and every poison control center in the world should be warned whenever a new drug emerges and causes harm. Speculation or not, I truly believe if there had been appropriate global communication in place, David might still be here. The more I questioned and the more I learned, the more obsessive I became. I even wrote a detailed letter to President Obama. I know! I also signed up to receive notifications for synthetic drug news, hoping to stay informed of current incidents and trends so that we could speak intelligently about the facts and how other communities were fighting this battle. Every day I checked my inbox. And every day it took a toll. It was difficult to read all of the stories and especially difficult to read the comments that followed. Seeing the turmoil it caused in me, Mike lovingly and protectively suggested turning off the notifications. It was a good call.

Early in 2011, we began working to educate our state representatives and senators on the dangers of these drugs and lobbying for legislation to protect the public. By that time, we had learned much more about the devastating effects of synthetic drugs and that our son was not the only person to take his life after smoking them. The Iowa Poison Control Center was receiving a growing number of calls related to synthetic drugs and these statistics were an important reminder to legislators that each frantic phone call represented a constituent, a precious life in grave danger. Other states had similar experiences. In fact, 18 states and all five branches of the U.S. military made the decision to ban one or more of the five synthetic substances.

Each time we went to the Statehouse, we stood outside the House and Senate chambers and filled out cards requesting to meet with as many representatives and senators as possible, praying that their eyes would be open to our message as we waited to see if they would accept our request to talk. We showed them pictures of David and handed them informative packets about K2, with the most up to date data, so that each representative and senator would be prepared to vote for current and upcoming synthetic drug bills. We attended many House and Senate committee meetings and were invited to speak at a few of them. It's fair to say that I was a fish out of water. Seriously. My nerves would kick in and so would my lack of self-confidence. Then, to top everything off, I was often flooded with thoughts about what brought us there in the first place . . . the death of our son. *We're here to share his story, Jan . . . to establish a positive legacy. You can fall apart later.* Our message was always short and to the point: proposed legislation will bring attention to the emergence of the dark and deadly world of synthetic drugs, which was increasingly affecting other families. We needed to protect Iowans. If the legislation didn't pass through assigned committees, that would be the end of it. And if that happened, we would have to wait until the next session to fight for it again.

I realize now that thinking it would be a slam dunk was naive. There wasn't anything easy about it, and I was so surprised by the opposition we faced. Surely, if it was their son or daughter, parent or grandparent, brother or sister . . . surely then they would be fighting the same fight. Wouldn't they? One state representative literally told friends who were with us that day, "My kids wouldn't be so stupid as to try K2." He later learned that this was becoming an issue in his precinct and changed his tune a bit. It was a crash course in government for us, and we learned a lot about the legislative process. To be honest, the "politics" of it was nauseating. It happened all the time: One party wanted a bill to pass and the other party disagreed. One didn't support the other unless they leveraged previous legislation of their own. The "newsy" word for this is gridlock. In my eyes, it's total negligence. The more time it took, the more Iowans were at risk. While debates lingered on, there was an increase in calls to Iowa poison control, and more kids were being seen in emergency rooms all across the country. At that time, doctors were unsure of how to treat patients displaying the effects of synthetic drugs because there was so little known about them. And sadly, people were dying as gridlock continued. This was so personal to me, and I took each dismissal as a dismissal of David's death, as well as those who died after him. When the process stalled, it felt like I was failing David. Thankfully, a friend of mine faithfully reminded me that we are not in control of the outcome . . . God is. Our calling is to share our story. Period. He will take care of the rest. Sounds simple, but it's so difficult to apply this to our lives on a daily basis.

Once the synthetic drug legislation passed through the State House committees in February 2011, our family and friends sat in the gallery to hear introduction and debate. Daniel was even invited to be present on the floor of the House as the bill was introduced. Talk about surreal. Later, as I stood in the lobby of the Statehouse, I noticed a group of elementary students taking a tour. Each one was gawking at the elaborate architecture and ornate paintings in our beautiful state house as they followed their guide. Immediately, it took me back to David's 6th grade field trip to the Capital. Same tour. Same elaborate architecture. Same spectacular dome. Same lawmaking process. I wanted to shout, "*This is where lives are protected! This is where elected officials speak on your behalf. This is where people will decide if my son's death will make a difference.*" These students had the same sense of curiosity and wonder that David had seven years before, walking on the same marble floors, and they had no idea that the men and women they visited in chambers were currently making a decision that would directly affect their future. As each student passed, I thought "This is for you . . . and you . . . and you." I prayed fervently that the legislation would pass. It just had to.

Meanwhile in Washington D.C., Senator Grassley introduced the David Mitchell Rozga Act, also known as the Dangerous Synthetic Drug Control Act of 2011. Mike was asked to testify on April 6th, along with a representative from the DEA and another from an anti-drug coalition from California. I will never forget the mixed emotions that flooded my mind as Daniel, my parents, and my brother took our seats in the hearing room. Just before it was Mike's turn to testify, one of Grassley's staffers brought in a poster of David's graduation picture. None of us was prepared for that, especially Mike, and it took him a moment to compose himself. You could have heard a pin drop.

Mike testifying before the U.S. Senate Caucus on International Narcotics Control.

Mike's testimony was personal and compelling, as he shared our family's experience. The committee members appeared shocked to learn of the K2 statistics he shared, and I prayed it would motivate them to take action. It was appalling that the manufacturers of these products had been able to distribute and sell them right under our noses. But now they were in the spotlight, and their dirty secrets were being revealed to the world.

Following the hearing, we were greeted by the producer of ABC's 20/20 and escorted to the Mayflower Hotel where Brian Ross would interview us for the show. We had known about the interview for some time and knew that we would be on display for the world to see. Our life. Our loss. Our David. It was necessary to get the word out about these drugs and the predators that make and sell them, but the thought of reliving everything so publicly was heartbreaking. A year ago, David was here and life was normal. Our grief was still so fresh, and we were very vulnerable. I remember telling my mother that I wasn't sure I could do it, and her response has never left me: "David's worth it, Jan. He would want you to help others." She was right. The interview started with questions about the day David died, and then Brian told us that the 20/20 team had also interviewed a distributor of K2, who referred to our family as ignorant idiots and suggested that K2 had nothing to do with David's death. *Really?* My blood boiled and I quickly pushed back. This from a guy who represented stores that sold K2 and Spice, substances that had already been connected to multiple deaths, and he had zero remorse or tact. It was appalling that he could be so insensitive about a situation–about people–he knew nothing about. Disgusting. Needless to say, we were all relieved when the interview was over.

I was so ready to unwind from the events of the day, so my brother who took on the role of social secretary, suggested we go to Bullfeathers, a popular restaurant in D.C. It was there that I met Jan. It's a rarity to meet someone with that name, so of course I had to comment. Jan and I were laughing together as Daniel walked up, and I introduced him to "my sister, Jan." The baffled look on his face said it all. My new friend, who was African American, smiled and quickly added, "Yes, we are sisters from the same Creator."

Then, the most amazing thing happened. Before moving on, Jan leaned in close to my face and quoted a scripture, "Oh, that you would bless me and enlarge my territory. Let your hand be with me, and keep me from harm so that I will be free from pain." (1 Chronicles 4:10) I hugged her and told her about David; explaining why we were in D.C. She hugged me tight and told me that our Heavenly Father loves me and to keep on fighting. Not only did she make my day, I felt the immediate and tangible encouragement of God–from a total stranger. *He is in this.*

After three days of activity in D.C., meeting with a variety of our nation's leaders and telling our story repeatedly, we arrived back in Iowa. Shortly after, a producer from 20/20 came to our hometown to finish taping for the interview that we started at the Mayflower. They took footage of David's memorial road sign in his high school hallway and interviewed his beloved band teachers. I took them to David's memorial tree and to the cemetery, and then we returned to our house for their interview with David's girlfriend, Carrie.

RAW JOURNAL ENTRY

Carrie told me that she was determined to make the interview real and from her heart, but not for entertainment purposes. There were tears during the interview, as she spoke about how losing David has changed her life, and all I could do was look at David's pictures on the bookcase. This cannot really be happening! It took so much courage to do what she did. I'm so proud of her and told her that David would be proud, too. I also gave her the 2010 White House Christmas ornament I purchased for her when we were in DC, and told her that, while it signifies the year we lost David, it also stands as a reminder of the beginning of our fight to rid the state and country of K2 and other synthetic drugs. Hopefully the 20/20 coverage will keep our mission alive.

In the end, our story on 20/20 was much briefer than we expected, and I was disappointed that more of David's story wasn't used. However, news cycles in television are fluid and can change in an instant. There have definitely been disappointing moments like this along the way, bringing frustration and emotional hurricanes, but we try to use each one as fuel for the fight. There's also frustration when elected officials fail to see the urgency of an issue that has already caused so much devastation for their constituents. To be completely honest, it makes me crazy. I'll never forget one visit to the Iowa statehouse, when a high-ranking senator left me speechless with his condescending words. It crushed me, but I saved my tears for the drive home. *Why doesn't he get it?!*

Despite opposition, Iowa's synthetic drug legislation passed the House in March, with a vote of 94–3, and a less-impressive version was eventually passed in the Iowa Senate in July, as part of a spending bill. It's not the overwhelming victory we hoped for, but the most important victory is that Governor Terry Branstad signed Iowa's first synthetic drug bill into law on August 1, 2011. We were very thankful to each lawmaker who acted to ban substances that were proven to be deadly. The following year, on May

25, 2012, we attended the signing of a bill strengthening this law, and additional amendments continue to follow as new information and new substances surface. Since 2011, all 50 states have passed laws banning synthetic substances and, while this is great news, the work is ongoing because new substances are continually emerging.

Governor Terry Branstad signs Iowa's first synthetic drug bill into law.

In January of 2012, we were contacted by our local medical examiner's office about an upcoming conference in Louisiana. He would be giving a presentation about how K2 has impacted our state and nation, and wanted our permission to discuss David's case. At the time of David's death, nothing was found in his system because testing for these substances hadn't been developed yet. We were told that labs are discarded after a year, but I asked if they could keep David's, just in case there were strides made in testing. Thankfully, they agreed to keep them indefinitely, and prior to the upcoming conference we agreed to have David's labs sent to Pennsylvania for testing. The Pennsylvania lab ran two tests, both with the same results. Of the five chemical compounds that were banned in the United States in 2010, substantial amounts of two of these compounds (JWH 073, JWH 018) were found in David's system. I asked the medical examiner if it would be common to obtain successful results after samples were eighteen months old, and he told me it was *uncommon*. We were given confirmation of what we already knew. It was a gift.

RAW JOURNAL ENTRY

A year ago, I felt so helpless and hopeless, thinking about the synthetic drug issue; how it contributed to David's death and threatened to harm so many other families. We agreed to be a voice for this cause, but I honestly didn't know how we would have the mental energy to fight such a difficult battle. I thought it was our family's fight, but I was wrong. I asked God to supernaturally put people in the right places, people with the power to help. I prayed for it often, and I was surprised when I began to realize, this is not the "Rozga family battle." It's God's battle. Always has been. Yes, it's personal and it always will be. But we are just soldiers in a bigger army, trusting God's marching orders, Right? "Lord, there is no one like you to help the powerless against the mighty. Help us O Lord, for we rely on you, and in your name, we have come against this vast army. O Lord, you are our God; do not let man prevail against you." (2 Chronicles 14:11) I want it all to move faster, and I get so angry when people don't understand the urgency. Then I have to remember that I am powerless, God, but you have proven yourself powerful . . . in so many ways. I will continue to trust you with the fight.

On July 10, 2012, two years after David died, President Obama signed the David Mitchell Rozga Act into law. We remain so grateful to Judge Mark Schlenker, Senator Grassley, Dave Bleich, Senator Feinstein, and a host of others for hearing our voice–for listening to David's story–and for joining us in the fight to prevent other families from experiencing the tragedy we suffered. As a result of our work in prevention and education on the dangers of synthetic drugs, the Office of National Drug Control Policy selected us as 2013 *Advocates for Action*. This led to an invitation to participate in kicking off the President's strategy for national drug control and to work with the Partnership for Drug-Free Kids, continuing to advocate for action on synthetic drugs.

Dale Woolery, Interim Director of the Iowa Governor's Office of Drug Control Policy, announcing us as 2013 Advocates for Action.

The journey has been a whirlwind at times, and over the years we continue to connect with local and national lawmakers, as well as first responders, to advocate for positive change on David's behalf. In 2014, we had a phone conversation with an undercover Des Moines police officer who just wanted to follow up with us after arrests were made following a local synthetic drug bust. He wanted to tell us that he was dedicating their success to us. Emotions welled up as he said, "We have not forgotten about David or your family." I miss David so much and I'm so thankful that he isn't forgotten. God continues to answer prayer.

Five years after passing Iowa synthetic drug legislation and four years after passing the David Mitchell Rozga Act, it was painfully clear to Mike and me that establishing these initial laws was only the tip of an ever-growing iceberg, and in 2016, we were invited back to Washington D.C. The use of synthetic drugs was becoming an even bigger epidemic and more deadly than ever, and the Senate Judiciary Committee asked Mike to testify, along with nine others. This hearing was far more publicized than the Senate Caucus of 2011, and we really felt the pressure of it. *What if they don't see the urgency? What if they refuse to take immediate action?* Quite frankly, I was afraid, so I reached out to Veronica Echhardt, one of our fellow warriors on the synthetic battle field, for support.

She gave me some of the best advice I've ever received. I had to stop focusing on the "justice" aspect of our trip. Instead, she urged me to focus on God's love and mercy while sharing our story and interacting with others. She and her husband Devin had plenty of experience with how all of this works. They have lobbied in their home state of California, testified before the U.S. House Judiciary Committee in Washington D.C., and even addressed the House of Lords in London. She encouraged me to release the outcome to God. After all, he placed us here for such a time as this. As we walk in obedience, the rest is up to him. The truth is good stuff, ya know? I needed that reminder.

I needed to release the results of our D.C. trip into God's hands and stop acting as if I had any power to control the outcome. Worrying wouldn't help. The other witnesses testifying before the panel would present professional opinions that pertained to their lines of work. Mike would present our hearts, as he spoke from his. Our focus was (and continues to be) to tell our story and pray that it makes an impact. As we made our way to D.C., I just prayed that Jesus would be glorified, regardless of the outcome. Our story, God's Glory. Period.

Mike sat at a long wooden table, alongside four other witnesses, and implored the Senate Judiciary Committee to increase their focus on manufacturers and distributors who continued to sidestep existing laws by hiding behind false advertising. He explained that more education is needed for the public to truly grasp the severity of the threat. Senator Grassley led the hearing, acknowledging the need for additional legislation against synthetic drugs and admitting that the battle against this ever-changing problem will be ongoing. Mike spoke flawlessly, and his voice was used powerfully once again.

Our family with Senator Grassley in Washington D.C.

The following year, Iowa's Governor Branstad would sign an updated version of the synthetic drug bill into law, just before accepting an appointment as the U.S. Ambassador to China. I really wanted to set up a meeting with him and a few of the families in Iowa who have lost children to K2 before he left. It was a big ask, but he agreed and it was so great to thank him personally for his support. (He actually agreed to two separate meetings because I got the calendar dates confused and gave the wrong dates to three of the six families. Way to go Jan!) This was an important part of our advocacy journey, and it's a memory that all of us will store in our hearts, knowing that the story of each loved one made a difference.

At that point, it had been seven years since David died . . . seven years of grief and the fight for raw survival. Seven years of being a voice for the dangers of the synthetic substances that caused him to take his life. But it was becoming clear that the fight was far from over. Even now, the battle rages on. Our wounds are less fresh and we've done a lot of healing, but reliving the horrible story of June 6th will always be painful. One thought keeps me going . . . *David's legacy is worth it.*

Your loved one is worth the fight, also . . . whatever that "fight" is. Somewhere in your loss is a story that will bring beauty from ashes. Is it an issue that needs your voice? Or comforting words that need to be shared with those who have experienced similar loss? Embracing the surviving legacy of your loved one doesn't require headlines or new legislation. Sometimes it's simply a kind word that offers the hope of survival. Advocacy that honors your loved one is the intentional act of sharing the positive lessons we learn in response to loss. If you told me that our family would have the emotional and mental capacity needed to fight an uphill battle against people who make, distribute, and sell the very thing that caused our son to take his life . . . I would have said it was impossible. God knew otherwise. He continues to be with us every step of the way, and he will continue fighting for us into the future. While the process has challenged our patience and endurance, it has also been an unspeakable joy to help others. My mom was right; as incredibly hard as it's been, it is all worth it because *David is worth it.* This will always be his legacy. My sweet boy, you did *not* die in vain.

FIRST AID FOR YOUR GRIEVING HEART

Healing Prayer

Lord Jesus, you know every terrible detail about the things that threaten to harm the people I love. Give me the emotional strength to seek understanding and show me when I need to speak up with a voice of wisdom. Help me to live with my eyes open to modern culture and my heart fully-filled with you.

Healing Truth

Visit the following pages to unleash God's healing power over the lies that threaten to defeat you: *Nothing good can come from this* (p. 239); *Telling my story is futile and/or self-serving* (p. 246).

Healing Words

Have you noticed any red flags about the culture surrounding your loved ones? What concerns do you have and have you shared them? What research might you need to do as you seek to understand these concerns? Maybe you don't have any concerns right now, but you know you need to have some purposeful conversations with your loved ones about modern culture and how it may be impacting them. What help do you need from God with all of this?

PART V

REDISCOVERING JOY

Rediscovering Joy

It's been more than a decade since David died. And since that day, I've been fighting for survival. It's a battle of ups-and-downs and utter dependence on God. I will never stop missing my son and though I've questioned God's timing and wondered if my joy will ever really be restored, I've learned to trust him in this messy and unfinished in-between . . . knowing that his perfect timing for lasting healing is worth the wait.

Ten years after David died, we spent the week after Christmas in Cabo San Lucas, Mexico. There is so much there to love: feeling the sun on my face, falling asleep to the rhythm of the waves crashing to shore, and waking to the sound of the barking seals. The beauty of God's creation is unmatched. The only thing I dreaded about the week was hearing the fireworks on New Year's Eve; the lingering smell of gunpowder that follows each burst . . . every pop mimicking the sound and smells of the day David died. I hated the thought of it.

For ten years, fireworks caused me anxiety, like clockwork, like a recurring emotional playlist of fear and anger and sadness. So, as a blanket of boats gathered in the Sea of Cortez bay and hundreds of people crowded the beachfront to bring in the new year with a bang, Mike and I headed to bed.

The first pop woke me up. I sat up and listened for the second and then the third. But instead of pulling the covers over my head, I did something that even surprised myself. I walked to our patio and began to watch . . . no rapid heartbeat . . . no anxiety. There were no recollections of the day David died. All I focused on was the most incredible display of fireworks I had ever seen in my life, like I was experiencing them for the very first time. I couldn't take my eyes off the picture postcard in the sky. Anxiety was replaced with awe, as the colors in the sky shined on my face and instead of feelings of

PTSD, I felt joy. Joy! The healing power of Jesus overwhelmed me. Tears filled my eyes and I heard God whisper to my soul, *it's time to put this part of your journey behind you, Jan.* He knew I needed this victory and my heart erupted in praise. *Thank you, Lord. Thank you!*

If you doubt that God will bring healing after so many in-between years, think again. God chose to bring healing in this area of my grief after nine and a half years. That's a long time to wait. It's a long time to pray for help and to avoid countless fireworks shows. But the joy that finally came, was absolutely worth the wait.

I don't know what my next victory will be, but God does. All I know is that I can absolutely trust it to come . . . at just the right time. As I continue to lean in to God's Word, to cry out to him in prayer, and to walk with him into each new day, and through every struggle with grief, I will continue to be restored and to find hope for the future. The Lord is faithful to those who trust in Him.

God sees your pain and he will never leave you alone in your fight for survival. Never. It may (who am I kidding–it *will*) take longer than you'd like, but victories will come and you will find healing . . . maybe when you least expect it. Mike and I continue to pray for each person who searches for hope in the pages of our story–including you–and we believe you will find the strength to persevere as you reject the lies that threaten to defeat you, claim the truth that brings healing, and face tomorrow knowing that Jesus loves you and you are not alone. Persevere, dear friend. Persevere.

> *"Blessed is the man who remains steadfast under trial, for when he has stood the test, he will receive the crown of life, which God has promised to those who love him." James 1:12*

PART VI

THE TRUTH COMPANION

Introduction to a Topical
Tool for Crushing Lies

*"If you abide in my word . . . you will know the truth,
and the truth will set you free."*

JOHN 8:31–32

God is never surprised by our pain, and the enemy never misses an opportunity to exploit it. The only way to heal our souls and survive loss is to
abide in the truth of God's Word. The Truth Companion is a survival tool.
"For though we live in the world, we do not wage war as the world does. The
weapons we fight with are not the weapons of the world. On the contrary,
they have divine power to demolish strongholds. We demolish arguments
and every pretension that sets itself up against the knowledge of God, and
we take captive every thought to make it obedient to Christ." (2 Corinthians
10:3–5) Time and time and time again, I am confronted with lies that cause
me to feel afraid and discouraged as I fight to survive the loss of our son.
And time and time and time again, God's Word provides powerful truths
that demolish those lies and bring healing to my heart. Thank you, Jesus, for
your weapon of Truth!

Each of the following topics identifies a lie that may be threatening to
defeat your grieving heart along with a powerful truth from God's Word
that crushes that lie and brings hope. This section is not intended to be read
in sequence. Rather, it is meant as a survival tool. What lie keeps you awake
at night and robs you of hope? Use the Table of Contents to find it, read
the brief introduction to the topic, and then set yourself free by engaging

155

in the seven days of scripture and prayer that follow. There is no expiration date. Still struggling? Reread the scriptures and reclaim the prayers. If you are able, commit the most meaningful scriptures to memory and meditate on them when you feel troubled. My prayer for each reader is that you discover peace, comfort, and even victory as you cling to the powerful Truth of God's Word. You are his precious child. You are fighting to survive your own, unique grief-storm. And you are not alone.

I Can't Pray

As Referenced in Chapter 1

The lie that defeats: I can't pray.

The truth that heals: God already knows my heart.

The lie that shouted to my soul, in the hurricane of losing our son, is that I could not pray. The truth I learned to cling to is that God already knows the darkest details of my heart. He knows my unspoken fears. He knows every desperate, ugly detail of my grief. And his Holy Spirit prays powerfully on my behalf. As you claim the truth of God's Word this week, I pray that the Holy Spirit will calm your troubled heart and overwhelm your soul with real and lasting peace. Pray only what you can and know that he hears more than you can say. He loves you deeply and his promises are real.

MONDAY

God's Truth: *I [Jesus] will ask the Father, and he will give you another advocate to help you and be with you forever–the Spirit of truth–for he lives with you and will be in you. John 14:16–17*
My Prayer: Dear Lord, your Spirit of truth is my Counselor forever, fighting for me when I can't fight for myself and never rejecting me because of grief. I trust you to fill my heart, God, with the promise that you know my pain even better than I know it myself and that you always will. Amen.

TUESDAY

God's Truth: *We do not know what we ought to pray for, but the Spirit himself intercedes for us through wordless groans . . . the Spirit intercedes for God's people in accordance with the will of God. Romans 8:26–27*
My Prayer: Oh God, I cling to the truth that your Spirit knows my grief completely and prays for me according to your perfect will, knowing exactly what I need for hope and healing. Help me in my weakness, at this very moment, and comfort my heart. Amen.

WEDNESDAY

God's Truth: *Record my misery; list my tears on your scroll. Psalm 56:8*
My Prayer: Dear Jesus, right now I choose to find rest for my soul, knowing the truth that you hold every tear close to your heart and that you understand every hurt I feel. Thank you that even when I have no words to pray, you know my deepest need. Amen.

THURSDAY

God's Truth: *You see the trouble of the afflicted; you consider their grief and take it in hand. The victims commit themselves to you; you are the helper of the fatherless. Psalm 10:14*
My Prayer: Oh God, you see my trouble and know every detail of my pain, so I choose to trust you with my grief. You are the only one who truly knows my thoughts and you love me anyway. Hold me in your hands, God, and help me through this day. Amen.

FRIDAY

God's Truth: *You have searched me, Lord, and you know me . . . you perceive my thoughts from afar . . . Before a word is on my tongue you, Lord, know it completely. Psalm 139:1–4*
My Prayer: Dear Lord, you know every ugly, fearful, and irrational thought that I have. Thank you so much for the truth that brings hope to my soul today . . . that nothing I think, feel, or say shocks you because you already know it completely. And you love me anyway. Amen.

SATURDAY

God's Truth: *Have mercy on me, Lord, for I am faint; heal me, Lord, for my bones are in agony. My soul is in deep anguish . . . All night long I flood my bed with weeping and drench my couch with tears . . . The Lord has heard my cry for mercy; the Lord accepts my prayer. Psalm 6:2–9*

My Prayer: Oh God, I'm so weak and I'm begging for your mercy. My soul suffers, my body hurts from the pain of this grief, and I'm completely worn out. Thank you that my tears are not in vain because they are like prayers to you; hear the cry of my heart and give me strength. Amen.

SUNDAY

God's Truth: *I waited patiently for the Lord; he turned to me and heard my cry. He lifted me out of the slimy pit, out of the mud and mire; he set my feet on a rock and gave me a firm place to stand. He put a new song in my mouth. . . Psalm 40:1–3*

My Prayer: Dear Jesus, I know that healing will take longer than I want it to, so I surrender every doubt and fear to you. I can't do this on my own. It's too big for me, but not too big for you. Thank you for the hope that you hear the cry of my heart and that, someday, I will sing a new song. Amen.

My Identity is Gone

As Referenced in Chapters 2 and 5

The lie that defeats: My identity is gone.

The truth that heals: My identity is in Christ.

My identity as David's mom was ripped away the day he died and it left me feeling empty and without purpose. The conspicuous void in my identity where he belonged shouted to my soul, "Your son is gone. You're no longer needed here." While it's true that David is gone, it is a lie that my identity as his mother is gone. Redefined? Yes. Less important? Never. Truth says that my true, eternal value is completely defined by who I am in Christ. Though hearing that truth may bring little comfort, I can't argue with God's Word. Right? Sometimes we must accept Truth simply because it's Truth.

As you claim the truth of God's Word this week, I pray you find peace in the only one who defines you . . . Jesus. It's natural to put all of our identity-eggs in one basket as we focus on our roles as mothers, fathers, wives, husbands, friends, etc., but our true identity is never tossed by the changing tide. Earthly relationships can be beautiful and blessed by God, but our eternal relationship as a child of the God of the Universe is where we find ultimate worth.

MONDAY

God's Truth: *But God chose you to be his people. You are royal priests. You are a holy nation. You are God's special treasure. You are all these things so that*

you can give him praise. God brought you out of darkness into his wonderful light. 1 Peter 2:9
My Prayer: Dear Lord, thank you for choosing me and for making me your treasure. As I struggle to find personal value in a new and difficult reality, I choose to seek you and to rest in my identity as your child . . . knowing that you are able to turn my darkness into light. Amen.

TUESDAY

God's Truth: *Yet to all who did receive him, to those who believed in his name, he gave the right to become children of God. John 1:12*
My Prayer: Oh God, I feel lost and without purpose. Still, I thank you for giving me the right to become your precious child and ask that you help this truth to flood my heart with comfort as I patiently wait for you to redefine my role on earth. Amen.

WEDNESDAY

God's Truth: *Set your hearts on things above, where Christ is, seated at the right hand of God. Set your minds on things above, not on earthly things. Colossians 3:1–2*
My Prayer: Jesus, my identity was taken when my loved one died and I desperately want it back. I feel incomplete, but you tell me to set my heart on you and on my identity as your child. Help me do that today and to remember that my value is not defined by earthly things. Amen.

THURSDAY

God's Truth: *For we are God's handiwork, created in Christ Jesus to do good works, which God prepared in advance for us to do. Ephesians 2:10*
My Prayer: Heavenly Father, I desperately miss the role I had in my loved one's life and I'm so thankful I had the opportunity to experience it. Still, I feel sad and out of sorts now that it's gone. Please help me to feel your assurance that I am still your masterpiece and that you still have a good purpose for me. Fill my human void, Jesus, as I choose to trust this. Amen.

FRIDAY

<u>God's Truth</u>: *You are no longer foreigners and strangers, but fellow citizens with God's people and also members of his household . . . And in him you too are being built together to become a dwelling in which God lives by his Spirit. Ephesians 2:19, 22*

<u>My Prayer</u>: Lord, the identity I knew is gone and I feel lost. Help me to focus on my eternal and unchanging identity as a member of your household–as a dwelling place for your Spirit–and to look at my loss through a lens of truth. By your grace, I still have a good purpose. Amen.

SATURDAY

<u>God's Truth</u>: *As a mother comforts her child, so will I comfort you. . .When you see this, your heart will rejoice and you will flourish like grass. Isaiah 66:13*

<u>My Prayer</u>: Oh God, sometimes I am consumed by what I've lost. Today, help me to focus on what cannot be lost . . . my identity as your beloved child. Help me to find rest in knowing that you are my comforter so that my heart will rejoice again. Amen.

SUNDAY

<u>God's Truth</u>: *God has placed the parts in the body. . .just as he wanted them to be. If they were all one part, where would the body be? As it is, there are many parts, but one body . . . Now you are the body of Christ, and each one of you is a part of it. 1 Corinthians 12:18–20, 27*

<u>My Prayer</u>: Dear Lord, though the role I had in my loved one's life was good and important and fulfilling, this is not the end for me. I am still a part of the body of Christ and I have a part to play. Help me embrace this truth for the future, God, to feel called to a new and great purpose, and to find joy in this truth. Amen.

I Could Have Stopped This

As Referenced in Chapters 3 and 8

The lie that defeats: I could have stopped this.

The truth that heals: It happened and I can't change it.

One of the most oppressive lies I struggle with, as David's mom, is that I could have somehow prevented this from happening. The *"what ifs"* can be consuming; What if I'd gotten off the phone earlier? What if I'd have said or done something different? It's an easy lie to get sucked into when facing irreversible devastation, and its goal is paralyzing guilt. If we dwell on the belief that we could have done something to prevent it from happening, or that it was our fault to begin with, then torment and guilt soon follow, making it impossible to move forward.

The truth is that nobody wins the *"what if"* game. It's a masterful trap from the father of lies and it's totally unwinnable. So, what does God say about this? He says to dwell on "whatever is true, whatever is noble, whatever is right, whatever is pure, whatever is lovely, whatever is admirable . . . And the God of peace will be with you." (Philippians 4:8–9) Every time I commit my mind to his truth and ask God to search my heart, he takes away thoughts that don't belong there . . . Every. Time.

As you focus on the Truth of God's Word this week, I pray you will find relief knowing that you have no control over what happened last year, last week, or yesterday. No amount of wishing will change the outcome. But peace will flood your soul as you let go of guilt and embrace your current reality . . . even when it's a devastating one. God uses our ugliest pieces to build new and beautiful things. We just need to pry our fingers from the *"what ifs"* and turn them over to him.

MONDAY

God's Truth: *Your eyes saw my unformed body; all the days ordained for me were written in your book before one of them came to be. Psalm 139:16*
My Prayer: Dear Lord, I am consumed by thoughts of what I could have done differently, to change the events of my loss. But you are the only one who sees the past and the future with perfect eyes. Help my soul to find rest in knowing that your ways are perfect, even when mine are not. Amen.

TUESDAY

God's Truth: *You do not even know what will happen tomorrow. What is your life? You are a mist that appears for a little while and then vanishes. Instead, you ought to say, "If it is the Lord's will, we will live and do this or that." James 4:14–15*
My Prayer: Oh God, as I navigate dark and unknown roads, your GPS is the only one that matters. Past circumstances are difficult to understand and impossible to change. The future is even more uncertain, so I choose to demolish any thought about changing the past and to focus only on today. Amen.

WEDNESDAY

God's Truth: *"I have told you these things, so that in me you may have peace. In this world you will have trouble. But take heart! I have overcome the world." John 16:33*
My Prayer: Father in heaven, you are never surprised by the trouble I have in this life and your Word tells me that you have overcome the world. You are sovereign. No matter how small and defeated I feel, help me to remember that you have the power to squash every lie that causes me to suffer. Amen.

THURSDAY

God's Truth: *It is God who arms me with strength and keeps my way secure. He makes my feet like the feet of a deer; he causes me to stand on the heights. He trains my hands for battle . . . You make your saving help my shield; your help has made me great. 2 Samuel 22:33–36*
My Prayer: Dear God, I'm standing in a battlefield, feeling defeated and desperately wishing I could do something to change what happened . . . to stop

what happened. Please Lord, train my mind for this battle, be my shield, and lead me into the future with peace in my heart. Amen.

FRIDAY

God's Truth: *Though I walk in the midst of trouble, you preserve my life . . . with your right hand you save me. The Lord will vindicate me; your love, Lord, endures forever—do not abandon the works of your hands. Psalm 138:7–8*
My Prayer: Oh Lord, I continue to relive this tragedy in my mind, hoping for a different outcome. Hold me in your loving arms as I choose to trust you with every detail of my grief and help me to accept the truth that I cannot change yesterday. Thank you that I can survive tomorrow because you love me and you will never abandon me. Amen.

SATURDAY

God's Truth: *Finally, brothers and sisters, whatever is true, whatever is noble, whatever is right, whatever is pure, whatever is lovely, whatever is admirable—if anything is excellent or praiseworthy—think about such things. Philippians 4:8*
My Prayer: Dear Jesus, today I choose to think about things that are true and lovely and praiseworthy, even though I don't feel like it. Thank you for granting me the strength to look at life through an eternal lens and the power to reject lies about the past. Amen.

SUNDAY

God's Truth: *When the Advocate comes, whom I will send to you from the Father—the Spirit of truth who goes out from the Father—he will testify about me. John 15:26*
My Prayer: Oh God, flood my mind with your Spirit of truth, at this very moment, so that I may experience relief from wrestling with reality. You are faithful always–and I desperately want your unexplainable joy to bring contentment to my troubled mind. Amen.

I Will Never Sleep Well Again

As Referenced in Chapter 3

The lie that defeats: I will never sleep well again.

The truth that heals: I can sleep in peace.

From the day my son died, I dreaded nighttime. I just knew that I would never sleep again, at least not peacefully. How could I? It didn't seem possible. So, the more I believed that lie, the more I stewed about going to bed. It was awful. The truth I learned to cling to is that peace wasn't going to force itself on me; I had to search for it. I had to take hold of it, intentionally. Jesus is the Prince of Peace. He's *my* Prince of Peace. He was there the whole time, waiting for me to surrender my spinning thoughts.

As you claim God's truth this week, I pray that you will purposefully search for the peace that surpasses understanding. Cry out to God for it. Fill your mind with scripture to meditate on as you lay in bed, and believe that *your* Prince of Peace will calm your mind and body as you trust him. He is faithful.

MONDAY

God's Truth: *In peace I will lie down and sleep, for you alone, Lord, make me dwell in safety. Psalm 4:8*
My Prayer: Father, because I trust you, I can lie down and sleep. You promise to protect my mind, even when the demons of grief compete for my attention. Nothing can take away the joy I have in you because you are my place of safety. Amen.

TUESDAY

God's Truth: *I call out to the Lord, and he answers me from his holy mountain. I lie down and sleep; I wake again, because the Lord sustains me. Psalm 3:4–5*
My Prayer: Father, you promise to hear my cries and to answer them. So today, I call out to you and ask that you grant me peaceful sleep when my head hits the pillow and that you sustain my body and mind with much needed rest. Thank you for working on my behalf. Amen.

WEDNESDAY

God's Truth: *The mind governed by the flesh is death, but the mind governed by the Spirit is life and peace. Romans 8:6*
My Prayer: Jesus, when I feel helpless and inconsolable, unable to sleep, remind me that your Holy Spirit is waiting to calm my anxious heart. No amount of obsessing will change my current situation, so I choose to place the chaos in your hands so that my mind can experience peace and that my body will have the rest it needs to face another day. Amen.

THURSDAY

God's Truth: *Whether you turn to the right or to the left, your ears will hear a voice behind you, saying, "This is the way; walk in it." Isaiah 30:21*
My Prayer: Oh God, it's so hard to surrender control and to stop my mind from spinning. Fill me with confidence that you are the only one who knows how my broken pieces can be made whole. I choose to listen to your voice at night and to trust you to silence the lies that keep me awake. Help me to get the rest I need to survive this storm. Amen.

FRIDAY

God's Truth: *The Lord your God is God; he is the faithful God, keeping his covenant of love to a thousand generations of those who love him and keep his commandments. Deuteronomy 7:9*
My Prayer: Father, nothing in my life feels secure right now. Give me eyes to see that your love is always secure. You are God and you are faithful. As I close my eyes tonight, I choose to focus on your faithfulness to a thousand generations and put my hope and trust in you. Amen.

SATURDAY

God's Truth: *Come to me, all you who are weary and burdened, and I will give you rest . . . for I am gentle and humble in heart, and you will find rest for your souls. Matthew 11:28–29*

My Prayer: Lord, I come to you with a weary and burdened heart, seeking rest and trusting your power to give me rest. Today, I choose to quiet my restless mind and to seek the powerful assurance of peace that only you can give. Amen.

SUNDAY

God's Truth: *And the peace of God, which transcends all understanding, will guard your hearts and your minds in Christ Jesus. Philippians 4:7*

My Prayer: Oh God, thank you for the times I experience peace. Help me not to lose sight of your goodness . . . ever. Remind me, as I lay down at night, that you promise to guard my mind with peace beyond all understanding, even when my world is crumbling. Guard my heart and mind from thoughts that wear me out and fill me with your perfect peace. Amen.

Fear Controls Me

As Referenced in Chapter 3

The lie that defeats: Fear controls me.

The truth that heals: Fear has no power over me.

The lie that haunted me after our son died was that I was paralyzed by fear. It wrapped itself around every thought and choked out any glimmer of hope. I was weak and broken by grief and fear demanded control by telling me that I was powerless to survive. Life without my son terrified me and fear convinced me that I couldn't do it.

The truth I continue to learn is that fear is not the boss of me. That sounds like a toddler, I know. But it's true. Fear is not my master and it's not yours either. The mission of fear is to destroy us, but we have a mighty defender who fights for us when we cannot fight for ourselves and makes peace possible. "God has not given us a spirit of fear but, of power and love and of a sound mind." (2 Timothy 1:7) We *are* powerless, but God's power in us is unstoppable. As you claim the truth of God's Word this week, I pray you find victory over fear by the power of his Spirit living in you. Believe this. Rely on it. Let Jesus reign in your life and crush the damning power of fear.

MONDAY

God's Truth: *But the Advocate, the Holy Spirit, whom the Father will send in my name, will teach you all things and will remind you of everything I have said to you. Peace I leave with you; my peace I give you . . . Do not let your hearts be troubled and do not be afraid. John 14:26–27*

<u>My Prayer</u>: Jesus, you knew I would experience trouble and fear so you sent your Spirit of peace to reign in my heart. Remind me of this every time I'm afraid. The world offers quick-fixes that never last, but your Holy Spirit promises lasting peace. Calm my troubled heart today and help me to face the future without fear. Amen

TUESDAY

<u>God's Truth</u>: *Therefore, do not worry about tomorrow, for tomorrow will worry about itself. Each day has enough trouble of its own. Matthew 6:34*

<u>My Prayer</u>: Lord, as you already know. . .I worry. All. The. Time. And I need your help to stop. When I stress about yesterday or fear for tomorrow, help me to take a deep breath and to rest in the truth that you hold *everything* in your hands so that I don't have to. Amen.

WEDNESDAY

<u>God's Truth</u>: *A furious squall came up, and the waves broke over the boat, so that it was nearly swamped. Jesus was in the stern, sleeping on a cushion. The disciples woke him and said to him, "Teacher, don't you care if we drown?" He got up, rebuked the wind and said to the waves, "Quiet! Be still!" Then the wind died down and it was completely calm. Mark 4:37–39*

<u>My Prayer</u>: Oh Jesus, your disciples were overwhelmed with fear and so am I. It feels like my boat is sinking and I'm struggling to trust you. So, just as you spoke to the waves and the wind and they stopped raging and were calm, speak into my storm today. Calm my fears, Jesus. Amen.

THURSDAY

<u>God's Truth</u>: *Though the mountains be shaken and the hills be removed, yet my unfailing love for you will not be shaken nor my covenant of peace be removed. Isaiah 54:10*

<u>My Prayer</u>: Lord, I feel like my whole world is unraveling, but you promise to demolish fear and replace it with peace. I choose to cling to you today, believing that I will find rest for my soul. Though I am shaken, you never are. Thank you for this promise. Amen.

FRIDAY

<u>God's Truth</u>: *Have I not commanded you? Be strong and courageous. Do not be afraid; do not be discouraged, for the Lord your God will be with you wherever you go." Joshua 1:9*
<u>My Prayer</u>: Oh God, when I am overwhelmed by fear, I will choose to desperately seek you and to trust that you are with me wherever I go. Help me to remember that you give me the power I need to be strong and courageous whenever I ask you for it. I'm asking for it now. Amen.

SATURDAY

<u>God's Truth</u>: *. . . neither death nor life, neither angels nor demons, neither the present nor the future, nor any powers, neither height nor depth, nor anything else in all creation, will be able to separate us from the love of God that is in Christ Jesus our Lord. Romans 8:38–39*
<u>My Prayer</u>: Dear God, regardless of my current pain and regardless of what my future holds, thank you for the assurance that nothing will ever separate me from your great love. I will cling to this promise today, believing that there really is nothing to fear because you are with me, you love me, and you never leave me alone. Amen.

SUNDAY

<u>God's Truth</u>: *I pray that the eyes of your heart may be enlightened so that you may know the hope to which he has called you . . . and his incomparably great power for us who believe. That power is the same as the mighty strength he exerted when he raised Christ from the dead . . . Ephesians 1:18–20*
<u>My Prayer</u>: When I feel paralyzed by fear, your power is the only thing that brings hope. The same power that raised Jesus from the dead lives in me and I am so thankful for the promise that your mighty strength is bigger than anything I face today. Fight for me, God, even when I can't fight for myself. Amen.

My Loved One May Not be in Heaven

As Referenced in Chapters 4 and 7

The lie that defeats: My loved one may not be in heaven.

The truth that heals: God is merciful, not wishing any to perish.

My son professed his love for Jesus often, with words and in worship. Even so, the enemy confronted me with doubt . . . repeatedly. Haunting doubt. And the only words that brought comfort in those moments came from Romans 10:9, ". . . if you confess with your mouth that Jesus is Lord and believe in your heart that God raised him from the dead, you will be saved." I believe that David's last breath on earth was his first breath in heaven. When fear comes, my only hope is to claim the promise of scripture.

But what if you don't have this confidence for your loved one? Death is the fate of every human being and our eternal destination is a matter of faith. The criminal hanging next to Jesus used his dying breath to profess belief that Jesus is Lord. And Jesus instantly rewarded his faith, "Truly I say to you, today you shall be with Me in Paradise" (Luke 23:43). God is merciful, anxious to save anyone who places their faith in his Son. We cannot presume that any person is eternally lost. And fearing that they're lost won't change a thing because eternity is only determined between our hearts and God's. So, the truth that brings comfort when we are unsure of our loved one's eternal condition is that God is merciful, not wishing any to perish.

As you claim God's Truth this week, I pray that you find peace in his mercy, strength to let go of what you cannot change, and power to cling to the eternal life he offers. This life is full of struggle, pain, and loss, but (Praise Jesus!) it is temporary. On the contrary, life in Christ is forever and it is perfect, with no more death and no more tears (Revelation 21:4).

MONDAY

God's Truth: *For God so loved the world that he gave his one and only Son, that whoever believes in him shall not perish but have eternal life. John 3:16*
My Prayer: Dear Lord, as my heart breaks over human loss I cling to your truth about eternal gain. You sent your only son to save anyone who professes their faith in Jesus, so I can be confident that my last breath on earth will be my first breath in Heaven. Fill my heart with hope today, that I will see my loved one again because of your great mercy. Amen.

TUESDAY

God's Truth: *Do not grieve like the rest of mankind, who have no hope. For we believe that Jesus died and rose again, and so we believe that God will bring with Jesus those who have fallen asleep in him. 1 Thessalonians 4:13–14*
My Prayer: Oh God, thank you that I am able to grieve with hope. Help me to find rest from my fears about my loved one's eternal condition. You died and rose again to save us from the ugliness of sin in the world, and even when my eyes are filled with tears, I can find comfort knowing that your mercy is offered to all who put their trust in you. Amen.

WEDNESDAY

God's Truth: *He will wipe every tear from their eyes. There will be no more death or mourning or crying or pain, for the old order of things has passed away. Revelation 21:4*
My Prayer: Heavenly Father, your truth brings moments of sweet relief to my fearful heart. Right now, I need your love to shine brighter than my pain and to help me stop worrying about things I cannot change. Wipe away my tears and help me to find rest knowing that, someday, there will be no more darkness or sadness. Amen.

THURSDAY

God's Truth: *Do not let your hearts be troubled . . . My Father's house has many rooms; if that were not so, would I have told you that I am going there to prepare a place for you? And if I go and prepare a place for you, I will come back and take you to be with me . . . John 14:1–3*

My Prayer: Lord Jesus, every time I worry about the eternal destiny of my loved one, please remind me that I cannot change it. Help me to focus on your truth and to find hope in knowing that you prepare a place for everyone who puts their faith in you . . . at any hour. Amen.

FRIDAY

God's Truth: *Jesus said to her, "I am the resurrection and the life. The one who believes in me will live, even though they die; whoever lives by believing in me will never die.* John 11:25–26
My Prayer: Dear God, Martha's belief that her brother would rise again was a reflection of her faith. I have faith too, but sometimes doubt takes over. Today, I choose to set aside everything causing fear and focus on the truth that you are the Messiah, the Son of God, who came to save the world. Amen.

SATURDAY

God's Truth: *If you declare with your mouth, "Jesus is Lord," and believe in your heart that God raised him from the dead, you will be saved.* Romans 10:9
My Prayer: Jesus, I miss my loved one so much and ache for just one more smile . . . one more hug. By your grace, I cling to the hope that we will see each other again. And when I feel unsure, I will choose to cling to your promise. . .that you eagerly save anyone who trusts you as Lord, even if it is with their last breath. Amen.

SUNDAY

God's Truth: *Then he said, "Jesus, remember me when you come into your kingdom." Jesus answered him, "Truly I tell you, today you will be with me in paradise."* Luke 23:42–43
My Prayer: Oh Lord, I'm so grateful that you never require fancy words or perfect behavior. You forgave the thief on the cross because you knew his heart. You know mine, too, and you knew the heart of my loved one. Calm my fears right now with the promise of Paradise and the hope of eternity with you. Amen.

I Will Never Feel Content Again

As Referenced in Chapters 2, 4, and 12

The lie that defeats: I will never feel content again.

The truth that heals: Contentment is possible because of Jesus Christ.

When my son died, I thought I would die too . . . not physically, but emotionally. I believed the lie that I would never experience happiness or contentment again. David was gone and a piece of me died with him, but the hard truth is that he should never have been the source of my contentment in the first place. My family and friends are my greatest blessings, but only Jesus can fill my emptiness. Truth is, my life will never be the same. But it's also true that the beauty and sufficiency of Christ still lives in me.

As you focus on God's truth this week, I pray that you will overflow with joy. Yes, *joy*. The quest for contentment is never-ending. You want it. You search for it. And it seems that all the searching leads to, well, more searching. When we finally choose to enter the presence of God, lean into our relationship with Jesus, and be filled with the power of the Holy Spirit . . . that is when we finally experience contentment. This week, as you read God's Word and share your heart with him, you just might find the sort of authentic contentment that you never thought possible. I pray that you do.

MONDAY

God's Truth: *The Lord is my shepherd, I lack nothing. He makes me lie down in green pastures, he leads me beside quiet waters, he refreshes my soul. He guides*

me along the right paths for his name's sake. Even though I walk through the darkest valley, I will fear no evil, for you are with me . . . Psalm 23:1–4
My Prayer: Oh Lord, you are my Shepherd and you give me everything I need. Today, I choose to focus on what I have and not what I wish I had. Thank you for walking with me through my darkest valley, and for providing the kind of contentment that refreshes my soul. Amen.

TUESDAY

God's Truth: *But he said to me, "My grace is sufficient for you, for my power is made perfect in weakness." Therefore, I will boast all the more gladly about my weaknesses, so that Christ's power may rest on me . . . For when I am weak, then I am strong. 2 Corinthians 12:9–10*
My Prayer: Dear Jesus, I don't have much to boast about these days. Help me to embrace my weakness as an opportunity to experience your grace and power in a way I've never experienced before. Fill my empty heart with life-giving joy that only you can give. Amen.

WEDNESDAY

God's Truth: *Humble yourselves, therefore, under God's mighty hand, that he may lift you up in due time. Cast all your anxiety on him because he cares for you. 1 Peter 5:6–7*
My Prayer: Heavenly Father, when humble desperation defines my day, there's nowhere to go but up. Today, as my anxious heart struggles to find contentment, lift me up and protect me with your mighty hand. Thank you for your perfect care and for the promise of healing. Amen.

THURSDAY

God's Truth: *And my God will meet all your needs according to the riches of his glory in Christ Jesus. Philippians 4:19*
My Prayer: Jesus, I need you! A part of me is missing and I can't imagine where my life will go from here. I feel lost and wonder if I will ever feel truly happy again. Right now, I choose to trust you to meet my needs according to the riches of your glory and to give me exactly what I need . . . when I need it. Thank you so much for this sweet hope. Amen.

FRIDAY

<u>God's Truth</u>: *I know what it is to be in need, and I know what it is to have plenty. I have learned the secret of being content in any and every situation, whether well fed or hungry, whether living in plenty or in want. I can do all this through him who gives me strength. Philippians 4:12–13*

<u>My Prayer</u>: Dear Lord, it's easy to feel content when life is going well, but this struggle with loss makes it hard to imagine that anything will ever fill the empty places of my heart. You tell me that the secret to contentment is finding my wholeness in you. Help me to believe this. Amen.

SATURDAY

<u>God's Truth</u>: *Look at the birds of the air; they do not sow or reap or store away in barns, and yet your heavenly Father feeds them. Are you not much more valuable than they? Matthew 6:26*

<u>My Prayer</u>: Oh God, as I struggle to accept this new reality, remind me that my life still has value. I still have value because you love me. Though I desperately wish my life was different right now, I boldly claim your promise to care for me and to help me feel content. Amen.

SUNDAY

<u>God's Truth</u>: *Praise be to the God and Father of our Lord Jesus Christ! In his great mercy he has given us new birth into a living hope . . . and into an inheritance that can never perish, spoil or fade. . . though now for a little while you may have had to suffer grief in all kinds of trials. These have come so that the proven genuineness of your faith—of greater worth than gold . . . may result in praise. 1 Peter 1:3–7*

<u>My Prayer</u>: Oh Lord, contrary to what the world gives, you give an inheritance that will never perish, spoil or fade. When I struggle to feel content, remind me that genuine faith is worth more than gold . . . more than any loss. I choose to praise you today and to believe that you are with me, filling my empty soul with inexpressible joy. Amen.

My Faith is Too Weak

As Referenced in Chapters 6, 9, and 11

The lie that defeats: My faith is too weak.

The truth that heals: God renews my faith.

The lie that tries to steal the joy of my salvation and even question it, is that my faith is too weak. Experiencing such devastating loss made my faith fragile and I was afraid it would continue to weaken. Feelings of fear, doubt, and even anger made me think I might lose it altogether. Did I still believe about God what I thought I believed before my son died? It was a constant battle in those early days. But the truth I learned is that God doesn't require strong faith. He simply requires faith. I am a child of God and doubt doesn't change that.

As you claim the truth of God's Word this week, think about the words Jesus spoke about faith the size of a mustard seed. These tiny seeds grow into 20-foot trees. In the same way, as you bring your weak faith to the living soil of truth, God will grow it into something stronger and more beautiful than ever before. Really! I pray you will see that the remnants of your faith are not insignificant. They are seeds of hope, preparing to bloom.

MONDAY

God's Truth: *Now faith is confidence in what we hope for and assurance about what we do not see. Hebrews 11:1*
My Prayer: God, I can't see an end to this pain and I don't feel hopeful today. My heart is weak and grief has destroyed my confidence. Still, I believe your

Word is true and ask you to increase my faith. Please God, give me the assurance I need to trust you completely. Amen.

TUESDAY

<u>God's Truth</u>: *He replied, "Because you have so little faith. Truly I tell you, if you have faith as small as a mustard seed, you can say to this mountain, 'Move from here to there,' and it will move. Nothing will be impossible for you." Matthew 17:20*

<u>My Prayer</u>: Jesus, grow my faith again and remind me that nothing is impossible for you. When I doubt, help me to claim this beautiful promise from your Word with confidence . . . that even the tiniest seed of faith is more powerful than I can imagine. So today, I choose to replant my mustard seed and trust you to bring the water. Amen.

WEDNESDAY

<u>God's Truth</u>: *Though you have not seen him, you love him; and even though you do not see him now, you believe in him and are filled with an inexpressible and glorious joy, for you are receiving the end result of your faith, the salvation of your souls. 1 Peter 1:8–9*

<u>My Prayer</u>: Lord, give me faith that brings inexpressible and glorious joy. You've saved my soul, so I choose to believe that you will also save me from this pit of grief. Though I may not feel your deliverance today, I trust that you are working and that hope will come. Amen.

THURSDAY

<u>God's Truth</u>: *"Lord, if it's you," Peter replied, "tell me to come to you on the water . . ." Then Peter got down out of the boat, walked on the water and came toward Jesus. But when he saw the wind, he was afraid and, beginning to sink, cried out, "Lord, save me!" Immediately Jesus reached out his hand and caught him. "You of little faith," he said, "why did you doubt?" Matthew 14:28–32*

<u>My Prayer</u>: Father, when I take my eyes off of you, my faith becomes weak and I am consumed by waves. You are the Son of God and my place of safety in times of trouble. Today, I choose to keep my eyes on you and to focus on your power to sustain me as I walk through grief. Amen.

FRIDAY

God's Truth: *Even youths grow tired and weary, and young men stumble and fall; but those who hope in the Lord will renew their strength. They will soar on wings like eagles; they will run and not grow weary; they will walk and not be faint. Isaiah 40:30–31*

My Prayer: Oh Lord, I'm tired. Will I ever soar on wings like eagles? Will I ever walk without growing weary? It doesn't feel like it. But your Word is true so I choose to trust you with what little hope I have left. You are the creator of the universe and I trust you to carry me until I'm able to run. Thank you for your patience and your incredible love! Amen.

SATURDAY

God's Truth: *Therefore, since we have been justified through faith, we have peace with God through our Lord Jesus Christ . . . And we boast in the hope of the glory of God. Not only so, but we also glory in our sufferings, because we know that suffering produces perseverance; perseverance, character; and character, hope. And hope does not put us to shame, because God's love has been poured out into our hearts through the Holy Spirit, who has been given to us. Romans 5:1–5*

My Prayer: Jesus, you have justified me through the kind of faith that brings peace. Boy do I need peace today! In my head, my hope is in you and I know that you love me. But in my heart, I wrestle with the reality of my pain and struggle to see the purpose in it. Lord, help my unbelief and give me hope again, by the power of your Holy Spirit living in me. Amen.

SUNDAY

God's Truth: *For it is by grace you have been saved, through faith—and this is not from yourselves, it is the gift of God—not by works, so that no one can boast. Ephesians 2:8–9*

My Prayer: Oh God, you never require me to jump through hoops to prove my love for you; you don't ask me to save myself. Help me to remember that as I struggle to trust. All you want is my undivided heart. Today, you have it–fully and completely–and I claim the truth that I have been saved by grace, through faith, and it is a precious gift from you. Amen.

I Am Alone in this Darkness

As Referenced in Chapter 5

> The lie that defeats: I am alone in this darkness.
>
> The truth that heals: It's dark, but I'm never alone.

This lie that swamped my soul, especially in the early days after losing David, didn't seem like a lie at all. The darkness was tangible. It engulfed me and I was so afraid it would never leave, but experiencing such horrific loss showed me that God is the only light that brings peace and hope in such dark times. Turning on a lamp shows us where to walk and where not to walk. God's light does the same. Choosing to walk in the light of his Word continues to guide me to comfort and healing, and it has been a vital tool in my fight for survival.

As you claim the truth of God's Word this week, my prayer is that you will see a glimmer of light, shining through your darkness and that it will direct you on your path to healing. May you know without a doubt that darkness has no power in the presence of God. His Word provides a lamp for your feet and a light for your path. Read it. Believe it. Claim it. Walk in it.

MONDAY

God's Truth: *You, Lord, are my lamp; the Lord turns my darkness into light. With your help I can advance against a troop; with my God I can scale a wall.* 2 Samuel 22:29–30

My Prayer: Dear Lord, I need your strength to fill me with confidence as I trust you to turn this darkness into light. With your help, I will find the energy to overcome the hopelessness that entangles me. Thank you for guiding me today and giving me the strength to make it to tomorrow. Amen.

TUESDAY

<u>God's Truth</u>: *Send me your light and your faithful care, let them lead me; let them bring me to your holy mountain, to the place where you dwell. Then I will go to the altar of God, to God, my joy and my delight. Psalm 43:3–4*

<u>My Prayer</u>: Dear Jesus, you promise to send light and truth every time I search for you. You are never far from my reach because your Word guides me and comforts me as I fight off the darkness of my grief. Though darkness seems to surround me, I know that I will find your joy again. Thank you, Jesus, for that hope. Amen.

WEDNESDAY

<u>God's Truth</u>: *"I have told you these things, so that in me you may have peace. In this world you will have trouble. But take heart! I have overcome the world." John 16:33*

<u>My Prayer</u>: God, sometimes life is good, but today it's dark . . . so dark. Even as fear overwhelms me, Jesus, I trust you to overcome this darkness. Thank you that fear has no power over me because you are with me; I can experience everlasting peace because you are my God and you walk with me. Amen.

THURSDAY

<u>God's Truth</u>: *Even the darkness will not be dark to you; the night will shine like the day, for darkness is as light to you. Psalm 139:12*

<u>My Prayer</u>: Heavenly Father, you are the only one who promises to free me from this trap of darkness; even my darkest night shines like day to you. Today, I claim the power of your Word to crush the lie that I am alone. Help me to find peace in the hope of your light and to believe that you are always with me . . . always. Amen.

FRIDAY

God's Truth: *When you walk, your steps will not be hampered; when you run, you will not stumble. Hold on to instruction, do not let it go; guard it, for it is your life. Proverbs 4:12–13*
My Prayer: Dear Lord, I will hold tight to your wisdom and instruction for my life. My mind is weak and I feel so alone, yet I believe I will overcome the lies that threaten to hold me captive because your truth breaks through the darkness of the storm and leads me to safety. Amen.

SATURDAY

God's Truth: *But you are a chosen people . . . God's special possession, that you may declare the praises of him who called you out of darkness into his wonderful light. 1 Peter 2:9*
My Prayer: Oh God, today I choose to declare your praise, knowing that you have called me out of darkness and into your light. I am your precious child and, even when I feel so alone, I can be confident that you are here. Thank you, Jesus, I am never alone. You are truth, you are life, and you will show me a way through this darkness. Amen.

SUNDAY

God's Truth: *Whoever dwells in the shelter of the Most High will rest in the shadow of the Almighty. I will say of the Lord, "He is my refuge and my fortress, my God, in whom I trust." Psalm 91:1–2*
My Prayer: Lord, I need to feel your protection in this darkness. You are my safe place even when I don't feel safe. And you are my strength when I don't feel strong. Help me to dwell in your presence right now and to feel your love and protection surrounding me. Amen.

I Can Get through this on My Own

As Referenced in Chapters 5 and 11

The lie that defeats: I can get through this on my own.

The truth that heals: I need help getting through this.

I was overwhelmed when our son died and I knew we would need professional help to get through it. However, I was indifferent about reaching out to friends for help. While I knew they would do anything for me, I was scared to ask them because I didn't want anyone to see the ugly truth of my grief. It seemed safer to keep them at a comfortable distance. And maybe it was, but it definitely wasn't helpful. The lie that hindered my healing was that I didn't need my friends . . . or anyone, really. But I have found such healing in the truth that God created me to be in community with others, especially in brokenness. He designed all of us to need one another.

As you claim the truth of God's Word this week, I pray you'll realize that your brokenness requires mending and that doing nothing, results in nothing. The anguish will continue to deepen until ultimately, you'll notice the years have flown by and you're still in the same place you were when you lost your loved one. I pray you allow yourself to be vulnerable with others; find help by leaning on friends, professional counseling, and even grief groups. Most of all, I pray that you lean into the compassionate arms of Jesus. The sooner you reject the lie that you can get through this on your own, the sooner you will find healing.

MONDAY

God's Truth: *The work is too heavy for you [Moses]; you cannot handle it alone. Listen to me and I will give you some advice . . . select capable men from all the people—men who fear God, trustworthy men who hate dishonest gain—and appoint them as officials . . . That will make your load lighter, because they will share it with you. If you do this and God so commands, you will be able to stand the strain. . . Exodus 18:13–23*
My Prayer: Dear Lord, just as Moses needed others to help him complete his work, so do I. Continually show me that grieving is too heavy to handle alone and that I need to share the load. Lead me to trustworthy friends so that I will be able to stand the strain of loss. Amen.

TUESDAY

God's Truth: *A friend loves at all times; a brother is born for times of adversity. Proverbs 17:17*
My Prayer: Oh God, it's so hard to let people into my mess, but you purposefully put friends and family in my life to help in times of adversity. This is a time of adversity! Please God, give me the strength to be transparent and to trust the people who love me most. Amen.

WEDNESDAY

God's Truth: *Ask and it will be given to you; seek and you will find; knock and the door will be opened to you. Matthew 7:7*
My Prayer: Jesus, you promise if we ask it will be given to us; if I seek then I will find and if I knock the door will be opened. Give me the emotional strength to ask and seek and knock. It seems so much easier to keep the ugliness of my loss hidden from others and to suffer alone, but this is not your plan. Provide relief, God, when I step out of my comfort zone and seek it. Amen.

THURSDAY

God's Truth: *With us is the Lord our God to help us and to fight our battles. And the people gained confidence from what Hezekiah the king of Judah said. 2 Chronicles 32:8*

My Prayer: Oh God, just as Hezekiah said, you are the Lord and you will help me to fight. I cry out for help today and accept the truth that I am too weak to do this alone. Lead me to people who will grow my confidence in your strength and help me heal. Amen.

FRIDAY

God's Truth: *Humble yourselves before the Lord, and he will lift you up. James 4:10*
My Prayer: Precious Father, my fear of letting others help me is so real, yet you promise to raise me up as I humble myself before you. Today, I will lay down my insecurities and trust you to send help through the hands and feet of my friends and family. Amen.

SATURDAY

God's Truth: *So in Christ we, though many, form one body, and each member belongs to all the others. Romans 12:5*
My Prayer: Jesus, your perfect plan is for your children to work together as one body, bearing one another's burdens. Protect me from anyone whose intentions aren't genuine and lead me to those who seek to bring light into my darkness . . . even when it shines light on my mess. Amen.

SUNDAY

God's Truth: *Let us consider how we may spur one another on toward love and good deeds, Hebrews 10:24*
My Prayer: Father, if I've ever needed encouragement it's now, yet nothing in me feels like being around others. Help me to recognize my need to spend time with other believers, especially when it hurts, because it is through fellowship that you provide love, encouragement, and hope. Amen.

I'm Failing to Meet the Needs of My Family

As Referenced in Chapter 6

The lie that defeats: I'm failing to meet the needs of my family.

The truth that heals: God is the only one who can meet the deepest emotional and spiritual needs of my family.

I'm the mom. It's in my DNA to comfort others. It's my job and my joy, but losing David made me question my ability to sufficiently help Mike and Daniel (my husband and son) with their grief. How could I when I felt so weak and discouraged myself? I pressured myself a lot . . . to be all things for them, when I couldn't even take care of myself. And when I felt like I failed, it filled me with guilt. The liberating truth is that God is the only one who can meet the deepest emotional and spiritual needs of my family . . . not me. It's horribly hard to watch them hurt, but losing my son didn't make me responsible for healing the hurts of everyone in my family.

As you search for wisdom this week, I pray you find freedom in knowing that the weight of the world–and even the grief of your family–doesn't fall on you. It falls on God. He already holds the world in his hands, and he doesn't need help carrying the burden of it. Right? So, take a deep breath, relax your shoulders, and lay down your need to mend the grieving hearts of everyone in your family. Stop pretending to be strong enough for everyone else and allow God to bear the weight. He's strong enough.

MONDAY

God's Truth: *The Lord is close to the brokenhearted and saves those who are crushed in spirit. Psalm 34:18*
My Prayer: Jesus, the truth is that you are near to the brokenhearted members of my family. Their spirits are crushed, God, please help them to feel your healing presence at this very moment. I can love them, but I can't heal them. You can . . . and I ask you to do just that. Amen.

TUESDAY

God's Truth: *My flesh and my heart may fail, but God is the strength of my heart and my portion forever. Psalm 73:26*
My Prayer: My flesh fails every day, Lord. My heart is broken and I need you to be strong for my family. You are sufficient to meet their needs and I desperately ask you to take care of them. Give me the strength to let go and the wisdom to trust you for their healing. Amen.

WEDNESDAY

God's Truth: *David also said to Solomon his son, "Be strong and courageous. . .Do not be afraid or discouraged, for the Lord God, my God, is with you. He will not fail you or forsake you until all the work for the service of the temple of the Lord is finished. 1 Chronicles 28:20*
My Prayer: Heavenly Father, it hurts more than I can bear to see members of my family hurting and to know that I am helpless to fix their pain. Help me not to fear or feel discouraged. I trust your promise to be with them and never to forsake them. Only you can heal their hearts. Amen.

THURSDAY

God's Truth: *God is our refuge and strength, an ever-present help in trouble. Therefore we will not fear, though the earth give way and the mountains fall into the heart of the sea. Psalm 46:1-2*
My Prayer: Father, you are my refuge and strength . . . my caretaker as I grieve. Remind me that you are these things for my family also. You offer them security and strength that I can't ever provide. Though the loss of our loved one has shattered our world, help me to rest in you as our only hope. Amen.

FRIDAY

God's Truth: *Peace I leave with you; my peace I give you. I do not give to you as the world gives. Do not let your hearts be troubled and do not be afraid. John 14:27*

My Prayer: Oh God, as much as I want to, I'm completely unable to give my family what they need right now. I'm powerless to take away their pain and I worry about them so much. Please overwhelm my mind with peace and drive out my fears. You are my God and I trust you to take care of each of us. Amen.

SATURDAY

God's Truth: *For the Spirit God gave us does not make us timid, but gives us power, love and self-discipline. 2 Timothy 1:7*

My Prayer: Jesus, you have not given me a spirit of fear, but of power and a sound mind. Any fear I have about my inadequacies comes from the enemy and I need your help to crush that lie. I am not the author of peace and healing; you are. I trust my loved ones to you today. Amen.

SUNDAY

God's Truth: *When Jesus came down from the mountainside, large crowds followed him. A man with leprosy came and knelt before him and said, "Lord, if you are willing, you can make me clean." Jesus reached out his hand and touched the man. "I am willing," he said. "Be clean!" Immediately he was cleansed of his leprosy. Matthew 8:1–3*

My Prayer: Lord, if you can heal the blind and the paralyzed and those filled with evil spirits, then you can certainly heal the hearts of my loved ones more completely. As I love them, help me to trust that you are sufficient to meet their needs and willing to heal their hearts. Amen.

If I Worry Enough Something Will Change

As Referenced in Chapters 5 and 6

The lie that defeats: If I worry enough something will change.

The truth that heals: Worry never makes things better.

Worry wart. Ask anyone in my family; I'm the worst. My Dad used to ask me, "Does worrying change anything about your situation?" In recent years, my husband has asked the same thing. And even though I *feel* like I can't help it, God's Word says that I do have the power to overcome worry when I fix my eyes on Jesus. The lie that kept me from having a calm mind after my son died is that if I worried enough, something would change. These words sound ridiculous when I read them on this page. Even so, it is clearly a struggle for me. Truth is, God is never the author of worry and worry never makes anything better.

As you claim the truth of God's Word this week, I pray that you hold tight to the promise that nothing good comes from worrying. All it does is complicate grief and prevent healing. Whatever tomorrow holds, you can trust God's promise to be with you always, guarding your heart and your mind. (Philippians 4:6–7) As you confront worry with the truth of scripture this week, may you experience peace in every aspect of your life!

MONDAY

God's Truth: *When anxiety was great within me, your consolation brought me joy. Psalm 94:19*

My Prayer: Lord, anxiety controls my mind and sometimes I wonder if I can even make it through another day. Right now, I choose to focus on you instead of the things that cause me to worry. You are the maker of the sky and the stars. Your creation is beautiful and it has the power to fill my anxious heart with peace. Amen.

TUESDAY

God's Truth: *Do not be anxious about anything, but in every situation, by prayer and petition, with thanksgiving, present your requests to God. And the peace of God, which transcends all understanding, will guard your hearts and your minds in Christ Jesus. Philippians 4:6–7*
My Prayer: Dear Jesus, thank you for your promise to guard my heart and mind. I worry about so many things, but today I choose to bring these anxious thoughts to you and ask you to fill me with your perfect peace . . . peace that exceeds all human understanding. Amen.

WEDNESDAY

God's Truth: *His divine power has given us everything we need for a godly life through our knowledge of him who called us by his own glory and goodness. 2 Peter 1:3*
My Prayer: Dear God, you have planted good things in me and you give me the power to live victoriously, even in the midst of grief. Right now, the worries and ugliness of this world are choking out this truth and making it difficult to see that there really is hope. Quiet my mind, God, and help me to focus on all that is good. Amen.

THURSDAY

God's Truth: *Consider the ravens: They do not sow or reap . . . yet God feeds them. And how much more valuable you are than birds! Who of you by worrying can add a single hour to your life? Since you cannot do this very little thing, why do you worry about the rest? Luke 12:24–26*
My Prayer: Father, you remind me that I cannot make a single thing better by worrying. I can't bring back my loved one or see into the future, but you love me more than I can imagine. You see yesterday, today, and forever. . .and you know exactly what I need. Help me to seek you and to trust you with tomorrow. Amen.

FRIDAY

God's Truth: *Since then, you have been raised with Christ, set your hearts on things above, where Christ is seated at the right hand of God. Set your minds on things above, not on earthly things. Colossians 3:1–2*
My Prayer: Heavenly Father, the bad stuff in life seems so much louder than the good right now, and there are so many uncertain things that flood my mind with worry and fear. But you desire so much more for me so I choose to set my mind on you and your eternal goodness. You are in control . . . not me. Amen.

SATURDAY

God's Truth: *. . . turn your ear to my words. Do not let them out of your sight, keep them within your heart; for they are life to those who find them and health to one's whole body. Above all else, guard your heart, for everything you do flows from it. Proverbs 4:20–23*
My Prayer: Oh Lord, your Word is life to my mind and body. With a worried heart, I choose to meditate on your truth today and to claim its power to demolish every lie that threatens to defeat me. Help me to guard my heart and to listen only to your voice. Amen.

SUNDAY

God's Truth: *Cast all your anxiety on him because he cares for you. Be alert and of sober mind. Your enemy the devil prowls around like a roaring lion looking for someone to devour. 1 Peter 5:7–8*
My Prayer: Jesus, you care for me more than I can even fathom, so I give you every anxious thought that clouds my mind and brings suffering, and I trust you to crush it. By the power of your Spirit, protect me from the enemy's attempts to devour me so that I can find contentment and live free of fear. Amen.

What Others Think of My Grief Matters

As Referenced in Chapter 6

The lie that defeats: What others think of my grief matters.

The truth that heals: God is the one I need to please.

Every time I ventured out of the house after my son died, it felt like I was on display. *There's the mother of the boy who. . . Poor dear, did you hear about. . .? She's a Christian, right?* It seemed impossible to ignore. And it wasn't just a feeling I had in public; it was every time I posted on social media or our story appeared in the news. The lie that kept me captive was that I should care what others think of my grief. But this is my journey. It's between God and me. And freedom only came when I focused on pleasing him. His opinion is the only one that matters.

As you claim the truth of scripture this week, I pray you find the strength to break free of feeling like your survival-story needs the approval of others . . . regardless of how much they love you. Their view is obstructed because they don't see all that God sees. If they believe a certain thing will help you to heal, commit it to prayer and ask for God's direction. This is your unique journey with the Lord. Focus on *his* approval, dear friend. He sees every ugly, messy, beautiful detail of you–inside and out–and he loves you fiercely. That is all that matters.

MONDAY

<u>God's Truth</u>: *He said to them, "You are the ones who justify yourselves in the eyes of others, but God knows your hearts. What people value highly is detestable in God's sight. Luke 16:15*

<u>My Prayer</u>: Oh God, you know my heart and you love me. When I feel judged by others, help me to remember that I am not justified by their opinions but by your grace and mercy. Your approval is all that I seek today. Amen.

TUESDAY

<u>God's Truth</u>: *Therefore, I urge you, brothers and sisters, in view of God's mercy, to offer your bodies as a living sacrifice, holy and pleasing to God—this is your true and proper worship. Romans 12:1*

<u>My Prayer</u>: Thank you, Jesus, for your mercy and strength to live in a way that is acceptable and pleasing to you, even when I feel like a mess. Though my heart is burdened by what others may or may not think of me, I choose to worship you. And I choose to focus on what pleases you. I'm all yours. Amen.

WEDNESDAY

<u>God's Truth</u>: *We continually ask God to fill you with the knowledge of his will through all the wisdom and understanding that the Spirit gives, so that you may live a life worthy of the Lord and please him in every way: bearing fruit in every good work, growing in the knowledge of God, being strengthened with all power according to his glorious might . . . Colossians 1:9–11*

<u>My Prayer</u>: Dear Lord, fill me with the wisdom of your Spirit so that I know how to behave in a way that pleases you. Thank you for giving me the strength and power to endure the pain of loss without worrying about the opinions of others. I claim that truth today. Amen.

THURSDAY

<u>God's Truth</u>: *But the Lord said to Samuel, "Do not consider his appearance or his height, for I have rejected him. The Lord does not look at the things people look at. People look at the outward appearance, but the Lord looks at the heart." 1 Samuel 16:7*

My Prayer: Lord, I'm valuable because I'm your child and not because I look or act a certain way. Help me to listen only for *your* voice telling me when it's time to push myself and when it's time to retreat. And help me to care only about having a heart that pleases you. Amen.

FRIDAY

God's Truth: *You do not delight in sacrifice or I would bring it; you do not take pleasure in burnt offerings. My sacrifice, O God, is a broken spirit; a broken and contrite heart you, God, will not despise. Psalm 51:16–17*
My Prayer: Father, if you take pleasure in a broken heart that seeks comfort in you, then you must feel pleased today! I'm so tired of trying to please others, but I don't seem to be able to stop. Thank you for the reminder today that you delight in me–mess and all–simply because I choose to draw near and you. Help this to be my focus every day. Amen.

SATURDAY

God's Truth: *I know, my God, that you test the heart and are pleased with integrity. All these things I have given willingly and with honest intent. And now I have seen with joy how willingly your people who are here have given to you. 1 Chronicles 29:17*
My Prayer: Dear Jesus, when it feels like others are judging the way I'm walking through grief, help me to turn to you for wisdom. You are the one who tests my heart and I trust you to reveal any change I need to make. Help me to find security only in your approval. Amen.

SUNDAY

God's Truth: *On the contrary, we speak as those approved by God to be entrusted with the gospel. We are not trying to please people but God, who tests our hearts. 1 Thessalonians 2:4*
My Prayer: Heavenly Father, I'm already approved because of Jesus and every imperfection is covered by your grace. As I walk through grief, I know I say things that don't make sense to others . . . sometimes because I'm misguided and sometimes because they don't understand my pain. Either way, thank you that I'm covered by your grace and that you love me. Amen.

Grieving During the Christmas Season Dishonors God

As Referenced in Chapter 7

The lie that defeats: Grieving during the Christmas season dishonors God.

The truth that heals: God understands my grief, even at Christmas.

After our son died, sadness shadowed the joy of Christmas. I tried to celebrate like before but it was just too hard. Would it always be that way? I didn't know. I told God that I was thankful for Jesus but my heart had a really hard time feeling thankful. And that made me feel so guilty. The Bible tells me that Jesus doesn't condemn us for our weaknesses. In fact, he has empathy for us and wants us to come to his throne with confidence, so that he can help us in our time of need. (Hebrews 4:15–16) This beautiful truth crushes the lie that God is dishonored–or offended somehow–by our grief at Christmas. He knows me, he understands, and he wants to help.

As you claim the truth of scriptures this week, I pray that you are able to release any guilt about feeling sad this Christmas so that you can welcome joy into your aching heart. It's an oxymoron, I know, but I also know that you will begin to feel authentic, life-giving joy as you lean into God's grace and accept that you can celebrate the birth of Jesus while still grieving the loss of someone you love. One baby step at a time. One prayer at a time. One victory at a time.

MONDAY

God's Truth: *Blessed are the poor in spirit, for theirs is the kingdom of heaven. Blessed are those who mourn, for they will be comforted. Matthew 5:3–4*
My Prayer: Oh Lord, I feel so bad about being sad during the Christmas season, when I should be celebrating your Son. Still, you promise to comfort those who mourn and I'm so grateful for this assurance. Help my mind and heart to focus on the gift of Jesus today, because he is the only reason I have for hope. Amen.

TUESDAY

God's Truth: *Heal me, Lord, and I will be healed; save me and I will be saved, for you are the one I praise. Jeremiah 17:14*
My Prayer: Dear Jesus, I choose to praise you this Christmas even though my heart hurts, because it's a season that reminds me that you are the only one who heals. You are the one who saves. And you are the only one who can restore my joy. Thank you, Jesus. Amen.

WEDNESDAY

God's Truth: *For this is what the high and exalted One says—he who lives forever, whose name is holy: "I live in a high and holy place, but also with the one who is contrite and lowly in spirit, to revive the spirit of the lowly and to revive the heart of the contrite. Isaiah 57:15*
My Prayer: Oh God, you are holy and perfect. You're the king of the universe, yet you sent your Son who humbled himself by coming to earth to renew broken spirits and to mend sorrowful hearts. Thank you for understanding my sadness and for working to make me whole again. Amen.

THURSDAY

God's Truth: *Though the fig tree does not bud and there are no grapes on the vines, though the olive crop fails and the fields produce no food, though there are no sheep in the pen and no cattle in the stalls, yet I will rejoice in the Lord, I will be joyful in God my Savior. The Sovereign Lord is my strength . . . he enables me to tread on the heights. Habakkuk 3:17–19*
My Prayer: Heavenly Father, though my world feels bleak and I have little joy, I choose to rejoice in Jesus this Christmas. I will respond with a joyful

heart because you understand my weakness and you give me the strength to get through even the most difficult days. Amen.

FRIDAY

God's Truth: *But I will sing of your strength, in the morning I will sing of your love; for you are my fortress, my refuge in times of trouble. You are my strength, I sing praise to you; you, God, are my fortress, my God on whom I can rely. Psalm 59:16–17*

My Prayer: Dear Jesus, you are my strength and protection. I sing praise to you today for coming to earth as a baby, living a perfect life, dying to forgive the sin of a broken world, and rising again to prepare a place for me in heaven. Even though my heart is filled with grief, I choose to seek joy in remembering the great things you've done for me. Amen.

SATURDAY

God's Truth: *And there were shepherds living out in the fields nearby, keeping watch over their flocks at night. An angel of the Lord appeared to them, and the glory of the Lord shone around them, and they were terrified. But the angel said to them, "Do not be afraid. I bring you good news that will cause great joy for all the people. Today in the town of David a Savior has been born to you; he is the Messiah, the Lord. Luke 2:8–11*

My Prayer: I praise you today, Jesus, because your birth brought good news that caused great joy for all people–even me and even now. Just as the angels glorified you from heaven, give me the strength to glorify you on earth and to find peace, even as I walk through grief. Amen.

SUNDAY

God's Truth: *But when the kindness and love of God our Savior appeared, he saved us, not because of righteous things we had done, but because of his mercy. He saved us through the washing of rebirth and renewal by the Holy Spirit, whom he poured out on us generously through Jesus Christ our Savior, so that, having been justified by his grace, we might become heirs having the hope of eternal life. Titus 3:4–7*

My Prayer: Jesus, you didn't come to earth to save me because I'm strong or blameless or because I have life figured out. You save me because of your mercy and you make my heart new by the power of the Holy Spirit, who justifies me by grace. Though it seems impossible to feel joyful this Christmas, I choose to celebrate because you love me . . . mess and all. Amen.

If I Don't Say *Yes* to Everything, then I'm Failing to Heal

As Referenced in Chapters 5, 7, and 10

The lie that defeats: If I don't say yes to everything, then I'm failing to heal.

The truth that heals: It's okay and even healthy to say no sometimes.

The lie that shouts to my overwhelmed heart is that I have to say yes to everything, even if it doesn't feel right or safe. If I don't, it surely proves that I'm not healing. It's a lie that is hard enough to combat under normal circumstances, but when dealing with loss it's even more exhausting–like being set on opposite sides of the same teeter totter. I should do it . . . I can't do it . . . I should do it . . . I can't do it. Finally, guilt takes over and I say *yes* purely out of obligation. It's no way to live. And it's no way to heal.

As you claim the truth of God's Word this week, I pray that you find the wisdom to discern between the things you need to skip, for the sake of your healing, and the things you need to walk through, for the sake of your healing . . . without guilt. Pace yourself. Truth is, it's okay and even healthy to say *no* sometimes. It doesn't mean you're failing to heal. It just means you're prioritizing your mental and emotional health. This too shall pass my friend. Give it time.

MONDAY

God's Truth: *[Martha] had a sister called Mary, who sat at the Lord's feet listening to what he said. But Martha was distracted by all the preparations that had to be made. She came to him and asked, "Lord, don't you care that my sister has left me to do the work by myself? Tell her to help me!"*

"Martha, Martha," the Lord answered, "you are worried and upset about many things, but few things are needed . . . Mary has chosen what is better . . ." Luke 10:39–42

My Prayer: Lord, I need your wisdom to "choose what is better." Help me to listen for your voice when making decisions about what to commit to and what to decline. My healing is way more important than pleasing others. Grief is complicated enough; help me not to make it more complicated by focusing on things that don't matter. Amen.

TUESDAY

God's Truth: *Therefore, we do not lose heart. Though outwardly we are wasting away, yet inwardly we are being renewed day by day. 2 Corinthians 4:16*

My Prayer: Oh God, the pain of loss is overwhelming and there are days when it feels like I'm wasting away. Help me to know when renewal will come through the love and presence of others and when it will come through being alone in your presence. I trust you to show me. Amen.

WEDNESDAY

God's Truth: *Look carefully then how you walk, not as unwise but as wise, making the best use of the time, because the days are evil. Therefore, do not be foolish . . . Ephesians 5:15–17*

My Prayer: Father, I want to be wise about how I spend my time but it's complicated sometimes. Either I feel guilty for declining opportunities to be with others or I feel discouraged because I've spent too much time alone. Quiet the noise, God, so I can hear your voice guiding me to what's best and then give me the strength to listen. Amen.

THURSDAY

God's Truth: *The apostles gathered around Jesus and reported to him all they had done and taught. Then, because so many people were coming and going that they did not even have a chance to eat, he said to them, "Come with me by yourselves to a quiet place and get some rest." So they went away by themselves in a boat to a solitary place.* Mark 6:30–32

My Prayer: Jesus, even you recognized the need to withdraw sometimes. Thank you so much for this example. Please give me the strength to follow it without guilt. There are times when it's good to get out of the house but it's also important to be still. Amen.

FRIDAY

God's Truth: *Therefore, since we are surrounded by such a great cloud of witnesses, let us throw off everything that hinders and the sin that so easily entangles. And let us run with perseverance the race marked out for us, fixing our eyes on Jesus.* Hebrews 12:1–2

My Prayer: Lord, there are so many people in my life who love me and want to help me heal. I never want to disappoint them but I also know that grief is a journey that takes extraordinary perseverance. Give me the wisdom to know when I need cheerleaders and when I need to curl up in a chair. . .alone. Both are needed sometimes. But not every time. I choose to fix my eyes on you today, Jesus, and to listen for your guidance. Amen.

SATURDAY

God's Truth: *Commit your way to the Lord; trust in him, and he will act.* Psalm 37:5
Whatever you do, work heartily, as for the Lord and not for men. Colossians 3:2

My Prayer: Dear God, I commit my way to you right now and trust you to act on my behalf. You are the only one who knows exactly what my heart needs to heal . . . more than I know it myself. I choose to follow you with my whole heart, so that I can say *yes* or *no* with confidence. Amen.

SUNDAY

God's Truth: *For everything there is a season, and a time for every matter under heaven: a time to be born, and a time to die . . . a time to break down, and a time to build up; a time to weep, and a time to laugh; a time to mourn, and a time to dance . . . a time to embrace, and a time to refrain from embracing . . .* Ecclesiastes 3:1–5

<u>My Prayer</u>: Precious Father, thank you for the freedom found in knowing that there is a time for everything. There is a time for me to withdraw from others and a time to push myself to engage with the world, even when I don't feel like it. Guide me, Jesus, to make healthy choices with my time as I walk through grief. Amen.

Death will Always Define My Life

As Referenced in Chapter 8

> The lie that defeats: Death will always define my life.
>
> The truth that heals: I am defined by the life of Jesus in me.

The lie that threatened to defeat me after David died, is that his death would not only control my life but define me . . . indefinitely. Losing my son has dramatically redefined my life, that's true and unavoidable, but so has the death and resurrection of Jesus. What a powerful truth! Because my hope is in a Savior who defeated death, I am defined by his life in me. The same power that raised Jesus from the dead, lives in me.

As you claim the truth of God's Word this week, I pray you find the strength in believing that Jesus has power over death and his free gift of eternal life is for anyone who places their trust in him. Your loved one is gone. You can't change that. It's awful and painful and it's part of your story forever. But Jesus is alive in heaven and he lives in the hearts of his children. Hope is found in life, not death, and the one who defines you is the same one whose death gives life. This week, choose life. If you are unsure what it means to have Jesus living in your heart, please visit Appendix A on page 251 to learn more about God's free gift of eternal life.

MONDAY

God's Truth: *I am the resurrection and the life. He who believes in me will live, even though he dies; and whoever lives and believes in me will never die.* John 11:25–26

My Prayer: Oh Jesus, it feels like the rest of my life will be defined by loss but your Word says that I am defined by your life in me. My hope is in life, not death. Help me to focus on this truth and to reject the lie that death consumes me. Amen.

TUESDAY

God's Truth: *Brothers, we do not want you to be ignorant about those who fall asleep, or to grieve like the rest of men. For since we believe that Jesus died and rose again, even so, through Jesus, God will bring with him those who have fallen asleep. 1 Thessalonians 4:13–14*
My Prayer: Lord, you don't leave us in the dark about matters of life and death. You make it very clear that those who proclaim Christ as Savior can live in the truth of your word and the light of your resurrection. . .to be defined by life and not death. I am so thankful for this bold assurance and choose to rest in it today. Amen.

WEDNESDAY

God's Truth: *If the Spirit of him who raised Jesus from the dead is living in you, he who raised Christ from the dead will also give life to your mortal bodies because of his Spirit who lives in you. Romans 8:11*
My Prayer: Oh God, from the moment I placed my trust in you, your Spirit took up residence in my heart and filled me with the same power that raised Jesus from the dead. My days are consumed with thoughts of death, as I fight my way through the pain of loss, but I have hope in your power to overcome the darkness and to breathe the promise of life into my mess. Amen.

THURSDAY

God's Truth: *For just as the Father raises the dead and gives them life, even so the Son also gives life to whom he wishes. John 5:21*
My Prayer: Thank you, Jesus, for loving me and defining me with everlasting life. I choose to find hope in the truth that you have overcome death. It has no power over you and so it has no power over your children. My pain is temporary but life in you is eternal. Amen.

FRIDAY

<u>God's Truth</u>: *Then Jesus spoke to them again, saying, "I am the Light of the world; he who follows me will not walk in the darkness, but will have the Light of life." John 8:12*

<u>My Prayer</u>: Heavenly Father, I choose to focus on the truth that you are the Light of life in my darkness. This truth crushes the lie that death defines me and reminds me that I am defined by life and hope, because you walk with me every day and you will never leave me. Amen.

SATURDAY

<u>God's Truth</u>: *The thief comes only to steal and kill and destroy; I came that they may have life, and have it abundantly. (John 10:10) For the law of the Spirit of life in Christ Jesus has set you free from the law of sin and of death. (Romans 8:2)*

<u>My Prayer</u>: Lord, I know the enemy's plan is for me to stay defeated in the darkness of his lies. But your plan is all that matters. Your voice is the only one I should listen to! Thank you for the promise that I have the power within me to experience abundant life, even as I grieve the loss of my loved one. Amen.

SUNDAY

<u>God's Truth</u>: *I have been crucified with Christ; and it is no longer I who live, but Christ lives in me; and the life which I now live in the flesh I live by faith in the Lord. Galatians 2:20*

<u>My Prayer</u>: Lord Jesus, I truly have been crucified with you. My sins were forgiven when you died, and my hope was restored when you rose again. You died so that I might live, and this changes everything. Every time I feel sad or discouraged, remind me of the tremendous comfort found in you. And help me to walk in faith with a grateful heart. Amen.

Grief Has Power Over Me

As Referenced in Chapter 8

The lie that defeats: Grief has power over me.

The truth that heals: Jesus gives me the power to overcome.

Grief has the power to keep you stuck in quicksand, unable to move. It shouts lies to your soul that threaten to destroy you. Can you hear them? *You will always feel like this. You will be sad for the rest of your life. Grief will always control you.* But praise Jesus! He has the power to crush every lie. He has power to defeat the enemy. And his power lives in you.

As you claim the truth of God's Word this week, I pray that you see his hand reaching for you and that you take hold of it. He is able to pull you out of the quicksand, to set your feet on solid ground, and to rescue you from the power of grief. Draw near to him in prayer and trust him for the power to overcome every single thing that threatens to defeat you.

MONDAY

<u>God's Truth</u>: *If the Spirit of him who raised Jesus from the dead is living in you, he who raised Christ from the dead will also give life to your mortal bodies because of his Spirit who lives in you. Romans 8:11*
<u>My Prayer</u>: Oh God, my mortal body is tired. When it's difficult to put one foot in front of the other, remind me that your Spirit lives in me and gives me the power to overcome the bondage of grief. Thank you for helping me to walk through difficult days with hope and grace. Amen.

TUESDAY

God's Truth: *The Lord is my light and my salvation— whom shall I fear? The Lord is the stronghold of my life—of whom shall I be afraid? Psalm 27:1*
My Prayer: Oh Lord, why do I forget that you're on my side? You fight for me and I never need to fear defeat. You are with me and you are for me! Thank you so much for shining light into my darkness and giving me the strength to soldier on. Amen.

WEDNESDAY

God's Truth: *I lift up my eyes to the hills. From where does my help come? My help comes from the Lord, who made heaven and earth. Psalm 121:1–2*
My Prayer: Jesus, my help comes only from you! Right now, I am in the crippling grip of grief but I know that you are near and able to overcome this pain. Help me to feel your presence today, God, and to experience the hope that tomorrow will be better. Amen.

THURSDAY

God's Truth: *He gives power to the weak and strength to the powerless. Isaiah 40:29*
My Prayer: Lord, I feel weak and powerless a lot these days, and I'm so thankful that even at my weakest, you become my strength. Thank you that I have the power to overcome . . . because of you. Today, I choose to focus on the comfort of this truth. Amen.

FRIDAY

God's Truth: *Be strong and bold; have no fear or dread of them, because it is the Lord your God who goes before you. He will be with you; he will not fail you or forsake you. Do not fear or be dismayed. Deuteronomy 31:6,8*
My Prayer: Thank you, God, that you are not surprised by anything that happens in my life. You know every detail of my grief and every thought that causes me to fear. Even so, I choose not to be dismayed today because I believe that you go before me, you walk with me, and you give me everything I need to overcome. Amen.

SATURDAY

<u>God's Truth</u>: *O Lord God of our fathers . . . You rule over all the kingdoms of the nations. In your hand are power and might, so that none is able to withstand you. 2 Chronicles 20:6*

<u>My Prayer</u>: Heavenly Father, I have no control. And though I never have, it's never been more evident than it is right now. Still, grief has no power over me because you are far more powerful and mighty and you rule the world. My heart praises you today and I trust you with every aspect of my life. You've got this. And you've got me. Amen.

SUNDAY

<u>God's Truth</u>: *God stretches the northern sky over empty space and hangs the earth on nothing . . . His Spirit made the heavens beautiful, and his power pierced the gliding serpent. These are just the beginning of all that he does, merely a whisper of his power. Who, then, can comprehend the thunder of his power? Job 26:7, 13–14*

<u>My Prayer</u>: Oh God, I find strength in the beauty of your universe, in the truth that you created the heavens and earth with a whisper, and that your power fights for me. . .for my survival. I can't comprehend such power but I'm so thankful for it. Please help me to rest knowing that victory will come in your timing, not mine. Amen.

Our Marriage Is Never Going to Make It

As Referenced in Chapter 9

The lie that defeats: Our marriage is never going to make it.

The truth that heals: God honors commitment.

Statistically, marriages impacted by the loss of a child face an uphill battle, but I didn't need to know the data to believe my marriage was at risk. We were devastated and I was taunted by the thought that it was just a matter of time before grief destroyed us for good. The tragic truth is that the enemy still wants grief to destroy our marriage and he will do anything to stop us from trusting God for restoration. We're in a battle and our marriage is worth fighting for. So is yours.

As you claim the truth of God's Word this week, I pray that you will intentionally take a stand against every lie that drives a wedge between you and your spouse. Stand firmly together and ask God for the strength and desire to recommit yourselves. He created marriage as a tool for survival, not destruction, and he will honor your commitment by giving you the will to survive even during the worst days. Nothing about it is easy, so make a decision this week to claim God's truth for your marriage and to walk through grief as one flesh . . . with patience, honesty, and grace. All day. Every day.

MONDAY

<u>God's Truth</u>: *God is our refuge and strength, an ever-present help in trouble.* *Psalm 46:1*

My Prayer: Dear Jesus, I am so afraid of the damage that grief is doing to our marriage. We are both grieving and we need to feel your protection and your strength so that we can press on together. Help both of us to turn to you during this dark time and to be gracious with one another every day. Amen.

TUESDAY

God's Truth: *No temptation has overtaken you except what is common to mankind. And God is faithful; he will not let you be tempted beyond what you can bear. But when you are tempted, he will also provide a way out so that you can endure it. 1 Corinthians 10:13*
My Prayer: Oh God, it's so tempting to be angry and impatient and selfish right now. Without your help, my spouse and I are not equipped to handle this path of grief. So, because you are faithful, give us the strength to pray for each other and to lean on the truth that you will provide a way for us to endure . . . together. Amen.

WEDNESDAY

God's Truth: *Keep me safe Lord from the hands of the wicked, protect me from the violent, who devise ways to trip my feet. Psalm 140:4*
My Prayer: Lord, our marriage is under attack and we need your protection from the lies that threaten to defeat us. Truth is, you help us to dwell in safety as we draw near to you and honor our commitment to each other. The enemy wants us to feel irritated and hurt and afraid, but none of this is from you. Today, help us to focus only on what is good and true. Amen.

THURSDAY

God's Truth: *Have mercy on me, my God, have mercy on me, for in you I take refuge. I will take refuge in the shadow of your wings until the disaster has passed. Psalm 57:1*
My Prayer: Father, as our marriage is pelted with the reality of pain and loss, I pray for your mercy. Thank you for being a place of safety; help us to be a place of safety for each other also. Encourage our hearts to believe that you are protecting us, even when we can't see it. Amen.

FRIDAY

<u>God's Truth</u>: *I know whom I have believed, and am convinced that he is able to guard what I have entrusted to him until that day. 2 Timothy 1:12*
<u>My Prayer</u>: Dear Lord, I don't know what grief will do to our marriage and it frightens me, but I choose to entrust it to you today. Fight for us and guard our love for each other. Give me the strength and patience to support my spouse, and to have a forgiving heart when I don't feel supported. Draw our hearts together as we draw near to you. Amen.

SATURDAY

<u>God's Truth</u>: *Let us not become weary in doing good, for at the proper time we will reap a harvest if we do not give up. Galatians 6:9*
<u>My Prayer</u>: Jesus, I am weary and it takes so much energy to grieve with my spouse because we are on different emotional pages nearly every day. . .each of us coping in different ways. Please don't let this divide us. Please help us to be a blessing to each other even though our hearts hurt. I choose to trust that we will reap a harvest if we don't give up. Amen.

SUNDAY

<u>God's Truth</u>: *Not that I have already obtained all this, or have already arrived at my goal, but I press on to take hold of that for which Christ Jesus took hold of me . . . one thing I do: Forgetting what is behind and straining toward what is ahead, I press on toward the goal to win the prize for which God has called me heavenward in Christ Jesus. Philippians 3:12–14*
<u>My Prayer</u>: Father, as my spouse and I struggle through the pains of grief we need your help to press on as one flesh. I believe that you will heal our hearts, individually and together, if we stay committed to loving each other and remain focused on the prize of a healthy and fulfilling relationship. Soften our hearts toward one another and strengthen our desire to survive. Amen

We Shouldn't Desire Sex When We're Grieving

As Referenced in Chapter 9

The lie that defeats: We shouldn't desire sex when we're grieving.

The truth that heals: Intimacy brings us together as one flesh.

The Bible says, "a man shall leave his father and mother and hold fast to his wife. And they shall become one flesh." (Genesis 2:24) The lie that threatened to defeat my marriage in the midst of grief is that our relationship should be put on hold; we shouldn't desire the whole "one flesh" thing. *I mean seriously, don't we have enough to deal with right now!* But God designed marital intimacy with healing power. He is pleased when we honor our commitment to love each other completely–for better or worse–to love and to cherish, even in the most tragic times.

As you claim the truth of God's Word this week, I pray that you will remember the incredible gift of covenant marriage. Emotional and physical intimacy in marriage isn't just "one more thing" to think about, it's God's beautiful, healing gift to you and it has the power to strengthen you both for your battle with grief and to deepen your love for one another. This week, crush the enemy's attempts to harm your relationship and trust God's perfect design. If there are issues in your marriage causing you to feel unsafe, I pray you will ask God to lead you to a professional Christian counselor who can provide additional guidance.

MONDAY

God's Truth: *The husband should fulfill his marital duty to his wife, and likewise the wife to her husband. The wife does not have authority over her own body but yields it to her husband. In the same way, the husband does not have authority over his own body but yields it to his wife. 1 Corinthians 7:3–4*

My Prayer: Dear God, grief has invaded every aspect of our marriage and redefined our relationship. We both struggle with selfishness, pride, and anger, and we need your help to offer ourselves unselfishly to each other—to love each other completely, both emotionally and physically. I trust you to help us heal as we honor our commitment. Amen.

TUESDAY

God's Truth: *Did he not make them one, with a portion of the Spirit in their union? So guard yourselves in your spirit, and let none of you be faithless to the wife of your youth. Malachi 2:15*

My Prayer: Lord, this is such a fragile time in our marriage. We are fighting the temptation to pull away from each other. So, as we fight to remain emotionally connected to one another, we need your Spirit to fight for us. Give us the desire to guard our marriage and to be available to one another in body, mind, and spirit. Amen.

WEDNESDAY

God's Truth: *Likewise, husbands, live with your wives in an understanding way, showing honor to the woman as the weaker vessel, since they are heirs with you of the grace of life, so that your prayers may not be hindered. 1 Peter 3:7–12*

My Prayer: Lord, your perfect design for marriage is for us to tackle life as a united team, as co–heirs of grace, and to be understanding with one another. This can be hard on ordinary days, but in the middle of the pain of loss, it seems almost impossible. Please, Lord, help us to see one another as teammates who are working for a common victory, and not as adversaries. . .so that our prayers will not be hindered. We can't do this without you. Amen.

THURSDAY

God's Truth: *Two are better than one, because they have a good return for their labor: If either of them falls down, one can help the other up. But pity anyone who falls and has no one to help them up. Also, if two lie down together, they will keep warm. But how can one keep warm alone? Though one may be overpowered, two can defend themselves. A cord of three strands is not quickly broken. Ecclesiastes 4:9–12*

My Prayer: Heavenly Father, you desire for our marriage to be a safe place . . . a place of mutual support. Grief is working to defeat us and we need your help to see this as an opportunity to help each other up, instead of tearing each other down. Together with you, we can survive this. Thank you for giving me hope. Amen.

FRIDAY

God's Truth: *With all humility and gentleness, with patience, bearing with one another in love, eager to maintain the unity of the Spirit in the bond of peace. Ephesians 4:2–3*

My Prayer: Oh Jesus, *bearing with one another* isn't possible without humility and I know I need to love my spouse with patience and grace. I need the same from my spouse, too. Soften our hearts today and give each of us a strong desire to maintain the unity of your Spirit . . . unity that brings peace and healing. Thank you for never leaving us alone. Amen.

SATURDAY

God's Truth: *Place me like a seal over your heart, like a seal on your arm. For love is as strong as death, its jealousy as enduring as the grave. Love flashes like fire, the brightest kind of flame. Many waters cannot quench love, nor can rivers drown it. If a man tried to buy love with all his wealth, his offer would be utterly scorned. Song of Solomon 8:6–7*

My Prayer: Lord, love is a gift from you and my spouse is a gift from you. Please help me to remember this, especially when it doesn't feel like it and help my spouse to recognize me as a gift as well. Your love is an indestructible force, and we need that force to work for us. Give us the desire to cling to one another and help our marriage to be a reflection of your unquenchable love as we continue to endure the pain of loss. Amen.

SUNDAY

God's Truth: *May the God who gives endurance and encouragement give you the same attitude of mind toward each other that Christ Jesus had, so that with one mind and one voice you may glorify the God and Father of our Lord Jesus Christ. Romans 15:5–6*

My Prayer: Jesus, you are the God of endurance and encouragement. We desperately need both today. Help our marriage to be one of harmony and desire, so we can glorify you and honor one another as we walk through the pain of grief. Show me any unmet need my spouse has and then give me the strength and wisdom to meet that need. And Jesus, I boldly trust you to give my spouse the same desire in return. Amen.

I Can't Celebrate Something that My Loved One Won't Get to Experience

As Referenced in Chapter 10

The lie that defeats: I can't celebrate something that my loved one won't get to experience.

The truth that heals: I can do all things through Christ.

Every college graduation announcement, wedding invitation, and baby shower is a reminder of what we won't ever get to celebrate with David. I want to be excited for others, truly, but it is such a battle to feel genuine joy for them. The lie that whispers (and sometimes shouts) to my soul is that I can't do it. I can't celebrate something that David will never get to experience. I just can't! But with the support of people who love me and the power of God's Spirit fighting for me, I've learned that I absolutely can. Even when it's gut wrenching, I can do it. And I need to do it.

As you claim the truth of God's Word this week, I pray that you find encouragement in God's promise to give you the emotional strength to do difficult things—things that you don't want to do—and that overcoming the fear of *repeat mourning* will give you a sense of comfort and even victory. Life doesn't wait for us to heal . . . it marches on with or without us. I pray that you will choose to move on with it, knowing that you can do anything through Christ who gives you strength.

MONDAY

God's Truth: *I can do all things through Christ who strengthens me. Philippians 4:13*
My Prayer: Oh God, it's so hard to keep it together when I see "whole" families going about their lives, enjoying time together, and celebrating milestones. Since I have absolutely no idea how to overcome this, I desperately depend on your promise that I can do all things with your strength living in me. Strengthen me today, God, and every day. Amen.

TUESDAY

God's Truth: *So do not fear, for I am with you; do not be dismayed, for I am your God. I will strengthen you and help you; I will uphold you with my righteous right hand. Isaiah 41:10*
My Prayer: Lord, why did this have to happen? Why is my loved one gone. . .never to celebrate the same milestones that others get to experience? I can wear myself out asking these questions but it will never help me heal. I know you tell me not to be dismayed, but I don't know how else to feel when confronted by the things my loved one is missing. Even so, I trust you to help me experience true joy for others as I lean on your strength to get me through. Amen.

WEDNESDAY

God's Truth: *Let us therefore approach the throne of grace with boldness, so that we may receive mercy and find grace to help in our time of need. Hebrews 4:16*
My Prayer: Jesus, thank you for the assurance of your grace and mercy in my time of need. Life feels so cruel when others are celebrating and I'm still filled with grief. Today, I boldly ask you to guard my heart against bitterness as life marches on around me and help me to feel genuine happiness for friends and family, even when their life–events reveal the pain in my heart. Amen.

THURSDAY

God's Truth: *And the God of all grace, who called you to his eternal glory in Christ, after you have suffered a little while, will himself restore you and make you strong, firm and steadfast. 1 Peter 5:10*

My Prayer: Father, my heart suffers and it's difficult to see a light at the end of the tunnel. When my eyes focus on the things that I don't get to experience with my loved one, help me to find rest in your promise to restore my soul and to find hope in your promise of eternal glory. Amen.

FRIDAY

God's Truth: *It is the Lord who goes before you. He will be with you; he will not fail you or forsake you. Do not fear or be dismayed. Deuteronomy 31:8*
My Prayer: Jesus, you know my grief and you know my future. Go before me and prepare my heart for the celebrations of friends and family that remind me of what I've lost. Thank you for never leaving me alone in my pain and for walking with me through every difficult situation. I choose to find peace knowing that you're by my side. Amen.

SATURDAY

God's Truth: *Do not fear, for I have redeemed you; I have called you by name, you are mine. When you pass through the waters, I will be with you; and through the rivers, they shall not overwhelm you; when you walk through fire you shall not be burned, and the flame shall not consume you. For I am the Lord your God, the Holy One of Israel, your Savior. Isaiah 43:1–3*
My Prayer: Oh God, some invitations and social media posts do make me feel as if I'm being flooded by rushing waters but your Word promises, when I call on your name, you will stand with me and keep me from being overwhelmed. You are the Lord my God, my Savior, and I'm calling on your name today to rescue my heart. Amen.

SUNDAY

God's Truth: *But the Lord is faithful, and he will strengthen and protect you from the evil one. 2 Thessalonians 3:3*
My Prayer: Dear Lord, the happy times my friends and family experience are good; strengthen me so that I can feel authentically happy for them. Protect me from the enemy's attempts to use the good times of other families as a weapon against me. I choose to rest in your faithfulness today. Amen.

I Don't Need to Socialize with Others

As Referenced in Chapter 10

The lie that defeats: I don't need to socialize with others.

The truth that heals: I need to experience community.

This is a lie that was especially hard for me to argue against. I simply didn't have the desire, need, or the patience to socialize with others. *Why allow myself into the seemingly normal lives of others when mine is such a mess?* But just as there was a time for me to withdraw and be still, there is also a time for me to engage with people who care about me . . . and who also miss my son. It often reopened wounds but it also nudged me out of my grief bubble and provided unique opportunities for healing. In his mercy, God designed us for each other. He designed us to engage in fellowship . . . especially when we're broken.

As you claim the truth of God's Word this week, I pray that you will recognize your need for community and that isolating yourself isn't healthy or helpful. You've heard it takes a village, right? Engaging with people who care about you, no matter where you're at in your grief, is a healthy way to renew your outlook on life and to strengthen you to embrace the future. Don't turn away from the love and encouragement that awaits you. Run toward it.

MONDAY

God's Truth: *I long to see you so that I may impart to you some spiritual gift to make you strong. . .that you and I may be mutually encouraged by each other's faith. Romans 1:11–12*

My Prayer: Dear God, I really don't want to have casual conversations about the "normal" families of others. I just don't. Still, my friends love me and you have given them to me as a gift so that we can experience mutual encouragement. Please give me the strength to engage with others, especially when I don't feel like it, and protect me from things that may be hurtful or discouraging. Amen.

TUESDAY

God's Truth: *Anxiety weighs down the heart, but a kind word cheers it up. Proverbs 12:25*

My Prayer: Jesus, the weight of grief is like a millstone around my heart and anxious thoughts are a constant companion. Give me the strength and desire to accept the kindness of others so that my heart can be cheered and my load lifted. Amen.

WEDNESDAY

God's Truth: *And let us consider how to stir up one another to love and good works, not neglecting to meet together, as is the habit of some, but encouraging one another, and all the more as you see the Day drawing near. Hebrews 10:24–25*

My Prayer: Lord, it's so easy to neglect spending time with friends because it takes emotional and mental energy that I don't have. The enemy wants me to stay isolated, but I choose to believe your truth that meeting together brings feelings of love and encouragement . . . and can even increase my energy. Show me how I can embrace this today. Amen.

THURSDAY

God's Truth: *For just as each of us has one body with many members, and these members do not all have the same function, so in Christ we, though many, form one body, and each member belongs to all the others. Romans 12:4–5*

My Prayer: Dear Jesus, your Word tells me that withdrawing from Christian friends and family prevents us all of us from carrying out our purpose to serve and encourage each other. Crush the lie that tells me to withdraw and give me the strength and wisdom to engage with others. Amen.

FRIDAY

God's Truth: *Pray that I may be kept safe . . . and that the contribution I take to Jerusalem may be favorably received by the Lord's people there, so that I may come to you with joy, by God's will, and in your company be refreshed.* Romans 15:32–32

My Prayer: Father, my heart definitely needs to be refreshed! So, why do I resist spending time in the company of friends and family? It feels easier to isolate myself and heal in private, but your truth says the opposite. Give me the wisdom and motivation to seek time with people who love me. Amen.

SATURDAY

God's Truth: *He died for us so that, whether we are awake or asleep, we may live together with him. Therefore encourage one another and build up one another, just as you also are doing.* 1 Thessalonians 5:10–11

My Prayer: Oh God, death doesn't separate you from your children, so it shouldn't separate us from each other either. Sometimes I feel like I should get a "pass" because of my loss, but I choose to focus on the truth today, that my loss makes it even more important to seek encouragement from others. Give me the strength to act on this truth. Amen.

SUNDAY

God's Truth: *For I have come to have much joy and comfort in your love, because the hearts of the saints have been refreshed through you, brother.* Philemon 1:7

My Prayer: Dear Lord, my heart is in desperate need of comfort and joy so I trust you to give me the strength and desire I need to accept opportunities to spend time with friends so that my heart can be refreshed. Thank you, Jesus. Amen.

I'm Too Broken to Help Others

As Referenced in Chapter 11

The lie that defeats: I am too broken to help others.

The truth that heals: God uses broken people to bring a message of hope to the world.

During my early days of grief, I felt like I should be wearing a sign around my neck: "I'm grieving. No loitering." *Who could possibly gain anything from being around someone who feels so empty, weak, and hurt? I have no energy and I'm definitely not qualified to help anyone.* The lie I believed is that I had nothing worthwhile to give. And even if I thought there was something to offer, I didn't want the responsibility of it. *There's no way God's choosing me to do anything good at a time like this.* The irony of this lie is that it is debunked over and over and over all through the Bible:

> Joseph was left for dead by his own brothers and then sold into slavery.
> Even so, God chose him to save Egypt from famine.
>
> Gideon was nearly paralyzed by fear.
> Even so, God chose him to lead an army.
>
> Ruth was grieving the loss of her father-in-law, brother-in-law, and husband.
> Even so, God chose her to be an example of uncompromised loyalty.
>
> Moses had a speech problem and had murdered an Egyptian.

Even so, God chose him to be the spokesperson for the freedom of the Israelites.

Paul was beaten, shipwrecked, imprisoned, and faced dangers of all sorts.
Even so, God chose him to bring the gospel to the Gentiles and his New Testament writings continue to spread the good news of Jesus.

Jesus himself was mocked, beaten, and betrayed.
Even so, God chose him to be the Savior of the world.

My son took his own life, leaving me shattered. *Even so*, I am called to share God's message of hope. As you claim the truth of God's Word this week, I pray that you feel him *choosing you.* You may be weak, fearful, unmotivated, betrayed, and even angry. You may believe that you've made terrible mistakes or that your weaknesses outweigh your strengths. *Even so*, God chooses your story to bring hope to others. Trust me! *Because of your brokenness*, you have something to give. People don't need polished presentations and they don't want to hear perfect stories. They just need to be cared for and listened to, and to see authentic examples of how God's faithfulness can get us through our darkest days. Ask God to help you. He will.

MONDAY

God's Truth: *As Jesus was getting into the boat, the man who had been demon-possessed begged to go with him. Jesus did not let him, but said, "Go home to your own people and tell them how much the Lord has done for you . . ." So the man went away and began to tell . . . how much Jesus had done for him. And all the people were amazed. Mark 5:18–20*
My Prayer: Jesus, I can't imagine how thankful this man was for your healing touch and it's easy to understand his enthusiasm for telling others about what you did for him. Help me to realize that you're doing the same for me. Because of you, I'm able to walk through grief without being destroyed and that is reason enough to tell my story! Please give me the strength. Amen.

TUESDAY

God's Truth: *[Joseph's] brothers came and threw themselves down before him . . . But Joseph said to them, "Don't be afraid. Am I in the place of God? You*

intended to harm me, but God intended it for good to accomplish what is now being done, the saving of many lives. Genesis 50:18–20
My Prayer: Lord, the enemy wants the loss of my loved one to defeat me. . .to hold me captive to pain and suffering. But you have the power to use tragedy to accomplish something good and I choose to believe that my story can save others from being defeated. Show me how. Amen.

WEDNESDAY

God's Truth: *Moses said to the Lord, "Pardon your servant, Lord. I have never been eloquent, neither in the past nor since you have spoken to your servant. I am slow of speech and tongue." The Lord said to him, "Who gave human beings their mouths? Is it not I, the Lord? Now go; I will help you speak and will teach you what to say." Exodus 4:10–12*
My Prayer: Oh God, I am so inadequate. My heart is shattered and it feels impossible to see beyond my own situation. But just as you helped Moses to speak and taught him what to say, you can do the same for me. Today, I choose to believe that I still have something to give and ask you to help me find the energy and desire to do so. Amen.

THURSDAY

God's Truth: *The Lord turned to [Gideon] and said, "Go in the strength you have and save Israel out of Midian's hand. Am I not sending you?"*
"Pardon me, my lord," Gideon replied, "but how can I save Israel? My clan is the weakest in Manasseh, and I am the least in my family."
The Lord answered, "I will be with you, and you will strike down all the Midianites, leaving none alive." Judges 6:14–16
My Prayer: Lord, I feel like Gideon. *How can I save anybody? I am too weak!* But just as you fought for him, I trust you to fight for me. Thank you for the truth that my grief can serve a good purpose by bringing hope to others. . .simply by sharing my own survival story. Thank you for this truth, God. Amen.

FRIDAY

God's Truth: *Christ suffered for you, leaving an example that you should follow. . .When they hurled their insults at him, he did not retaliate; when he suffered, he made no threats. Instead, he entrusted himself to him who judges justly. "He himself bore our sins . . . by his wounds you have been healed." 1 Peter 2:21–24*

My Prayer: Precious Savior, you suffered more than I ever will and you responded with grace and love. Remind me of your example every time I feel too broken to think of others above myself. Thank you for choosing me—for choosing my survival—to bring hope to others. Amen.

SATURDAY

God's Truth: *Now I [Paul] want you to know . . . that what has happened to me has actually served to advance the gospel. As a result, it has become clear throughout the whole palace guard and to everyone else that I am in chains for Christ. And because of my chains, most of the brothers and sisters have become confident in the Lord and dare all the more to proclaim the gospel without fear. Philippians 1:12–14*

My Prayer: Father, every survival story has the potential to inspire others. Paul survived dangerous and painful circumstances by boldly proclaiming his faith in you, and his testimony caused others to put their confidence in you as well. By the power of your Spirit, help me to boldly tell others how you walk with me through even the darkest days of grief. Amen.

SUNDAY

God's Truth: *. . . bestow on them a crown of beauty instead of ashes, the oil of joy instead of mourning, and a garment of praise instead of a spirit of despair. They will be called oaks of righteousness, a planting of the Lord for the display of his splendor. Isaiah 61:3*

My Prayer: Oh God, it's hard to believe that I could ever be an example of your splendor, when I feel more like a frightened child who's hiding under the covers. Even so, I trust you to bring beauty from ashes and praise from despair . . . one day at a time. Make me willing, God, to share the hope I have in you so that it will encourage others to find hope in you as well. Amen.

Nobody Will Ever Understand or Make Me Feel Better about My Loss

As Referenced in Chapter 11

The lie that defeats: Nobody will ever understand or make me feel better about my loss.

The truth that heals: God demonstrates his love for me through the love of others.

The lies that have posed the greatest threat to my survival are the ones that keep me in emotional and physical isolation, in a place where it's easy to stay convinced that nobody understands my situation and nobody can make me feel better about losing my loved one. Thankfully, I've experienced the healing truth that God does use the presence of others to demonstrate his love and care for me. Truth is, they don't understand my pain and they can't change my situation but allowing them to be the hands and feet of God refreshes my soul and brings healing to my heart.

As you claim the truth of God's Word this week, I pray that you find the courage to step out of your comfort zone and trust those who love you; allow them to meet you where you are. There are few things as healing as opening up about our struggle . . . even if the other person never speaks a word in return. Trust God to use those who love you, not only to listen, but to offer gracious words that are sweet to your soul and healing to your bones. (Proverbs 16:24)

MONDAY

God's Truth: *For where two or three gather in my name, there am I with them.*
Matthew 18:20

My Prayer: Jesus, most of your adult life was spent with your closest friends and there was no way that they could possibly understand your emotions or your personal struggle. My friends can't understand mine either. Still, there is power in gathering together and sharing our deepest needs because you show up . . . every time. Thank you for the assurance that there is healing power in spending time with people who love and care for me. Amen.

TUESDAY

God's Truth: *Rejoice with those who rejoice; mourn with those who mourn.*
Romans 12:15

My Prayer: Lord, you have such a powerful purpose for Christian community. The love and comfort I receive from others is a tangible expression of your love for me, showing me that you care about the details of my life. When grief causes me to withdraw in isolation, help me to seek time with people who care about me. Protect me from any words that cause additional pain and show me that I am loved, I'm not alone, and there is hope. Amen.

WEDNESDAY

God's Truth: *My goal is that [Christians] may be encouraged in heart and united in love, so that they may have the full riches of complete understanding, in order that they may know the mystery of Christ, in whom are hidden all the treasures of wisdom and knowledge. Colossians 2:2–3*

My Prayer: Father, your Word tells me that spending time with Christian friends will increase my understanding of your wisdom and knowledge. Why wouldn't I want that? Help me to embrace this truth so that spending time with others will grow my faith and to remind me of the treasure we have in Jesus. Amen.

THURSDAY

God's Truth: *I [Jesus] have given them the glory that you gave me, that they may be one as we are one—I in them and you in me—so that they may be brought to complete unity. Then the world will know that you sent me and have loved them even as you have loved me. John 17:22–23*

My Prayer: Lord Jesus, you understand that human relationships are complicated so you prayed that we would always have unity with one another—not just when life is good but always. Thank you that I can experience your love and encouragement through others, even when they can't understand my struggle, and help me to find healing when I spend time with others. Amen.

FRIDAY

God's Truth: *Since God so loved us, we also ought to love one another. No one has ever seen God; but if we love one another, God lives in us and his love is made complete in us. 1 John 4:11–12*

My Prayer: Thank you, God, for loving me and for creating me to experience healing through fellowship. Please lead me to healthy relationships and make me mindful that the love and encouragement I receive from others is a gift from you. It's your way of breaking through the isolation and using others to mend my heart. Amen.

SATURDAY

God's Truth: *Bear one another's burdens, and so fulfill the law of Christ. Galatians 6:2*

My Prayer: Father, you didn't design me to suffer alone. You designed me to bear the burdens of others and to let them do the same for me. I don't get a "pass" just because others may not understand my pain. Please help me to tear down any walls I've built-up and to embrace the truth that you demonstrate your love for me through the love of others. Amen.

SUNDAY

God's Truth: *God is love. Whoever lives in love lives in God, and God in them. This is how love is made complete among us . . . In this world we are like Jesus. 1 John 4:16–17*

My Prayer: Oh God, though it feels safer to withdraw in isolation, help me to trust that you work through others to love me when I am shattered. Thank you for putting my burdens on their hearts; help me to receive their love and kindness with a grateful heart and to find strength in their presence. Amen.

I'm Forgetting My Loved One

As Referenced in Chapters 2 and 12

The lie that defeats: I'm forgetting my loved one.

The truth that heals: With a thankful heart, I will always remember my love for the one I lost.

My mind plays tricks on me sometimes, causing me to fear that I'm forgetting David. Ridiculous, right? *He's my son! Of course I'm not forgetting him!* The heartbreaking reality is that I have forgotten some of the details about life with him, as any parent does, but the truth is that I will never forget how much I love him and I will always be grateful for the time we shared. Thinking about life with David is a healthy part of my grief journey, but only when I choose to focus on the good stuff. I'm thankful for so many things, and that is what I try to think about most . . . not with bitterness because of what I've lost but with gratitude for what I had.

As you claim the truth of God's Word this week, I pray that you find peace in remembering the good times you shared with your loved one. Maybe time was brief and you are haunted by the memories you never got to make. Maybe you have a lifetime of memories—some good and some challenging. Whatever memories you have, hold on to the best of them. Talk about them. Ask others to share memories of your loved one. Never feel like you have to leave your loved one behind . . . just find the strength to let go of what hurts and hold tight to the love you will always treasure.

MONDAY

God's Truth: *The thief comes only to steal and kill and destroy. I came that they may have life and have it abundantly. John 10:10*
My Prayer: Heavenly Father, the "thief" tries to rob me of the joy in my memories. But you want me to live abundantly. Help me to remember my loved one with a joyful heart, not with bitterness or despair. When things seem fuzzy, help me to hold tight the love that I will never forget. Amen.

TUESDAY

God's Truth: *I will give thanks to the Lord with my whole heart; I will recount all of your wonderful deeds. Psalm 9:1*
My Prayer: Oh God, even though grief consumes me, help it not to shadow the many blessings you've given me or the good times I shared with my loved one. When I'm weighed down by what I've lost, help me to purpose-fully recount the good stuff and to give you thanks with my whole heart. Amen.

WEDNESDAY

God's Truth: *I thank God for you whenever I think of you. Philippians 1:3–6*
My Prayer: Lord Jesus, thank you for the time I had with my loved one. Though I wanted more, I choose to believe that the blessing of the memories I do have and the love that will never fade will bring healing and not keep me trapped in sorrow. Amen.

THURSDAY

God's Truth: *I [Paul] thank God, whom I serve, as my ancestors did, with a clear conscience, as night and day I constantly remember you in my prayers. Recalling your tears, I long to see you, so that I may be filled with joy . . . 2 Timothy 1:3–4*
My Prayer: Jesus, just as Paul longed to see members of his spiritual family, I long to see my loved one, too. . .to have one more hug, one more smile, one more conversation. Thank you for the assurance that this desire is not wrong and help the memories to bring me joy. Amen.

FRIDAY

<u>God's Truth</u>: *But joyful are those who have the God of Israel as their helper, whose hope is in the Lord their God. Psalm 146:5*
<u>My Prayer</u>: Lord, when I feel like I'm forgetting my loved one it makes me desperately sad, but you are my helper and your Word tells me that drawing near to you will bring joy to my heart. Please help me today to find joy in the memories I have and to rest in knowing that the love we shared will never fade. Amen.

SATURDAY

<u>God's Truth</u>: *Now stand here quietly before the Lord as I remind you of all the great things the Lord has done for you and your ancestors. 1 Samuel 12:7*
<u>My Prayer</u>: Oh God, you have been doing great things for generations and there is so much in my own life to be thankful for as well. When my heart is heavy, help me to remember that. Flood my soul with gratitude today: for the time I had with my loved one, for the love we shared, and for the promise of a future that is still filled with purpose. Amen.

SUNDAY

<u>God's Truth</u>: *He caused the storm to be still so that the waves of the sea were hushed. Then they were glad because they were quiet and he guided them to their desired haven. Let them give thanks to the Lord for his lovingkindness. . . Psalm 107:29–32*
<u>My Prayer</u>: Jesus, a storm of anxiety rages in my mind and I need your powerful voice to quiet my fears. When I hear your voice, my heart will be glad and I will give you thanks for the time I had with my loved one and for your lovingkindness. Amen.

I Just Need to "Get Over It"

As Referenced in Chapter 12

> The lie that defeats: I just need to "get over it."
>
> The truth that heals: God is making a way through.

Whether spoken literally or simply implied, my healing process can be halted by the lie that I need to "just get over" my grief. If only I could! Grief is such a personal emotion and I need the freedom to walk through it at my own pace, trusting God to guide me. Sure, there are times when I need a nudge from others to push through certain struggles that are holding me back, but this is quite different than being told to simply be done grieving. I might as well try to stop the rain. Truth is, God is making a way through my pain and he is healing my heart as I follow him.

As you claim the truth of God's Word this week, I pray that you will trust him with the pace of your grief. He doesn't ask you to "get over it." He asks you to trust him and to follow where he leads so he can heal you in his perfect timing. Though grief doesn't have an expiration date, it also doesn't have to consume you. It's haphazard and repetitive and messy . . . and that's okay. Cling to the promise this week, that God will make a way through the pain.

MONDAY

<u>God's Truth</u>: *He heals the brokenhearted and binds up their wounds. He determines the number of the stars and calls them each by name. Great is our Lord and mighty in power; his understanding has no limit. Psalm 147:3–5*

My Prayer: Lord Jesus, I trust your mighty power to heal my broken heart and bind up my wounds in your perfect timing. Thank you for always understanding me, even when I don't understand myself. And help others to be patient with me also. Amen.

TUESDAY

God's Truth: *I waited patiently for the Lord; he turned to me and heard my cry. He lifted me out of the slimy pit. . .he set my feet on a rock and gave me a firm place to stand. He put a new song in my mouth, a hymn of praise to our God. Psalm 40:1–3*

My Prayer: Jesus, *you* are my only hope for complete healing. *You* are the one who rescues me from the pit of grief. *You* are the one who will put a new song in my heart. I choose to praise you today for the truth that you hear my cries for help and that you will restore my joy as I continue to follow *your* voice. Thank you for sustaining me through the journey. Amen.

WEDNESDAY

God's Truth: *For he is the living God and he endures forever; his kingdom will not be destroyed . . . He rescues and he saves; he performs signs and wonders in the heavens and on the earth. He has rescued Daniel from the power of the lions. Daniel 6:26–27*

My Prayer: Oh God, you shut the mouths of the lions and miraculously saved Daniel's life. In the same way, I trust you to stop the pain of grief from devouring me. Save me from being destroyed and help me to be patient as I trust you to get me through. Amen.

THURSDAY

God's Truth: *Trust in the Lord with all your heart, and do not lean on your own understanding. In all your ways acknowledge him, and he will make straight your paths. Proverbs 3:5–6*

My Prayer: Heavenly Father, I choose to trust you with my whole heart today because I will never understand how to do this on my own. Make the path to healing straight before me and give me the strength and wisdom to follow you as I trust your perfect timing. Amen.

FRIDAY

God's Truth: *Forget the former things; do not dwell on the past. See, I am doing a new thing! Now it springs up; do you not perceive it? I am making a way in the wilderness and streams in the wasteland. Isaiah 43:18–19*

My Prayer: Dear Lord, thank you for the promise that you are doing a new thing in my heart each day; you are making a way through this wilderness as I put one foot in front of the other. Make it clear when I need to stop dwelling on the past and slow me down when I'm rushing to please others. Amen.

SATURDAY

God's Truth: *But they who wait for the Lord shall renew their strength; they shall mount up with wings like eagles; they shall run and not be weary; they shall walk and not faint. Isaiah 40:31*

My Prayer: Oh Lord, I wait on you to renew my strength and to get me through, no matter how long it takes. And I find hope in knowing that you have greater plans for me than I can even imagine. Help me to embrace the truth that feeling strong isn't an insult to my loved one; it's a testimony to your healing power and it's what they would want for me. Amen.

SUNDAY

God's Truth: *Do not fear, for I have redeemed you; I have summoned you by name; you are mine. When you pass through the waters, I will be with you; and when you pass through the rivers, they will not sweep over you. Isaiah 43:1–2*

My Prayer: Jesus, you know me, you know the loss I've suffered, and you promise to get me through. I choose to trust you today for protection and deliverance. Help me not to fear the future because I know that you will be with me every step of the way. Amen.

People Don't Care Anymore

As Referenced in Chapter 12

The lie that defeats: People don't care anymore.

The truth that heals: God never stops caring for me.

The woe is me mentality fuels a host of lies. One of which is that people don't care anymore. *They don't care about David and they don't care about me. They've moved on . . . without us.* I admit, it's a particularly lame lie, but it's not easy to fight off. The truth is that people do care. They just don't have the same intensity of compassion they once did, and as the years march on questions about how I'm doing are asked far less often. I don't resent it; I just wish it was different. Thank you, Jesus, that your interest in me never fades and your mercies are new every single day.

As you claim the truth of God's Word this week, I pray that you will experience how deep and wide the Father's love is for you. His care for you never fades and he will never stop fighting for you. He created your loved one, he remembers your loss, and he knows the pain it continues to cause. When people feel distant or indifferent, resist the temptation to pout. They still care. It's just different now. Let it go and cling passionately to the truth that the Lord is always near and he remains intimately interested in your journey . . . no matter how long you've been walking through it.

MONDAY

God's Truth: *Why, my soul, are you downcast? Why so disturbed within me? Put your hope in God, for I will yet praise him, my Savior and my God. Psalm 42:11*
My Prayer: Oh God, it hurts my feelings when friends and family seem distant or indifferent. Help me to remember that they really do care even when they don't show it the way I wish they would. And remind me that my hope shouldn't be in them anyway . . . but only in you. You are never distant and you are never indifferent. Amen.

TUESDAY

God's Truth: *Whatever you do, work heartily, as for the Lord and not for men, knowing that from the Lord you will receive the inheritance as your reward. You are serving the Lord Christ. Colossians 3:23–25*
My Prayer: Dear Lord, help me to draw near to you and reject the lie that people don't care about me anymore. They shouldn't determine my value anyway. Thank you for always caring passionately about every detail of my grief and help me to serve you with all of my heart. Amen.

WEDNESDAY

God's Truth: *He tends his flock like a shepherd: He gathers the lambs in his arms and carries them close to his heart. Isaiah 40:11*
My Prayer: Father, my heart feels alone today and I needed this reminder. A shepherd never leaves his sheep and you are my shepherd. Every day, you gather me in your arms and carry me close to your heart. What a beautiful comfort! Thank you that I am never alone in grief. Amen.

THURSDAY

God's Truth: *Humble yourselves, therefore, under the mighty hand of God so that at the proper time he may exalt you, casting all your anxieties on him, because he cares for you. 1 Peter 5:6–7*
My Prayer: Jesus, when I feel like friends have moved on and they're no longer interested in my struggle, hold me in your mighty hand. Today, I choose to humble myself by turning every hurt feeling and every anxious thought over to you. Thank you for loving me. Amen.

FRIDAY

<u>God's Truth</u>: . . . *neither death nor life, neither angels nor demons, neither the present nor the future, nor any powers, neither height nor depth, nor anything else in all creation, will be able to separate us from the love of God that is in Christ Jesus our Lord. Romans 8:38–39*

<u>My Prayer</u>: Father, it's so easy to feel hurt by human relationships. Even though I know in my heart that my friends and family love me, there are times when they make me question my worth. Thank you for the powerful reminder that nothing will ever separate me from your perfect love. You never walk away when my grief is repetitive or my attitude stinks. Thank you, Jesus. Amen.

SATURDAY

<u>God's Truth</u>: *And therefore, I have hope: The steadfast love of the Lord never ceases; his mercies never come to an end; they are new every morning; great is your faithfulness. Lamentations 3:21–23*

<u>My Prayer</u>: Faithful God, though I wish for more from friends and family sometimes, they should never be my primary source of comfort or hope. Only your love is steadfast. Only your hope lasts. Only your faithfulness is unceasing. Thank you that I never have to question whether you care or not, because the truth is that you care more than I can ever imagine. Amen.

SUNDAY

<u>God's Truth</u>: *See what great love the Father has lavished on us, that we should be called children of God! And that is what we are! 1 John 3:1*

<u>My Prayer</u>: Dear Jesus, you make me safer, give me greater hope, and make me feel more loved than any human ever can. Please help me to keep my expectations for human relationships in check by keeping me focused on the emotional strength and support that you lavish on me. I am so thankful to be cared for as your child. Amen.

Nothing Good Can Come from This

As Referenced in Chapters 13 and 14

The lie that defeats: Nothing good can come from this.

The truth that heals: In time, good will come.

Truth is, saying goodbye to my son was the most cruel and unfair thing I've ever had to do . . . and there was nothing good about it. I'd bring him back in an instant if I could, but I can't. And the only way to experience something good from such a painful reality is to treasure the love I have for my son and to put new energy into the future. My son is gone, but my life isn't over. And having hope for what comes next doesn't mean I'm forgetting him. It just means I'm healing. By God's mercy and in his perfect timing, there is more to my tragic story than suffering. Praise Jesus for this healing truth!

As you claim the truth of God's Word this week, I pray that you are filled with mental and emotional energy to face the future with hope. I know how difficult it is. Trust me! Your heart is breaking and nothing about losing your loved one feels good. But please keep fighting! Hold tight to the truth that God is able to bring something good—beautiful even—from your loss. He loves you so much. He is good and his tender mercies are yours. (Psalm 145:9)

MONDAY

God's Truth: . . . *being confident of this, that God who began a good work in you will carry it on to completion until the day of Christ Jesus. Philippians 1:6*

<u>My Prayer</u>: Oh God, it's so hard to believe that anything good can come from this but your Word says that there is a purpose for my life . . . and grief hasn't change that. No matter what happens in my life, you will never give up on me. Thank you that I can trust you to bring good again. Amen.

TUESDAY

<u>God's Truth</u>: *And we know that in all things God works for the good of those who love him, who have been called according to his purpose.* Romans 8:28
<u>My Prayer</u>: Jesus, I surrender my doubting heart today and trust you with these words. There's nothing good about my loved one being gone and I need help to accept the truth that good can come from it. I love you and ask you to shine your light into the fog that surrounds me. Amen.

WEDNESDAY

<u>God's Truth</u>: *You intended to harm me, but God intended it for good to accomplish what is now being done, the saving of many lives.* Genesis 50:20
<u>My Prayer</u>: Lord, I'm so thankful that there is more for me than just this life . . . this pain. Because you are the author of hope, you bring eternal good out of even the most devastating situations and you can use my story of survival to bring hope to others. Thank you for this hope. Amen.

THURSDAY

<u>God's Truth</u>: *. . . my only aim is to finish the race and complete the task the Lord Jesus has given me—the task of testifying to the good news of God's grace.* Acts 20:24
<u>My Prayer</u>: Heavenly Father, give me the energy I need to press on and to finish strong. Your view of what is good is a heart that is willing to testify to your faithfulness. I trust you to make me willing and to help me see that every time I take a step forward—however small—it is evidence of your faithfulness . . . and that is something good. Thank you for this truth, God. Amen.

FRIDAY

<u>God's Truth</u>: *For our light and momentary troubles are achieving for us an eternal glory that far outweighs them all. So, we fix our eyes not on what*

is seen, but on what is unseen, since what is seen is temporary, but what is unseen is eternal. 2 Corinthians 4:17–18
<u>My Prayer</u>: Oh Lord, nothing about my loss feels light or momentary but compared to what you suffered to save us from the punishment of sin, that's exactly what they are. Right now, all I can see is pain but by faith I choose to focus on what I cannot see: on your power to bring beauty from ashes and on the promise of an eternity that far outweighs my earthly struggle. Amen.

SATURDAY

<u>God's Truth</u>: *The sufferings of this present time are not worth comparing with the glory that is to be revealed to us. Romans 8:18*
<u>My Prayer</u>: Lord, my heart continues to suffer and the future feels dark. Help me to cling to your truth today and to really believe that my pain is nothing compared to the glory you have in store for me. Thank you that no matter how dark life gets there is always hope on the horizon. Amen.

SUNDAY

<u>God's Truth</u>: *Praise the Lord, my soul; all my inmost being, praise his holy name. Praise the Lord, my soul, and forget not all his benefits . . . who redeems your life from the pit and crowns you with love and compassion, who satisfies your desires with good things so that your youth is renewed like the eagle's. Psalm 103:1–5*
<u>My Prayer</u>: Father, I offer you a sacrifice of praise today. You are compassionate and good and you have the power to heal. Flood my heart with your goodness and renew my hope. This darkness won't last forever because you redeem me from the pit, crown me with love, and—in your perfect timing—you will satisfy my desires with good things. Thank you, Jesus. Amen.

It's Easier Not to Know the Dangers that Threaten My Family

As Referenced in Chapter 13

The lie that defeats: It's easier not to know the dangers that threaten my family.

The truth that heals: It is wise to seek understanding.

Mark Twain said it best; denial ain't just a river in Egypt! Would you rather relax on a floatie in the waters of denial than face harsh reality? *My kids know better. They'll never . . . (fill in the blank). It's so sad that other families have to deal with that.* Believe me, I get it. We talked to our boys about drinking, drugs, sex and every other topic we knew we needed to cover. But we couldn't talk to them about what we didn't know existed. How could we? David chose to smoke a four–dollar packet of so–called *incense,* bought from a store at the mall, and 90 minutes later he was gone. I can't turn back time, but I can implore you to reject the temptation to ignore the dangers that threaten your kids and to act on the truth that it is wise to aggressively seek understanding about current youth culture. I beg you to be proactively informed—not so that you will live in fear but so you will walk in wisdom. Take it from me, ignorance is not bliss.

As you claim the truth of God's Word this week, I pray that you will be encouraged to set aside time to boldly pursue your kids. Go beyond, *"How was school? Please pass the potatoes,"* and dive into uncomfortable topics. Tell them what you've heard or learned about certain dangers and ask what they know about them. Talk to other parents, read school emails, research the newest drug trends and trending dares and pranks. Contact local law enforcement and ask what dangerous activities they are seeing in your community. Be hungry to understand the culture surrounding your kids. Most importantly, draw near to God daily, praying for guidance and protection and seeking wisdom from his Word.

MONDAY

<u>God's Truth</u>: *Have nothing to do with the fruitless deeds of darkness, but rather expose them . . . everything exposed by the light becomes visible. . .Be very careful, then, how you live—not as unwise but as wise, making the most of every opportunity, because the days are evil. Ephesians 5:8–16*
<u>My Prayer</u>: Dear Lord, protect me from wearing blinders that make me oblivious to the dangers that threaten my family. By your wisdom, show me any people, things, or activities that are unsafe for my children and then prepare their hearts to receive the truth from me. Amen.

TUESDAY

<u>God's Truth</u>: *The beginning of wisdom is this: Get wisdom. Though it cost all you have, get understanding. Proverbs 4:7*
<u>My Prayer</u>: Oh God, I must choose every day to live in wisdom and not denial. Give me the mindfulness to search for wisdom and not to act on emotional whims. Protect my family from any unhealthy desires to be culturally popular and make us alert to anything that is contrary to your best. Amen.

WEDNESDAY

<u>God's Truth</u>: *Beloved, do not believe every spirit, but test the spirits to see whether they are from God, for many false prophets have gone out into the world. 1 John 4:1*
<u>My Prayer</u>: Jesus, everybody has an opinion but only your truth is without fault. Give me the wisdom to listen for any lies or deceptions that are influencing my kids and to use your Word as a guide for making wise parenting choices. By the power of your Spirit, instruct my children in your ways, convict their hearts when they go astray, and crush any attempt by the enemy to harm my family. Thank you, Jesus. Amen.

THURSDAY

God's Truth: *For the protection of wisdom is like the protection of money, and the advantage of knowledge is that wisdom preserves the life of him who has it. Ecclesiastes 7:12*

My Prayer: Father, ignorance is not bliss. It is wise to chase after wisdom that comes from you because your wisdom preserves life. Direct me to people and resources that reveal potential dangers and then help me to respond with wise action. . .and not with fear or denial. Amen.

FRIDAY

God's Truth: *Be sober-minded; be watchful. Your adversary the devil prowls around like a roaring lion, seeking someone to devour. 1 Peter 5:8*

My Prayer: Lord, please don't allow me to get too comfortable or to let my guard down to the evil threatening to devour my family. Keep my eyes and ears alert and then give me the strength and wisdom to fight back so that we are not blindsided. Thank you for the truth that you are mightier than any danger and you will fight for us. Amen.

SATURDAY

God's Truth: *Without guidance a nation falls. But many good advisers can bring victory to a nation. Proverbs 11:14*

My Prayer: Dear God, help me to be humble when seeking guidance from others and to know that there is wisdom in learning from experience. I want to know the truth. I want to know the dangers that threaten my family. And I don't want to be destroyed by the thought that we are immune from evil or poor judgement. Protect me from pride so that the wisdom I gain from you can protect my family. Amen.

SUNDAY

God's Truth: *For there is nothing hidden that will not be disclosed, and nothing concealed that will not be known or brought out into the open. Luke 8:17*

My Prayer: Oh Father, help me not to be deceived! I don't want to find out about danger when it's too late. Your Word says that evil will be exposed. As

I search to intentionally understand the culture my kids are growing up in, lead me to people, websites, and conversations that will bring evil to light and equip me to advocate on behalf of my family and the families of others. Amen.

Telling My Story is Futile and/or Self–Serving

As Referenced in Chapters 11, 13, and 14

The lie that defeats: Telling my story is futile and/or self–serving.

The truth that heals: Jesus calls me to tell my story so he may be glorified.

When I talk with others about our loss—whether in casual conversation, from a stage, or in writing—I am sometimes discouraged by the lie that sharing my grief story is futile and self-serving. *Do they even care about this? Do I just want them to feel sorry for me? Am I just shamefully trying to keep David's memory alive?* Lies! Every heartbreak has the potential to bring hope to others . . . even mine. Even yours. Truth is, Jesus calls us to tell our stories of heartbreak and survival so that he may be glorified and others may find hope.

RAW JOURNAL ENTRY

Three years after David died: Lord, I want to help people because you have helped me. It's as simple as that. I have a lot to say. I could write a book! Lol. So, I'm going to. And I'm going to trust you with the process and the outcome. People need to know that there is hope even when everything seems hopeless. That is what you're showing and it's what I want to show others. When I finally sat at my computer this morning, I was so afraid that you wouldn't guide me like you have in the past, but I shouldn't have doubted you. You showed up. Thank you for guiding my heart today. Regardless of where this goes, I will not doubt what you have already done in my life, and what you will continue to do tomorrow, and the next day, and the next, and the next. Thank you, Lord. Same time tomorrow?

As you claim the truth of God's Word this week, I pray that you will see how he is helping you to survive, how far you've already come, and that no matter where you are on the healing scale, your story of survival can encourage others. It can! Maybe you're not ready yet, but as you draw near to him this week, I pray that you will find new purpose and strength to search for ways that your story can bring hope and healing to others. It's not a story you asked for, I get it, but it's uniquely yours and nobody can tell it as masterfully as you. It's always worth it when you help others to believe that they aren't alone and that there really is hope.

MONDAY

<u>God's Truth</u>: "*Return home and tell how much God has done for you.*" *So the man went away and told all over town how much Jesus had done for him.* Luke 8:38–39

<u>My Prayer</u>: Jesus, in your lovingkindness you healed so many people during your ministry on earth and you wanted them to share their excitement about what you had done. It's no different now. You continue to sustain me through unthinkable pain and to bring hope into a hopeless situation. Why wouldn't I want to share that with others! Give me the words and direct my steps to the people who need to hear it most. We all need to know that we're not alone. Amen.

TUESDAY

<u>God's Truth</u>: *As the rain and the snow come down from heaven, and do not return to it without watering the earth and making it bud and flourish . . . so is my word that goes out from my mouth: It will not return to me empty, but will accomplish what I desire and achieve the purpose for which I sent it.* Isaiah 55:10–11

<u>My Prayer</u>: Oh God, I'm living a story I didn't want but I choose to believe that you will use it to accomplish something good. My story is for your glory. You want me to use the words of my mouth to tell others the truth about Jesus and to testify to all he has done for me. . .especially in the midst of unbelievable heartache. May my words bring glory to you! Amen.

WEDNESDAY

God's Truth: *So do not be ashamed of the testimony about our Lord . . . He has saved us and called us to a holy life—not because of anything we have done but because of his own purpose and grace. 2 Timothy 1:8–9*
My Prayer: Dear Lord, strengthen me to share my testimony of your faithfulness unashamedly. Crush every fear that my story is too religious or too painful or too . . . whatever. It's mine and I'm the only one that can tell it. Ultimately, it's not about anything I've done but about Christ in me and about his purpose and grace. Thank you for this reminder. Amen.

THURSDAY

God's Truth: *You are the light of the world. A town built on a hill cannot be hidden. Neither do people light a lamp and put it under a bowl. Instead they put it on its stand, and it gives light to everyone in the house. In the same way, let your light shine before others, that they may . . . glorify your Father in heaven. Matthew 5:14–16*
My Prayer: Oh God, nothing about grief makes me feel like the light of the world but your Word tells me that I absolutely have the opportunity to be just that. As you shine light into my darkness, you ask me to share that light to others. Give me the strength to do that. May I never shy away from letting others hear me glorify your name. Amen.

FRIDAY

God's Truth: *It is my pleasure to tell you about the miraculous signs and wonders that the Most High God has performed for me. How great are his signs, how mighty his wonders! Daniel 4:2*
My Prayer: Heavenly Father, there are days when simply getting out of bed in the morning is miraculous. Others may not see this as a mighty wonder but it's mighty to me and it is proof that you have carried me through times of desperation . . . even when my faith is weak. Others need this hope, too, so help me to share the things you've done for me with confidence. Amen.

SATURDAY

God's Truth: *The Spirit of the Sovereign Lord is on me, because the Lord has anointed me to proclaim good news . . . to comfort all who mourn . . . to bestow on them a crown of beauty instead of ashes, the oil of joy instead of mourning, and a garment of praise instead of a spirit of despair. Isaiah 61:1–3*

My Prayer: Lord Jesus, despair has defined much of my grief journey but every time I've called on you, you've shown up. Help me to boldly tell others how you continue to replace my spirit of despair with a garment of praise. May my story of survival comfort others who mourn and restore their hope for the future. Amen.

SUNDAY

God's Truth: *My mouth will tell of your righteous deeds, of your saving acts all day long—though I know not how to relate them all. I will come and proclaim your mighty acts, Sovereign Lord; I will proclaim your righteous deeds, yours alone. Psalm 17:15–16*

My Prayer: Loving God, you continue to write my survival story as I continue to trust you with my heart, and your Word tells me that you are glorified when I proclaim your faithfulness. Lead me to those who need to hear this truth and help me to share it in a way that brings glory to you. I'm not surviving because I'm strong and wise; I'm surviving because your power lives in me. Thank you so much for this truth and for the emotional energy to share it with others. Amen.

Appendix A

God's Free Gift of Eternal Life

If you stood before God today and he asked why he should let you into heaven, how would you answer? Maybe you would tell him that you go to church every Sunday or that you try to be a good person. Maybe you would say that a loving God should let everyone into Heaven or perhaps you wouldn't have an answer at all. Dear friend, it's great for us to go to church and try to be good people. And it's true that he is a loving God who wants everyone to spend eternity with him, but none of these answers will get you through the door of heaven. There is only one way, and it has nothing to do with your accomplishments. The only answer is Jesus.

GOD LOVES YOU SO MUCH.

God desperately loves you, cares about the details of your life, and wants a relationship with you. In Jeremiah 31:3 God says, "I have loved you with an everlasting love; I have drawn you with unfailing kindness." There's nothing you can do to make him love you more and nothing you can do to make him love you less. John 3:16 says, "For God so loved the world (you) that he gave his one and only Son, that whoever believes in him shall not perish but have eternal life."

YOU CAN'T EVER BE GOOD ENOUGH TO EARN ETERNAL FORGIVENESS.

Romans 3:23 says, "For all have sinned and fall short of the glory of God." Romans 6:23 says, "The wages of sin is death. . ." Even though God loves you, the consequence of sin is death (eternal separation from him) and no amount of good behavior is enough to pay that debt. Your only hope to escape the consequence of sin is Jesus. In John 14:6, Jesus says, "I am the way, and the truth, and the life. No one comes to the Father except through me."

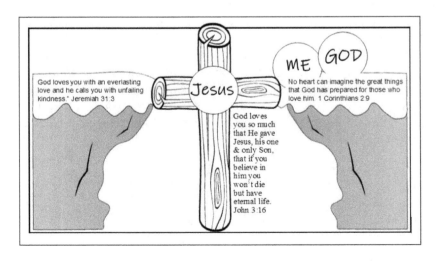

JESUS PAID THE FULL COST OF YOUR SIN.

Even though "the wages of sin is death," Romans 6:23 goes on to say that "the gift of God is eternal life through Jesus our Lord." He didn't wait until you were good enough, because he knew you never *could* be good enough. Instead, Romans 5:8 says, "But God demonstrates his own love for us in this: While we were still sinners, Christ died for us." Jesus came to earth, lived a perfect life, died a torturous death, then raised to life again and lives with his Father in heaven. . .all of this so that you can be eternally forgiven. What a profound expression of love!

AND GOD'S GIFT OF ETERNAL FORGIVENESS IS WAITING FOR YOU.

When you receive a gift, it doesn't belong to you until you reach out and take it. The same is true for God's gift of eternal life. You must take hold of it by admitting your own sinfulness, believing that you cannot save yourself, and proclaiming complete trust (faith) that Jesus paid the full cost of your sin when he died on the cross. Romans 10:9–10 says, "If you declare with your mouth, 'Jesus is Lord,' and believe in your heart that God raised him from the dead, you will be saved. For it is with your heart that you believe and are justified (made right with God), and it is with your mouth that you profess your faith and are saved (delivered from the penalty of sin)."

A PRAYER FOR SALVATION.

When you're ready to receive God's gift of eternal life through faith in His Son, Jesus, let this prayer be the cry of your heart:

> *Dear Jesus, I know that I am a sinner and that I need your forgive-ness. I believe that you are the Son of God, and that you came to earth, lived a perfect life, died on the cross for my sin and rose again so that I can be saved. Please forgive my sins, and come into my life. I am ready to trust you as my Savior because I believe that your Word is true, that you have a good purpose for my life, and that you will always be with me, even for all eternity. Amen*

NOW WHAT?

I am so excited for you. Becoming a Christian isn't a quick fix for your problems, but it is a promise that you will never walk alone. As you enter your
new relationship with God, I encourage you to spend time doing these three
things:

1. Listen to him. Read the Bible with a desire to understand more about
   him. Whether reading the book of John or another book, remember
   that you are on a new and beautiful, life-long journey to know God,
   so simply make it a daily habit to open his Word and read. As you
   seek him, his Holy Spirit will fill you with strength and wisdom for an
   abundant life. For online resources to grow your faith, visit Our Daily
   Bread at www.odb.org or download the free New Life devotional series
   at www.guidelines.org.

2. Talk to him. Just as human relationships depend on two-way communication, God wants you to do more than just listen. He wants you to
   talk to him through prayer and to share your hurts and fears, questions
   and desires. Tell him when you mess up and ask him for forgiveness.
   As you are honest with him and trust him to listen, his Spirit will speak
   to you and strengthen you for whatever life brings your way.

3. Listen and talk to others who love him. While accepting God's eternal forgiveness through Jesus seals your eternal condition, attending
   church and spending time with other believers (people who love Jesus) is all about your earthly condition. God promises that you will be
   strengthened as you worship and pray with others, enjoy life together,
   serve each other, and share life's ups and downs. If you need help finding a church in your area, visit www.churchfinder.com and then visit
   church websites to learn what they believe, how they encourage Christian community, and how they are telling others about Jesus.

BUILDING A HABIT OF PRAYER.

Whether you have known Jesus as your Savior for many years, you just
trusted him as your Savior today, or you're still unsure about his role in your
life, consider praying these daily truths as you draw near to him and seek
wisdom.

MONDAY

God's Truth: *Behold, God is my salvation, I will trust and not be afraid; For the Lord God is my strength and song, And He has become my salvation. Isaiah 12:2*

My Prayer: Thank you, Jesus, for being my salvation! Thank you for suffering and dying to save me from the punishment of sin and for being my strength during every difficult thing. Because of you, I can trust and not be afraid and I can look to the future with hope. Amen.

TUESDAY

God's Truth: *Therefore, if anyone is in Christ, he is a new creation. The old has passed away; behold, the new has come. 2 Corinthians 5:17*

My Prayer: Oh Lord, thank you for your promise of new things. My soul is tired from grieving day and night, but your sacrifice—your salvation—brings new hope for tomorrow and reminds me that this earthly life, even with all of its struggle, is not the end. I know that I will be with you in Heaven someday and that there will be an end to my tears. Amen.

WEDNESDAY

God's Truth: *The LORD is my light and my salvation; Whom shall I fear? The Lord is the defense of my life; Whom shall I dread? Psalm 27:1*

My Prayer: Heavenly Father, thank you for bringing light into this dark world and for being my safe place. I have nothing to fear because you have already conquered death and you have given me the promise of eternal life in heaven with you. Amen.

THURSDAY

God's Truth: *The LORD is my strength and song, And He has become my salvation; This is my God, and I will praise Him; My father's God, and I will extol Him. Exodus 15:2*

My Prayer: Jesus, your salvation gives me a song of hope. I choose to praise you today, even as my heart is grieving, because you have overcome the world and your strength lives in me. Amen.

FRIDAY

<u>God's Truth</u>: *Blessed be the Lord, who daily bears our burden, The God who is our salvation. Psalm 68:19*
<u>My Prayer</u>: Oh Lord, thank you that I am not alone in my grief. Not only have you saved my soul, but you promise to carry the weight of my burdens as I trust you with them. Help me to trust you today. . .right now. . .and to find comfort in your salvation. Amen.

SATURDAY

<u>God's Truth</u>: *Praise be to the Lord my Rock . . . He is my loving God and my fortress, my stronghold and my deliverer, my shield, in whom I take refuge. . . Psalm 144:1–2*
<u>My Prayer</u>: Oh God, I choose to praise you for being my strength and my place of safety. You rescue me from the darkness of this world and give me hope for the future, knowing that the pain of this world is temporary. Thank you for loving me, for understanding my grief, and for never giving up on me. Amen.

SUNDAY

<u>God's Truth</u>: *God so loved the world that he gave his one and only son. Anyone who believes in him will not die but have eternal life. John 3:16*
<u>My Prayer</u>: Thank you, God, for loving me so much that you sent Jesus to suffer and die, to save me from the penalty of sin. Though my heart aches because of the death of my loved one, it rejoices in the promise of eternal life with you. Amen.

Appendix B

Resources for Walking through Grief and Understanding Youth Culture

GRIEFSHARE

griefshare.org

GriefShare is a 13-week support group and features Biblical teaching on grief and recovery for those who have lost a spouse, child, friend or other loved ones to death. Whether your loss is recent or from previous years, it can still hurt and be difficult to work through. GriefShare can help. Find a GriefShare support group or event near you.

FOCUS ON THE FAMILY

focusonthefamily.com

Focus on the Family is a global Christian ministry dedicated to helping families thrive. We provide help and resources for couples to build healthy marriages that reflect God's design, and for parents to raise their children according to morals and values grounded in biblical principles.

THE CENTER FOR PARENT/YOUTH UNDERSTANDING (CPYU)

cpyu.org

This faith-based site provides information, resources, and analysis on today's youth culture. Clicking on the Resources tab takes visitors to audio, PDF, links, list, and videos about more than 300 topics influencing our kids.

COMMON SENSE MEDIA

commonsensemedia.org

The Parent tab on this site takes visitors to reviews of movies, television shows, books, apps, video games, and websites. Parents can search by child's age or desired topic, and the social media page provides information about trends, definitions of social media terms, the issue of sexting, descriptions of social media platforms, and specific apps parents should watch out for.

THE SOURCE4PARENTS

thesource4parents.com

This is a free resource specifically for parents, offering articles, book reviews, and website links dealing with a variety of youth culture topics. It also has music discussions that include scripture and engaging questions to discuss with your kids.

NATIONAL INSTITUTE ON DRUG ABUSE

teens.drugabuse.gov

This is a source of science-based information for teens and parents, created to give facts about drugs and their effects on the brain and body. The resources promote learning and encourage critical thinking so teens will make informed decisions.

JUST THINK TWICE

justthinktwice.gov/drugs

This is a government website that provides information about current drug trends, a drug and paraphernalia index, true stories, resources about potential consequences, and a wide variety of up-to-date news and media reports related to the current drug culture.

THE PARENT RESOURCE PROJECT (YOUTH SUICIDE PREVENTION)

prp.jasonfoundation.com

The purpose of this site is to educate teens and parents about the issue of youth suicide. It includes articles, videos, and a resource page with links to dozens of external sites dealing with topics such as suicide, bullying, mental health, substance use, parenting, and teen relationships.

DRUG ENFORCEMENT ADMINISTRATION NATIONAL DRUG THREAT ASSESSMENT

dea.gov (search: national-drug-threat-assessment)

This report provides comprehensive federal, state, and local data about the threat posed to U.S. citizens by domestic and international drug trafficking and the abuse of both licit and illicit drugs. It also shares which substances and criminal organizations represent the greatest threat.

TEEN-SAFE

teen-safe.org

Teen-safe's goal is to provide the latest science and true-life stories as educational materials to parents, teens, and pre-teens to foster better family communications, promote resilience and healthy activities, and to reduce risky behaviors in teens with the goal of preserving their futures.

SUBSTANCE ABUSE AND MENTAL HEALTH SERVICES ADMINISTRATION (SAMHSA)

samhsa.gov

The Substance Abuse and Mental Health Services Administration (SAMHSA) is the agency within the U.S. Department of Health and Human Services, leading public health efforts to advance the behavioral health of the nation. SAMHSA's mission is to reduce the impact of substance abuse and mental illness on America's communities.

Bibliography

Fetterman, Anne, Joseph Campellone, and Kent Turley. "Understanding the Teen Brain." University of Rochester Medical Center Encyclopedia. University of Rochester Medical Center. Accessed December 20, 2020. https://www.urmc. rochester.edu/encyclopedia/content.aspx?ContentTypeID=1.

Griffith, Mary Bess, Joanne M. Hall, and Becky Fields. "Crying That Heals." *Journal of Holistic Nursing* 29, no. 3 (2011) 167–79. https://doi.org/10.1177 /0898010110393355.

Moisse, Katie, and Ray Sanchez. "DEA Bans Sale of K2, Synthetic Marijuana, and Five Chemicals Used to Make It." ABC News. ABC News Network. Accessed December 20, 2020. https://abcnews.go.com/Health/Wellness/k2-crackdown-drug-enforcement-administration-bans-fake-pot/story?id=13027548.

Stevenson, Sarah. "There's Magic in Your Smile," June 25, 2012. https://www. psychologytoday.com/us/blog/cutting-edge-leadership/201206/there-s-magic-in-your-smile.

Zuccino, David. "Scientist's Research Produces a Dangerous High," September 28, 2011. https://www.latimes.com/world/la-xpm-2011-sep-28-la-na-killer-weed-2011 0928-story.html.

CPSIA information can be obtained
at www.ICGtesting.com
Printed in the USA
LVHW012239020422
714985LV00002B/2